T0196741

SODOM'S

THRESHOLD

SODOM'S

THRESHOLD

THE DESIRE FOR THE UNTHINKABLE

Isaac B. Rosler, PhD

SODOM'S THRESHOLD
THE DESIRE FOR THE UNTHINKABLE

Scripture quotations marked KJV are from the Holy Bible, King James Version (Authorized Version). First published in 1611. Quoted from the KJV Classic Reference Bible, Copyright © 1983 by The Zondervan Corporation.

iUniverse books may be ordered through booksellers or by contacting:

iUniverse
1663 Liberty Drive
Bloomington, IN 47403
www.iuniverse.com
1-800-Authors (1-800-288-4677)

Because of the dynamic nature of the Internet, any web addresses or links contained in this book may have changed since publication and may no longer be valid. The views expressed in this work are solely those of the author and do not necessarily reflect the views of the publisher, and the publisher hereby disclaims any responsibility for them.

Any people depicted in stock imagery provided by Thinkstock are models, and such images are being used for illustrative purposes only. Certain stock imagery © Thinkstock.

ISBN: 978-1-5320-2175-6 (sc)
ISBN: 978-1-5320-2174-9 (e)

Library of Congress Control Number: 2017909065

Print information available on the last page.

iUniverse rev. date: 06/30/2017

"Rosler's ambitious project to recuperate the unnamable and unsacrificeable excess of passion represented by Sodom is a virtuosic deconstruction and an important ethical intervention. By resisting a narrative and naming of wickedness, Rosler's study reveals the survival of a resilient surplus, which exceeds the sustained homophobic attempt to equate Sodom with deviance, so as to originate there a narrative of an otherly community. Working across sacred and secular texts, from the literary to the cinematic, Rosler reminds us that no matter how oppressive and repressive any given cultural, ideological and political moment is, there is a surplus in every community that always exceeds the capacity of those in power to demonize, exclude and elide what is exorbitant, silent, and other. Ranging from Job to Heidegger, Pasolini to García Márquez, Rosler's argument relies on close nuanced readings across time, language, and society so as to offer painfully exact accounts of how a mutating linguistic space is recurrently usurped and haunted by hatred and prejudice. For Rosler, whether meditating on the State of Israel or the meaning of true hospitality, Sodom is that othering other that opens the necessary borderless space for all to be able to become themselves, always in transit, always strange and singular. Readers with a Derridean turn, with an appreciation of ingeniously subversive Biblical criticism, and a host of other materials connected by their foregrounding of trespass, will find in this study a lyricism of expression and an intensity of ethical engagement that cannot be forgotten and certainly not erased."

-Elizabeth Richmond-Garza, PhD
Director, Program in Comparative Literature at UT, Austin.

FOREWORD

Tales of the Sodomites' wickedness have been mobilized to condemn homosexuality and other forms of perceived sexual deviancy, to exclude "sinners," to inspire fear in potential sinners, and to establish distinct boundaries between self and other. Turning to the destruction of Sodom, Isaac Rosler recognizes that there is an indestructible alterity in the narrative, a surplus that remains untouched as the story unfolds. He approaches the biblical story by raising a series of questions, creating entry points to deconstruct it. His work steps toward, identifies, and interrogates the boundaries between what the text includes and what it excludes. Poking at its textual limits and peeking into its margins, Rosler creates space to wonder who the Sodomites were and what they did, why the narrative was written as it was, and how and what it has made possible.

Sodom's Threshold deconstructs the story of Sodom's erasure to seek out the trace of its indestructible and unsacrificeable passion. The Sodomites had a taste for the foreign and the strange. Rosler invites the reader to think and sense the excess of the Sodomites associated with their desire to touch and "penetrate" the coming of the other. *Sodom's Threshold* is an invitation to reflect upon what or who mesmerized the Sodomites and if that surplus is anything that a law can forbid or oppose. Lingering over these questions, setting them aside, and circling back to them, Rosler's work revolves around an "unseemly" intoxication, a "deviancy" ascribed to Sodom. Who were the Sodomites? What does this name nominate and abominate? What do we see in them when we approach their specters without an assumption of deviancy? What is this line or threshold from which deviation and contamination emerge? Rosler's work circles around the revolting revolt of the Sodomites, around the multiplying metaphors turning against a surplus that is forbidden to name, around a sin so "very grievous" that may not be represented, and around a disruption that seems to deserve absolute extermination and oblivion. It is toward that inenarrable and exorbitant surplus that Rosler's work orbits around and opens up.

Rosler underlines how the story of Sodom establishes and mediates concepts of deviancy and contamination through an affirmative alterity that is not dialectical, does not oppose, and is not opposable. Rosler demonstrates that the moral imperatives that emerge from the biblical story can never amount to the alterity that makes them possible in the first place. The biblical story founds a series of orthodoxies meant to determine who belongs in a certain community of chosen people; however, Rosler exposes that the passion that impassions the Sodomites, the passion that is the foundation of any communal law, remains without community, without law, and without name. Underlining these forms of community creation, Rosler also recognizes them as boundaries, indicators of a limit, a space, a threshold that can never be properly presented, represented, dominated, and nominated. Rosler explores the desiring impetus that can never overlap with any given law or community, the altering passion that impassions and alters every law, the surplus that partakes in any community as it departs untouched. He orbits around the exorbitant desire of the Sodomites, an ecstatic affirmation that embraces the dangers and joys of the coming of what is completely other and foreign. His work hovers around a law that emerges from Sodom, a law that prohibits to think what cannot be represented (a "very grievous desire"). The law of Sodom prohibits to represent the unthinkable, an excess that has always already surpassed representation.

Drawing from Genesis, films like *Midnight Cowboy*, and the novel *Il Bell' Antonio* by Vitaliano Brancati, among others, Rosler creates a rich dialogue between several narratives and genres, which reveals how Sodom continues to influence a range of contemporary forms of thought and cultural productions. His careful attention to the texts in close readings, as he weaves them together in a deconstructive analysis, reveals the scope of his project beyond the story of Sodom to the broad and pervasive forms of thinking that it bolsters. His insightful and skilled studies of texts originally written in biblical Hebrew, modern Italian, and contemporary English point toward an overabundant remanence, an idiom of passion that transfers to every language but remains without analogy, thereby exacerbating the passion to name, touch, and "penetrate" an idiom that partakes in every text but remains untouched and unsacrificeable.

Sodom's Threshold is an invitation to more open and humane responses to otherness, a call to heterogeneous forms of thought, a movement toward a shifting self-awareness. It highlights how concepts like nature, culture, and tradition absorb, usurp, repress, and incorporate otherness (the strange, the foreign, and the desire for the unthinkable) in the service of replicating our own visions of intolerance and reinforcing the recurring positions of "we" against the other. This book represents a necessary intervention in the seemingly endless outpouring of shortsighted legislation, unapologetic phobias, and extreme nationalism rising anew in today's world. It also offers a tender and powerful homage to the victims of violent acts in the service of racism, homophobia, and nativism, among other hate-driven isms. The evil that could drive such acts is also the legacy of the misunderstood story of Sodom, a town destroyed in the name of absolute truths and unquestionable decrees. What is it about the other and the strange that inspires such destruction? How might this frenzied, disorienting encounter with the other lead to a desire for its annihilation?

Raising these questions, Rosler turns back to the story of Sodom, often cited in acts of hatred toward "deviant" and "threatening" sexualities. He turns back to those otherly Sodomites whose sin was an excess, a surplus that was "very grievous." He recognizes that efforts to annihilate such "deviancy" only make it more a part of us, more revealing of our limitations that part and depart from an alterity that is inviolable, untouchable, and indestructible. Blurring the line between "us" and "them," internal and external, Rosler's work reveals a surplus in the threshold of the senses that will never coincide with a hegemonic identity, or a coherent self.

In spite of the recent tendency to bring democracies to the extreme right, the alterity that orbits around every democracy in the world will never completely escape the untranslatable idiom, the excess that makes democracies turn toward an impassioned future of possibilities and singularities that is yet to come. It is this excess that will make every democracy turn again and anew toward a desire for an alterity that is absolutely other, that is other than norms and models. He calls for multiple translations of a surplus that will continue to turn democracy into something unprecedented, to an affirmation that will always aim toward laws that legislate how to take care of each other, how to bring justice to whomever is other and any other. Such openness sacrifices beliefs and narratives that we might hold dear, and yet it also makes possible new, critical forms of being to emerge.

Raelene C. Wyse
Austin, Texas

The desire of God is God as the other
name of desire.
—Jacques Derrida. *On the Name*

And with my own flesh, I will see God.
—Job

Something unstilled, unstillable is within
me, it wants to be voiced.
A craving for love is within me;
it speaks the language of love.
—Friedrich Nietzsche, "The Night
of Song," *Thus Spoke Zarathustra*

Thinking guides and sustains every
gesture of the hand.
—Martin Heidegger, *What Is Called
Thinking?*

Pero la tribu de Melquíades había
sido borrada de la faz de la tierra
por haber sobrepasado los límites del
conocimiento humano.
[But Melquíades' tribe had been erased
from the face of earth for having exceeded
the limits of human knowledge.]
—Gabriel García Márquez, *One Hundred
Years of Solitude*

Ecce Homo

Yes, I know from where I came!
Ever hungry like a flame,
I consume myself and glow.
Light grows all that I conceive,
Ashes everything I leave:
Flame I am assuredly.
—Friedrich Nietzsche, "Joke, Cunning and
Revenge," *The Gay Science*

CONTENTS

The Grasp of the Coming of the Other

Why is the story of Sodom and Gomorrah included in the book of Genesis? What does it initiate and touch? Who are these people? What do they desperately try to grasp and "penetrate"? To whom or to what do they aim their passion? The narrative has recurred with renewed interest throughout the centuries. There is both rejection and fascination toward those "sinful" individuals that God wanted to eliminate from the face of the earth. Their passionate mark still lingers, and their desiring impetus still flows quietly from ashes.

Pandemonium erupts in Sodom when two guests (two angel-messengers) arrive to Lot's home. Their arrival impassions the Sodomites with mesmerizing desire. The revolting people of Sodom are in revolt. Who are these strangers without name and without country that come from nowhere and bring, on the one hand, a message of death and, on the other, a provocation of joy and pleasure? Who are these otherly figures, these newcomers who tempt the Sodomites, contaminate their senses, traverse their bodies, and distort their impressions? Who/what are these unfigurable silhouettes who overflow the Sodomites' bodies and senses and immolate their hands in a paralyzing dream?

The Sodomites perceive the arrival of an "outside" provocation, of two angel-specters-visitors that bring the town to pandemonium and frenzy. An ineludible event unfolds: the arrival of an unconditional alterity contaminates from the "outside" the Sodomites' perceptions, impressions, and emotions. The Sodomites' frenzy multiplies at the threshold of Lot's door as they sense the contours of a foreign figure, an exteriority that resonates in their senses, a foreignness that does not belong to any known knowledge.

A maddening desire insinuates to them from an elsewhere and brings them to force themselves into Lot's home in order to "know" (נדעה)[1] the "people" (אנשים)[2] visiting his home. The word in Hebrew for Lot's guests translates as "people" (without specifying their gender). In a second that splits, all the town becomes other than themselves, strange, as they sense an exteriority that multiplies their desire to touch, embrace, penetrate a rare and foreign texture that insinuates to them in passing through the threshold of Lot's door.

The untranslatable passion of the Sodomites is unspeakable and unseemly, an indefinite desire that does not

---

[1] Torah, Genesis, 19:6, Hebrew-English Edition (Skokie, Illinois: 2012), 31.
[2] Ibid., 19:5.

know the name of what or who is desired. Out of Sodom and Gomorrah, everything has been said without affecting their ecstatic secret. It seems that any attempt for a reinterpretation will find its way to a duplication and multiplication of sorts that will circulate a "proper" knowledge already known, unless one focuses on a repetition that is forgotten, on a recurring surplus, a dream of dreams that is excluded from religion and its history, the remains of an ineludible but quiet exuberance without which religion would not have a chance. This book is about this residue, this remnant without religion that does not make itself present, that remains in the antechamber of religion, in the threshold of sense, between outside and inside. This book does not unveil "the secret" of Sodom but brings awareness that there is a secret, that religion could not do without that secret, that we all partake in the secret, that it is without religion, that it is unsacrificeable, and that there is no mystery in their secret:

> Wherever knowledge can only be supposed, wherever, as a result, one knows that supposition cannot give rise to knowledge, wherever no knowledge could ever be disputed, there is the invisible production (for no one ever witnesses it) of a *secrecy effect*, of what we might call a *speculation on the capital secret or on the capital of the secret*. The calculated and yet finally incalculable production of this secrecy effect relies on a simulacrum. This simulacrum recalls, from another point of view, the situation described at the beginning of *Raymond*

> *Roussel*: the risk of "being deceived less by
> a secret than by the awareness that there is
> a secret."[3]

This book is about writing and rewriting with the passion of the Sodomites about their unpronounceable secret, about their penetrating grasp.

The tale does not clarify if the Sodomites saw the strangers (face-to-face) arriving to town. What it affirms is that everyone sensed their spectral arrival. Some translations refer to them as men; however, the direct translation is "people." The Sodomites did not see the "people" (אנשים) but anticipated their exuberant and foreign presence. What they saw, assuming that they in fact visualized something, appeared without appearing, between their senses at the threshold of Lot's door. At the same time, whatever Lot perceives in his guests drives him to a mad frenzy, to the point of offering his virgin daughters to the Sodomites for the sake of protecting the strangers:

> And Lot said: Behold now, my lords, turn
> in, I pray you, into your servant's house, and
> tarry all night, and wash your feet … And
> the angels said, Nay; but we will abide in the
> street all night. And Lot pressed upon them
> greatly; and they turned in unto him, and
> entered into his house; and he made them a
> feast … But before they lay down, the men of
> the city, even the men of Sodom, compassed

---

[3] Derrida, *Resistances of Psychoanalysis*, trans. Peggy Kamuf, et al. (Stanford: Stanford University Press, 1998), 92.

the house round, both old and young, all the people from every quarter: And they called unto Lot, and said unto him, Where are the men (אנשים) which came into thee this night? Bring them out unto us, that we may penetrate (נדעה) them. And Lot went out at the door unto them, and shut the door after him, And said, Behold now, I have two daughters which have not known man; let me, I pray you, bring them out unto you, and do ye to them as is good in your eyes: only unto these men do nothing; for therefore came they under the shadow of my roof. (Genesis 19:2–8)

In this scene, Lot must have also sensed that there was something otherly and foreign (external) about the foreigners. What is it that obsesses Lot to the point of offering his virgin daughters to the crowd? He must have also perceived some kind of an overflowing excess in them, something that was other than human. What kind of surplus message did the specters/angels carry, and why did he respond and correspond by sending his daughters "out" to the crowd? Is it possible to substitute and supplement one excess with another? Would the crowd be satisfied by this substitution, by penetrating the virginity of Lot's daughters, or would they rather penetrate another kind of virginity? The Sodomites yearn to grasp, capture, embrace, and penetrate (נדעה) an overabundant excess.[4] The messengers communicate something that

---

[4] "*Nehedah*" "(נדעה)" is literally translated as "to know." In the biblical sense, "to know" is associated with penetration of knowledge and/

mesmerizes and blinds both Lot and the crowd. Like the Sodomites, Lot perceives a foreign heterogeneity, an external figure, a communication without analogy that he in turn figures (translates) into an insufficient analogy through the offering of his daughters. Lot and the Sodomites desire the strangers with a desire that surpasses their desires, a multiplying desire that unleashes, unfolds, and contaminates the shores of expressible language. The otherly skin of the specters is in excess of any language, and its surplus speaks through analogies that provoke a passion for a syncopal space, for an affirmative dispersion that remains exterior, out of touch, and without analogy in the perception of the Sodomites and Lot, and in the impressions of the reader of the story. Every analogy attempted with the spectral excess becomes equivocal, ruined, and imperfect. Without this desire for what remains out of grasp, there is no desire in motion:

> Without this desire for virginity no desire
> whatever would be set moving, likewise
> without Necessity and without what comes
> along to interrupt and thwart that desire,
> desire itself would not unfold ... the desire

---

or physical penetration of a person. Knowledge is the penetration of that whom/which one desires to know (metaphorically or/and literally). According to Derrida [*Of Hospitality*, trans. Rachel Bowlby (Stanford: Stanford University Press, 2000)], the people of Sodom want to see the strangers/visitors, "in order to 'penetrate' them, says one translation (Chouraqui's: 'Get them to come out to us: let's penetrate them!'), to 'get to know' them, another modestly puts it (Dhorme's in the Pléiade collection: 'Get them to come out to us so that we can get to know them')," 151.

for virginity is what makes possible the kernel desire itself—the intact desire for intactness.[5]

If the Sodomites desired the angels only because they were men, then Lot would have never offered his daughters to those who only preferred men. The Sodomites desired (to know) to penetrate a virginity that was other than virginity, one that remains untouched even through the senses of touch. They were driven to those unfigurable figures that disoriented, distorted, and disorganized the Sodomites' senses. They had a desire to "know," "penetrate," and "grasp" a spectral presence in passing, a surplus that was neither "natural" nor "nature" or human but was in excess of them.

The figure of hospitality becomes pivotal in the story, as a desire to welcome and know (נדעה) a living presence in passing, an external texture that is separated by an infinitely small threshold from which all passions flow. The threshold only enhances, increases, and supplements the passion that extends, the passion caught between the thresholds of perception, between the sensible and the intelligible, inside and outside. The figure of the threshold is the genesis of a border (which could both receive or reject, communicate or neutralize), a mediating space through which something external and exterior is grasped and, at the same time, interrupted. In between spaces, a hand touches an exterior and untouchable foreign figure. But the threshold is a passage to that which is without passage, a trespassing that opens, on the one hand, the possibility of knowledge, ethics,

---

[5] Derrida, *The Ear of the Other,* ed. Christie McDonald, trans. by Peggy Kamuf, (Nebraska: University of Nebraska Press, 1988), 116.

responsibility, and economy and, on the other, the constant questioning of their (familiar and established) truths:

> The fact that there is … neither continuity of passage nor interruption or mere caesura, that the motifs of passage of what passes and comes to pass [*passe et se passe*] in history belong neither to a solid foundation nor to a founding decision, that the passage has no grounding ground and no indivisible line under it, requires us to rethink the very figure of *threshold* (ground, foundational solidity, limit between inside and outside, inclusion and exclusion, etc.). What the texts we have read call for is at least a greater vigilance as to our irrepressible desire for the threshold, a threshold that *is* a threshold, a single and solid threshold. Perhaps there never is a threshold, any such threshold. Which is perhaps why we remain on it and risk staying on the threshold for ever.[6]

The threshold of Genesis is a multiplying limit of what cannot be surpassed, of what has already been surpassed without surpassing because it is not really a limit. The figure of the threshold in Lot's door resists the limit and at the same time establishes it. The house of Lot marks the beginning of a biblical architecture associated with the homely, the sacred,

---

[6] Derrida, *The Beast & the Sovereign Volume I*, ed. Michael Lisse, et al., trans. Geoffrey Bennington (Chicago and London: University of Chicago Press, 2011), 333–334.

community, and truth. It is the genesis of preservation. It preserves the safety of the religious home and the temple, which are the architectural grounds out of which religious investments, political authority, and cultural influences unfold. This safe architectural design, this sacred space, however, comes from a space that is both inhabitable and unassailable, a region that in Sodom is not only kept at bay, as something external and foreign, but also as something brought into ruins and cinders. The recurrent idiom of Sodom, its ineffable region, is what haunts the immunity of the sacred, its faint saved space.

Is there such a thing as the coming of angels? Indeed there is. Angels are from this world. They are specters arriving all the time; they are the other to whom we give hospitality; they take the form of the unknown that we welcome in our senses and our thoughts. Angels are shadows and shades of desire for the unknown. Whether addressed like men or not, the spectral visitors incarnate a hybrid excess, an alterity that is untranslatable through the senses alone. The anticipation for an unknown form provokes the Sodomites' senses to a referent without reference. A mute language of desire imperfectly aligns with an infinite text that hopes to give form to a who or a what that impassions, a discourse in which one secret word is (always) missing. What is the sex of angels? Are they a "who," a "what," or something in between? How is one attracted to the hybrid texture of an angel, a specter who is either, or, both and none? Do the angels in Sodom have a face, a body, or a sex? The Sodomites' desire yearns for a foreign form that crosses through all kind of identities and through all kinds of knowledge. One can perhaps speculate that they turn their senses toward:

> A call which addresses and provokes *above all* else, above and beyond whatever says "me," my "body," as a "man" or a "woman," or my sex. They turn to the other when it speaks to "whom," to "what," to this "who" which has not yet been assigned an identity or, to either one sex or the other?[7]

The vague name "angel" does not name anything in particular; it only alludes to some hybrid notion. One may risk saying that the attraction of the Sodomites is a fascination associated with something in between a "who" or a "what," a figure whose configuration is uncertain and for this very reason disperses and distorts the perception and emotions of the Sodomites. They want to "know" (נדעה) that "who" or "what" that speaks to them with a strange murmur. The hybrid nature of the specters causes a disorganizing impetus in the Sodomites who yield to the immediateness and indefiniteness of an otherly texture, a surface that remains without analogy. The event of their arrival, their "happening" is in excess of every known grasp, word, texture, vision, or presence. The Sodomites' dispersing and dissembling desire comes from the other. Their exuberant passion addresses an incalculable X without analogy, a specter without an ultimate predication, sex, or face. This figure that surpasses all figures exceeds the concept of fraternization:

---

[7] Derrida, "Voice II," in *Points … Interviews, 1974–1994*, ed. Elisabeth Weber, trans. Verena Andermatt Conley (Stanford: Stanford University Press, 1995), 163.

> Fraternization is always caught up, like
> friendship itself, in a vertiginous process
> of hyperbolization. There is always
> someone, something more fraternal than
> the brother, more friendly than the friend,
> more equitable than justice and law—and
> the measure is given by the immensity and
> incommensurability of this "more."[8]

Could it be that the orgiastic people of Sodom are at the same time the most virtuous for desiring the unknown, for contemplating in passion the Absolute Other, for wanting to grasp an incorruptible texture? They entered an alliance with a nonknowledge, an alliance without alliance, without pact or history. These pre-Jews and pre-Christians experience an inexpressible religion without religion. Who can rule upon this formless-forming trace? Is it possible to govern? Who can bring justice to the writing of the impossible, the writing of disaster, rupture, rapture, partition, and departure? Who can keep the secret safe, the secret known through extreme destitution, blindness, and incineration? Who can write with burning hands, with a writing in ruins and cinders, with a writing other than writing about their rapturing and rupturing desire? Who can give form to a grasp that is never at hand?:

> The hand does not only grasp and catch,
> or push and pull. The hand reaches and
> extends, receives and welcomes—and not

---

[8] Derrida, *Politics of Friendship*, trans. George Collins (London, New York: Verso, 1997), 239.

just things: the hand extends itself, and receives its own welcome in the hands of others. The hand holds. The hand carries. The hand designs and signs, presumably because man is a sign.[9]

Is such syntax of silence, fire, embers, and cinders possible? A circular syntax departs in Genesis, a circle of passion desires to grasp incessantly what is neither near nor far, what lets itself be bound into a self-forming/self, a multiplying/self that is relentlessly parting from and departing toward an unexpected pleasure. In Hebrew, "*Sdom*" "(סדם)", the initial and final consonants encircle empty voids [the first S (ס) and the last M (ם)]. The empty spaces "ס" "ם" are interrupted by the other two letters. The name "Sodom" "(סדם)" forms through its empty spaces, voids that disrupt, distort, and interrupt its own name. Two consonants, the first and the last one, seem to draw from erasure. The flow of those empty consonants repeats in different places without saying anything. In this movement of spacing and repetition, a silent grasp both draws and withdraws an evanescent trace in a name that signifies through its erasure. "What is Sodom? What does it name? What do we name when we say Sodom? What do we love or hate when we say Sodom סדם?"

The arousal of the Sodomites' passion rests ad infinitum in a diffuse anticipation, in a disorganizing etymology. The specters' texture in the hands of the Sodomites opens an indeterminate "maybe," a "perhaps" of multiplying possibilities that entice the Sodomites to an impassioned

---

[9] Martin Heidegger, *What Is Called Thinking?*, trans. J. Glenn Gray, intr. J. Glenn Gray (New York: Harpers & Row, 1968), 16.

frenzy. How does the Sodomites' gender or sexual desire react to an "X" that exceeds gender and surpasses representation? Their unsatisfied desire craves an X, and it is precisely this inaccessibility that multiplies their yearnings. The longing for an X, with a desire beyond binary oppositions (feminine versus masculine), unsettles genders, sexual desire, and all centers of passion. The craving for X frees their impressions and perceptions, displaying multiple and incalculable choreographies of desire. As desires are multiplied and distorted, the Sodomites abandon themselves to a determinate indetermination, to a craving for a "who" or a "what," foreign figures in passing. The exposure to the wholly other is as unbearable as it is mesmerizing:

> The sex of the addresser awaits its determination by or from the other. It is the other who will perhaps decide who I am—man or woman. Nor is this decided once and for all. It may go one way one time and another way another time. What is more, if there is a multitude of sexes (because there are perhaps more than two) which sign differently, then I will have to assume (I—or rather whoever says I—will have to assume) this polysexuality.[10]

The "messengers" (heralds of the strange and the uncanny) entice the frenzy of the Sodomites. The trace of (a) God (the irruption of an otherly exteriority) is gathered and divided in the Sodomites' disjointed desires, at the edge

---

[10] Derrida, *Ear,* 52.

of their senses. The angelic texture participates without participation in the enticement of the Sodomites and summons them to a multiplying ecstasy, a blinding agitation at the edge of their senses, an edge that is ominous and hopeful, dreadful and loving, violent and tender, consuming and liberating, a hinge where "more" interrupts "more" and calls for more than more:

> Interruption occurs at the edge, or rather it constitutes the edge where beings touch each other, expose themselves to each other and separate from one another, thus communicating and propagating their community. On this edge, destined to this edge and called forth by it, born of interruption, there is a passion. This is, if you will, what remains of myth, or rather, it is *itself the interruption* of myth.[11]

The passion that impassions the Sodomites is a tale of frenzy in a town that cannot control the desire for specters. But who is not mesmerized by the announcement of the arrival of a coveted indetermination, and could we not assume that one is at all times anticipating and expecting the advent of an X that is yet to be known? The coming of the other intoxicates, distorts, and contaminates the senses because its advent may not be calculated with any known desire. Their exceeding desire will have existed before the Sodomites, before there

---

[11] Jean-Luc Nancy, *The Inoperative Community,* trans. Peter Connor et al., ed. Peter Connor (Minneapolis: University of Minnesota Press, 2006), 61.

was a God, or any gods. This longing for what is yet to come puts in motion the invention of God(s). The coming of the X-other ignites their affections, infects their impressions, and distorts their response:

> The other, the arrival of the other is always incalculable. Once one accepts its principle and gives oneself over to this exposure to the other—to the event that comes to affect us, and therefore to the affectivity by which life is defined—at that moment, it is necessary to be prepared to invent the coming of a discourse capable of taking this into account.[12]

The Sodomites are affected by the incommensurability of the other, and this moment reveals an impetus that not only can survive any catastrophe but also will repeat recurrently, without religion, even without memory, throughout the history of the world.

In Genesis 19:6, the future tense of the verb "to know" reads "נדעה," which, as it was pointed before, means "to penetrate" or "to know." At the same time, the present tense of "נדעה" is "ידעה," which associates both with the concept "to know" and "יד," which means hand. "Knowing," "penetration," "grasping," "hand," and "at hand" form a manifold unity of knowledge in this passage that fuses the sense of touch (to sense) with knowledge (to grasp, to penetrate, and to know).

---

[12] Derrida and Elizabeth Roudinesco, "Unforeseeable Freedom," in *For What Tomorrow ... A Dialogue*, trans. Jeff Fort (Stanford: Stanford University Press, 2004), 58.

"God" starts with the letter " י" followed by another letter "י" forming "יי." The hand senses and grasps the threshold from out of which the desire to name what is not at hand unfolds. Is it possible to touch a space that makes possible the grasp of touch? Everyone in Sodom is trembling with anticipation; everyone is a little bit like God in the instant they want to "penetrate" an inviolable secret:

> The trembling of the formula "every other (one) is every (bit) other" can also be reproduced. It can do so to the extent of replacing one of the "every others" by God: "Every other (one) is God," or "God is every (bit) other." Such a substitution in no way alters the "extent" of the original formulation, whatever grammatical function be assigned to the various words. In one case God is defined as infinitely other, as wholly other, every bit other. In the other case it is declared that every other one, each of the others, is God inasmuch as he or she is, *like* God, wholly other.[13]

They are impassioned by an alterity that overwhelms them, by an uncanny exteriority that puts itself into motion from a dispersion that is interior to them.

The entrance of the angels to Sodom and the trance that they stir up reverberates in the form of a desire for specters, for the strange and the dangerous, and for whatever or whoever

---

[13] Derrida, *The Gift of Death*, trans. D. Willis (Chicago: University of Chicago Press, 1992), 87.

is coming. In the threshold of Lot's home, supplicating hands leave a burning trace without anagoge, without analogy, and without a known language. They leave an immemorial trace that makes everyone want to speak its hyperbolic secret. This writing of desire, of a desire that loves the unknown, will expand and contract, part and depart, divide and multiply in a thousand tales and a million metaphors. This is not only an excessive writing at the threshold but also a writing without measure that is in excess of destruction and oblivion. At the threshold, the distance toward the desired specter incarnates a finite infinitude of contortions and adorations, a feast of metaphors that add up while copulating toward an unfinished ecstatic writing, one that is at the threshold of our senses:

> Just as the end of writing passes beyond writing, its origin is not yet in the book. The writer, builder, and guardian of the book posts himself at the entrance to the house. The writer is a ferryman and his destination always has a liminal signification. *"Who are you? —The guardian of the house. — ... Are you in the book? —My place is on the threshold."*[14]

The living presence "right there" is conceivable through the difference of spaces. Without the difference established through the threshold of touch, there is no anticipation of the "there," and the living presence would be unimaginable

---

[14] Derrida, "Edmond Jabès and the Question of the Book," in *Writing and Difference,* trans. Alan Bass (Chicago: University of Chicago Press, 1978), 76.

in its absolute present.[15] What escapes from Sodom's absolute destruction is precisely the difference between spaces, an absolute difference that is at the service of an absolute presence that is always the supplement of a supplement, a presence subtracted (at the threshold) and infinitely restituted as it is surpassed:

> A radical difference remains, which has nothing in common with any other difference. This is a difference which in fact distinguishes nothing, a difference which separates no being, no lived-experience, no determinate signification. This is a difference however which, without altering anything, changes all the signs, and it is a difference in which alone the possibility of a transcendental question holds, that is, the possibility of freedom itself. This is, therefore, the fundamental difference without which no other difference in the world would make sense or even have a chance of appearing *as such*.[16]

The passing of the living presence can only be imagined "as such" through the threshold, through the separations of spaces. The threshold of touch is a space of dislocation and

---

[15] "The Living Present (lebendige Gegenwart) is the universal and absolute form of transcendental experience to which Husserl refers us." Derrida, *Of Grammatology*, trans. Gayatri Chakravorty Spivak (Baltimore: The Johns Hopkins University Press, 1976), 62.

[16] Derrida, *Voice and Phenomenon*, trans. Leonard Lawlor (Evanston, Illinois: Northwestern University Press, 2011), 10.

deferral overloaded with an endless impetus, an ungraspable language that may not be substituted with any name. Their desire desires the exteriority of the living presence grasped through a threshold that is other than presence or nonpresence, that adds up ad infinitum the presentation and representation of the advent of an arrival that is without arrival and out of touch. In this realm of awe and transgression, proximity and distance, the Sodomites stand before their erotic and hyperbolic experience, a display of auto-affection that opens all their senses, unfolds multiplying significations, and disorganizes them. The Sodomites are before the deferred texture of the (אנשים) angelic messengers who awaken their senses and traverse the Sodomites with a sense other than sense, with a sense that wants to touch what remains suspended in an interval that is out of touch. They have an ecstatic yearning for a "what" or "who" in passing, a figure that is never completely at hand.

They are caught in a "passage" to an unexpected elsewhere. The more they approach the threshold, the more incalculable becomes the hiatus between them and the strangers. The secret of the destruction of Sodom is kept in the threshold, in the spaces that it displaces, all of which leave a trace of passion for an indestructible interval of touch. The nonpassing, nontrespassing hiatus is indestructible; it is a region of ecstatic dislocation. It returns through a difference and deferral of spaces, a play of proximity and distance at the service of a desire for an absolute presence.

The secret of their passionate trace, the contamination that it puts into motion, is everywhere and anywhere. What or who impassioned the Sodomites? That question is recurrent, not only from the threshold but also from the buried ruins of Sodom and its silent ashes. The threshold of touch puts in motion an indescribable passion, a love that loves more than love. One may say that everyone is born with this errant and disproportionate sentiment, with "a love more loving than love"[17] that crosses the senses and is in excess of gender, sexual orientation, family, nation, and everything that has a name that touches the world. One may speculate as well that every second in everybody's life depends on an untranslatable desire that continually transports the individual to a region of adoration and hope for an incommensurable love for specters, for whomever and whatever, for what is without equivalence and comes from the other (any other who is other), for an X that remains out of grasp, for a nonobject, a voice, a region, a space that ignites an associative pleasure that is insatiable:

> To the braided polyphone which is coiled up in every voice, to a vocal *difference* rebellious to any *opposition* and which is not derived from anything else: it belongs to no one, it carries spacing and does not let any space be assigned to it. As organ or signifying power, it cannot remain at the disposal of either a person or a self, either a consciousness or an unconscious, either one of the two sexes. Even bisexuality is insufficient for it. Nor does it "express" a community, if we mean by that a totality of subjects, a "we," a collection of *egos*, men or women ("we men," "we women"). This writing of voice represents nothing, it is not

---

[17] Derrida, *Politics of Friendship*, 64.

the representative of a "drive," a "word," or a "thing." This voice lets itself be heard, and it speaks otherwise, watching out for all these violent assignations, of which there are always more to come.[18]

Strangers to an X specter that cannot be touched or named, the Sodomites grasp the other between spaces, through a proximity that makes all proximities possible. They open up the transit of passion and the transitivity for every thread of love. This impetus to love the unknown, to love what is not yet, what is yet to come (this transitivity toward the sensible) exists in all the books of the world, in every language, as the figure of an unavowable stranger in passing, as the specter that one would like to touch and grasp, as the dreamlike texture that no text can fully describe but every text will attempt to write about, as the murmur that promises the proximity to an ecstatic secret that arrives through a disappearing trace. The mark of the Sodomites, their extreme passion buried in a lost desert, is an "archi-originary" trace:

> [A]rchi-originary, the most anarchic and anarchivable place possible, not the island, nor the Promised Land, but a certain desert, that which makes possible, opens, hollows or infinitizes the other. Ecstasy or existence of the most extreme abstraction. That which would orient "in" the desert, without

---

[18] Derrida, "Voice II," 162.

> pathway and without interior, the possibility
> of a *religio*, of a *relegere*, and of a *religare*.[19]

What is the name of that evanescent love that seems to take place only one time every time?

> How can one adjust a name to what could take place only once, perhaps, for the first and last time? How can one name an event? For this love that would take place only once would be the only possible event: as an impossible event. Even if the right name for this unique love were to be found, how would one convince everyone else of its appropriateness?[20]

The coming/sending of the other in Sodom consists in an arrival that fails to arrive, a sending that is grasped through its deferral. It is a mandate that arrives by not arriving because the strangers remain unknown (to the Sodomites) as they deliver a message of catastrophe, disappearance, and oblivion. The Sodomites are driven toward figures that are other than human, specters that come as erasure and are sent to erase. The Sodomites desire to know/touch/penetrate this nonknowledge, this foreign exteriority that erases, that arrives by erasing. Their desire is caught in a threshold of touch that is twofold: the physical threshold of Lot's door (which defers the instant of erasure through an infinite proximity) and the

---

[19] Derrida, "Faith and Knowledge," in *Acts of Religion*, ed. Gil Anidjar (New York: Routledge, 2002), 55.
[20] Derrida, *Politics of Friendship*, 66.

threshold of their own senses (a sense other than the sense of touch that multiplies in the limit of the senses in order to reach for a spectral living presence). The Sodomites aim,

> toward something other than itself, which is
> not to say that this desire has an "object" in
> the normal sense of the term: it goes toward
> what cannot feature as an object. One could
> say that this drive goes toward greater being
> or greater sense, toward the increase that it
> truly "is" itself.[21]

The Sodomites grasp an immemorial archi-desire, a surplus known through its deferral and erasure, a secret guarded and kept in a knot, in a knot that is religiously knotted. The secret of the impassioned Sodomites is accessible through its very inaccessibility, through what is anticipated and, at the same time, through what remains after catastrophe and erasure. The knot is associated with a "not," a "do not pass," a usurpation of the orgiastic secret of Sodom that welcomes a "contamination" that existed before God and without God, a "virus" that multiplies the anticipation of an abysmal desire to approach a foreign exteriority, a spastic interval. There is an unspeakable word, a surplus grasped in the burning hands of the Sodomites.

The testimony that emerges from ashes cannot be testified and may not be obliterated. The passion of Sodom, the infinite agitation of the surplus that escapes the senses but

---

[21] Nancy, *Adoration: The Deconstruction of Christianity II*, trans. John McKeane, ed. John D. Caputo (New York: Fordham University Press, 2013), 62.

entices them to unfold, lives through the secret contortions of a repetitive rhythm. Sodom leaves an insatiable mark, an immemorial memory of passionate torsions and contortions from which a voracious writing will continue to emerge among lovers, religious people, and atheist thinkers. The community of lovers responds to an impossible exigency, an alterity that is in the origin of every language. They are exposed, "to death's dispersal. A death, by definition, without glory, without consolation, without recourse, which no other disappearance can equal, except perhaps for that disappearance that inscribes itself in writing..."[22]

To hear or sense the rhythm of this fragile and uncanny affection implies to revive its mandate through the pulse of writing. What comes from the other is an exteriority that watches, calls, approaches, provokes, distances, and entices from within an interiority with multiple edges and borders, none of which exhausts the desire to embrace an errant specter.[23] But the question always remains: who or what is that exteriority? Is it outside? Is it inside? Is it me? Is it (a) God?

The advent of Judeo-Christian-Muslim scriptures would play against the background of this overflowing and "contaminated" limit. The desire for what or who is absolutely other is impossible to cancel or govern through multiplying decrees. The conductivity of the coming of the

---

[22] Maurice Blanchot, *The Unavowable Community*, trans. Pierre Joris (New York: Station Hill Press, 1988), 46.

[23] "It is all that suffices to provoke the *mysterium tremendum*, inscribing itself within the order of the gaze. God sees me, he looks into me in secret, but I don't see him, I don't see him looking at me..." Derrida, *Gift of Death*, 91.

other is impossible to repress by any concentration of political discourses, by any overdetermined and attentive religious or national force, and, in the best-case scenario, the coming of the other is impossible to reveal "as such" in a dogma, a concept, or a determinate desire:

> *The other* always responds, by definition, to the name of the figure of the *incalculable*. No brain, no neurological analysis, however exhaustive it's supposed to be, can render the encounter with the other. The coming of the other, *l'arrivance de l'arrivant*—the "arriving-ness" of the arrival—this is *what happens*, this is the one *who or which arrives* as an unforeseeable event.[24]

No sacrifice, genocide, or law could extinguish the remaining remains, the remaining ashes of the coming of the other in Sodom, a mark of a desire that is undefeatable. The excess exercised by the Sodomites and exorcised infinitely by a multiplicity of sorts remains intact and always comes back through the very decrees and religions that contain, forbid, repress, and dissimulate the desire that is in excess of every touch. To articulate this rupture is the rapture of every religion, its anticipated wish, which comes, in passing, too soon or too late through a certain diction and contradiction, through a certain benediction (stolen from a contaminated curse in course). That errant excess summons sources and sorceresses to dominate and denominate what remains to be grasped, what remains without denomination through nominations,

---

[24] Derrida and Roudinesco, "Unforeseeable Freedom," 50.

denominations, and abominations. With names or without a name, this incommensurable desire announces an event of what is yet to be known and, in that sense, reformulates a persistent question associated with an "exteriority" with the recurring advent of who or a what. This question, this desire for the unknown (or desire for the question) is a call "to know" (to penetrate) the unformed. The destruction of Sodom is about the trace of this indestructible passion for the unknown, about a passion that exceeds passion, and about the survivance of the "name" of this excess:

> Some trace remains right in this corpus, becomes this corpus as *sur-vivance* of apophasis (more than life and more than death), survivance of an internal onto-logico-semantic auto-destruction: there will have been absolute rarefaction, the desert will have taken place, nothing will have taken place but this place. Certainly, the "unknowable God," the ignored or unrecognized God that we spoke about says nothing: of him there is nothing said that might hold ...[25]

Is there something even more powerful than God in the godless town of Sodom? "What if 'God' were only the name of an exorbitant excess, of an infinite relation to infinity?"[26] If such a strange place existed, could it be possible to erase

---

[25] Derrida, *On the Name*, ed. Tomas Dutoit, trans. D. Wood et al. (Stanford: Stanford University Press, 1995), 55.

[26] Nancy, *Adoration*, 20. (Quote slightly modified.)

the town from the memory of people, or would it come back to haunt all the names of God, all gods, and each belief? Is there something in the story that remains untold but keeps coming back, even after the destruction and the millennial defamation of Sodom and Gomorrah? When trying to surpass the threshold, the Sodomites are instantly blinded. They reach their hands ecstatically, with adoration and supplication, attempting to palpate something or someone absolutely foreign, a texture, region, or adventure that disorganizes their senses. Could this rare passion disappear in the ashes of their holocaust? Would their disappearance have the mark of enamored ashes floating in a forgotten desert?

"What are 'enamored ashes'?" The cinders of Sodom part from a forbidden tomb, a cenotaph without memory, a passion ignited by its consuming destruction. Who has not experienced secretly the gift of Sodom, its enamored ashes, a trace for a desire that lacks everything and is in excess of every expectation? "There are cinders" in Sodom, traces of enamored ashes that transmit the experience of incineration, which is experience itself: "I am cinder that darkens in the flame/ nothing that remains to consume the fire/that in amorous conflagration is dispersed," that "will be cinder, but will remain sentient/ will be dust but amorous dust."[27] What remains (as enamored ashes) is a nonthing, a space that gives itself to be bound to the other, to whomever and whatever is coming. The Sodomites speak their ecstatic secret from the grounds of their abysmal silence, from the very whisper of enamored ashes:

---

[27] Poem by Francisco de Quevedo cited by Derrida, in *Cinders*, trans., ed., and int. Ned Lukacher (Nebraska: University of Nebraska Press, 1987), 75.

Cinders is an absolute non-memory, so to speak. Thus, it communicates with that which is the gift, for example, does not even seek to get recognized or kept, does not even seek to be saved. Well, to say that there are cinders there, that there is some cinder there, is to say that in every trace, in every writing, and consequently in every experience (for me every experience is, in a certain way, an experience of trace and writing), in every experience there is this incineration, this experience of incineration which is experience itself.[28]

The surplus of Sodom remains as a binding and bonding conduct, a conductivity that is without memory, presence, and truth. Through the impasse of the threshold, the multiplicative limit drawn by their hands touch an "exteriority" constitutive of every interiority in the limit of grasp. If one speculates that the Sodomites were an orgiastic town with contaminated and forbidden desires, then what was the excess that they were capable to experience? What sense did they have that surpassed all their senses? What did the Sodomites perceive in the limit (of their senses)? What kind of communication, sending, or mandate exceeded their genders or, for that matter, any genre or classification? What kind of surplus surpassed their impressions?:

---

[28] Derrida, "There is No *One* Narcissism," in *Points … Interviews, 1974–1994*, ed. Elisabeth Weber, trans. Peggy Kamuf et al. (Stanford: Stanford University Press, 1995), 209.

The very experience of this limit is a bliss greater than my bliss, it exceeds both myself and my sex, it is sublime, but without sublimation. If there is a sublime, it would be there where there might be no more sublimation, *n'est-ce pas*. And in order to be sublime, sexual difference must no longer be subject to dialectics.[29]

Everything was extinguished in Sodom but what is left after fire: cinders, enamored ashes. What remains without residue is a space/hiatus that sends, transfers, binds, anticipates, and supplements. What remains is a region of absolute contingency where passions come into play again, where a sense other than sense recurs, infecting the sense of limit, the sense that separates interiority from exteriority,

which amounts to annulling the ethical qualification and to thinking of writing beyond good and evil; yes above all, in as much as we designate the impossibility of formulating the movement of supplementarity [of the surplus] within the classical logos, within the logic of identity, within ontology, within the opposition of presence and absence, positive and negative, and even within dialectics ...[30]

---

[29] Derrida, "Voice II," 164.

[30] Derrida, *Of Grammatology*, 314. (My parenthetical emphasis.)

If there is a narrative that would describe what happened in Sodom, it would be a writing that deconstructs itself aiming through its consumption, toward the consummation of a pure event, an event that would take place through its disappearance. The contours of Sodom's story exceed programmed and programmatic languages, traverse all genres, and surpasses all religions. It is a story of an exteriority that is always already interior to the senses, a border that multiplies and that cannot be accommodated in any specific genre, gender, passion, sexual desire, or religious enthusiasm. The story of Sodom is a fable between fictions because its contours can never be described as a thing "as such," as a reality, or as a legitimate truth; however, what unfolds through its open contours (the drawing and withdrawing surplus in Sodom) may be understood as the most real of all realities. The most real of all realities takes place when the grasp of the Sodomites reaches a multiplying limit a hiatus that exceeds words and disjoins them, leaving a murmur that remains oscillating between fable, abstraction, and dream:

> The trait (the trait of the face, the line or the limit) that then runs the risk of being effaced in the sand would perhaps also be the one that separates an end from itself, thereby multiplying it endlessly and making it, once again, into a limit: the self-relation of a limit at once erases and multiplies the limit; it cannot but divide it in inventing it. The limit only comes to be effaced—it only comes to efface itself—as soon as it is inscribed.[31]

---

[31] Derrida, *Resistances*, 110.

The people of Sodom are impassioned by an ecstatic "yes," an archaic "yes" before religion, before categorical imperatives, before regulative laws, and before "shall nots." A mute, positive, and sublime "perhaps" opens the desire to grasp the incommensurable and indeterminate other, a passion for something or someone, a capacity to love anybody that is any other and anybody. The Sodomites' love for specters is unsacrificeable, finite, and mortal.[32] All forms of expression are at play for this desire that overflows every and any knowledge. A spastic space in passing flows through the threshold, a recurring opening that opens, an inexpressible and inextinguishable hiatus that releases the difference between inside and outside without being either. The external thing that they want to grasp and penetrate is within reach and out of reach, right "there" and right "here," enticing their sense of touch. The threshold binds the world of meaning and sense with nonmeaning and nontruth (with the anticipation for touching and seeing the "yet to come" and the "perhaps").

The relentless and infallible desire that comes from the other is impossible without the threshold, without the space of "no pass," which also calls, invites, entices toward a restless "yes," "yes come," "yes come closer and take a leap ... of faith," "yes, if only ..." This space of "no pass" is not a prohibition, but it marks the pace/space without step, the rhythm toward a continuous anticipation for the evanescent and consuming

---

[32] "The purported love for the immortal (the passion for 'my God' as the one I love above all) is reinscribed as a love for the mortal. As Derrida writes, 'you stand in for anybody, my god.'" Martin Hägglund, *Radical Atheism, Derrida and the Time of Life*, ed. Werner Hamacher (Stanford: Stanford University Press, 2008), 147.

figure of the coming of the other. The charged threshold, its space without steps remains virginal, impossible to penetrate, a space of difference, indifference, differentiation, and deferral. This spectral space is where the promise of the grasp for the future (a desire that is in excess of any desire) opens the possibility and impossibility of its iteration. If there is an event in Sodom, it is not its destruction but the arrival of the other in passing, the arrival that fails to arrive, the arrival that succeeds in not arriving. The destruction of Sodom erases what had already arrived, what arrives only to erase itself. The destruction of Sodom not only does not destroy the indestructible but gives movement to its eternal return.

The threshold of Lot's door is a limit in which a surplus of desire gathers, disperses, and surpasses. It is a limit that calls and commands one to advance while making the entrance impossible, to advance beyond steps and without any possibility of stopping. The limit is passage and pathway, a double invitation to trespass and not to pass. Sodom is the limit and the promise, the door and the pathway toward an exorbitant alterity that translates (into a multiplicity of desires) but remains without translation, without arrival, without steps, and without archive. The tale of Sodom is about the experience of a "heterogeneity without accomplishment."[33] Sodom is madness. It is the madness of

---

[33] "Is there not a messianic extremity, an *eskhaton* whose ultimate event (immediate rupture, unheard-of interruption, untimeliness of the infinite surprise, heterogeneity without accomplishment) can exceed, *at each moment*, the final term of a *phusis*, such as work, the production, and the *telos* of history? The question is indeed 'whither?' Not only whence comes the ghost but first of all is it going to come back? Is it not already beginning to arrive and where is it going? What of the future? The future can only be for ghosts. And the past."

an unfulfilled desire that remains unfulfilled. The desire to found any law, to iterate and grasp its opening will be other than the evanescent hiatus from which it departs because, "the foundation of law—law of the law, institution of the institution, origin of the constitution—is a 'performative' event that cannot belong to the set that it founds, inaugurates or justifies."[34]

The threshold cannot be ruined; it is unsacrificeable, and its disproportional pace where no steps are possible dance eternally and silently in the remains of the remains of Sodom, in its embers and ashes, in an anonymous desert without name, without country, without presence, and in its disappearing trace: "The trace is produced as its own erasure. And it belongs to the trace to erase itself, to elude that which might maintain it in presence. The trace is neither perceptible nor imperceptible."[35] The threshold of Sodom touches the limit of thought and multiplies it. There is no distance in this faraway-ness and proximity but just a hiatus that never ceases to occur, a syncopeic texture that although untouchable makes possible the anticipation of every touch. The ecstasy of the Sodomites is a reaction to a form of absolute inhospitality and uninhabitability. "A true messianic in general, if there is one, would have the form of absolute inhospitality, of uninhabitability."[36] If there is sexual desire

Derrida, *Specters of Marx: The State of Debt, the Work of Mourning, and the New International*, trans. Peggy Kamuf (New York: Routledge, 1994), 37.

[34] Ibid., 57.

[35] Derrida, "*Ousia* and *Grammē*," in *Margins of Philosophy*, trans. Alan Bass (Chicago: University of Chicago Press, 1982), 65.

[36] John D. Caputo, *The Prayers and Tears of Derrida, Religion without Religion* (Bloomington: Indiana University Press, 1997), 142.

at the threshold, it is one that is always in excess of itself, in excess of all desires and passions. Sodom does not engender or give birth but eternally salutes to a blend of voices, to a multiplicity of desires that flow toward an exteriority without contours. As Sodom vanishes, it salutes the departure of multiplicative desiring voices that leave their unsacrificeable mark in immemorial ashes:

> I would like to believe in the multiplicity of sexually marked voices. I would like to believe in the masses, this indeterminable number of blended voices, this mobile of non-identified sexual marks whose choreography can carry, divide, multiply the body of each "individual," whether he be classified as "man" or "woman" according to the criteria of usage.[37]

In their spasmodic salute-farewell, the Sodomites exceed all cultures, all religions, all languages, and all communities, including the concept of what is human in humanity. This spasm, this trait and retreat, this contamination is always born anew through an eternal expenditure of mute ecstasy, which is free from every sovereignty, from every rule of faith, from every power and state.[38] This spasm is relaunched in

---

[37] Derrida, "Voice II," 156.

[38] "This is the classic Hegelian moment of absolute freedom (and terror) when everything, every rule of faith, every power of law and the state, is swept away and suddenly everything is free of every constraint, free of every sovereignty but that of freedom itself ..." Gerald L. Bruns, *Blanchot: The Refusal of Philosophy* (Baltimore: The Johns Hopkins University Press, 2005), 41.

any desert region; it speaks of an experience that grasps the impossible. Without saying anything, this contaminated spasm makes one speak of unfulfilled messianisms, of a desire that desires what or who has to be yet invented:

> One should not simply consider contamination as a threat, however ... Possible contamination must be assumed because it is also opening or chance, our chance. Without contamination we would have no opening or chance. Contamination is not only to be assumed or affirmed: it is the very possibility of affirmation in the first place ... Threat is chance, chance is threat—this law is absolutely undeniable and irreducible.[39]

Sodom's threshold, its blinded grasp, and its enamored ashes constitute the idiom that opens the future of religion and maintains its vibrancy through a consuming and disappearing trace that in turn dissociates from religion or any form of social bound that attempts to program, unify, or usurp the multiplicative excess of their grasp. The trace of Sodom withdraws from all the names of religion, including those that religion assigns to it through multiple visions, revisions, reversions, inversions, and perversions. Their consuming, contaminated, and degenerating desire is always at work in every law and in the core of religious belief. "The

---

[39] Derrida, "Nietzsche and the Machine," in *Negotiations, Interventions and Interviews 1971–2001*, ed. and trans. Elizabeth Rottenberg (Stanford: Stanford University Press, 2002), 248.

orgiastic mystery recurs indefinitely, it is always at work: not only in Platonism, but also in Christianity and even in the space of secularization in general."[40] The foreign and uncanny exuberance of its trace (impossible to annihilate and never completely grasped) flows into every language, and it translates into multiple discourses of freedom, into a desire for revolution, democracy, and justice. The orgiastic impetus goes on in spite of (or because of) multiple conversions, prohibitions, persecutions, repressions, and exterminations:

> Although it is incorporated, disciplined, subjugated, and enslaved, the orgiastic is not annihilated. It continues to motivate subterraneously a mythology of responsible freedom that is at the same time a politics, indeed the still partly intact foundation of politics in the West; it continues to motivate such a freedom after the second turnaround or conversion that is Christianity.[41]

The secret kept by this fable, by this "fabulous" tale, is that the "literal" sacrifice and extermination of the Sodomites does not annul their orgiastic impetus, which is unsacrificeable.[42]

---

[40] Derrida, *Gift of Death*, 21.

[41] Derrida, *Gift of Death*, 19.

[42] "Historical conversions to responsibility, such as Patočka analyzes in both cases, well describe this movement by which the event of a second mystery does not destroy the first. On the contrary it keeps it inside unconsciously, after having effected a topical displacement and a hierarchical subordination: one secret is at the same time enclosed and dominated by the other. Platonic mystery thus *incorporates* orgiastic mystery and Christian *mystery* represses Platonic mystery.

The desire that is in excess of desire, the impetus that is erased from the story erases itself without sacrifice only to be reborn again anytime, for anybody, and in any epoch. The ruin of Sodom does not eradicate the excess that withdraws before any catastrophe, before any departure or arrival. The adoration of the Sodomites, their unconditional readiness to sense the foreign and embrace it, to pay heed to the strange, and to welcome what or who is coming happens everywhere and at any instant, with or without religion, with or without catastrophe. The adoration that hopes for or anticipates the coming of the other starts at the beginning of any letter, any strophe, or any grasp independently of any catastrophe and any knowledge.

Sodom's tale is about a contamination that comes from the "outside," a corruption that is even stronger than God or any "natural" laws established by Him. Their unconditional and mad wantonness is finite even though it measures against what or who is incalculable, and their contaminated passion is inscribed in the flow of life and hope.[43] Their anonymous passion without name is an excess that impassions and will be renamed ad infinitum; it will be the name grasped by no

---

That, in short, is the story that would need to be 'acknowledged,' as if confessed!" Ibid., 9–10.

[43] "'The incalculable is there, but we ought not exempt ourselves from counting—counting with it, though not on it—from measuring ourselves against time always our adversary…. There is no need to invoke our certain death. Finitude is inscribed in the very structure of life, in the fragile destiny of the planet as well as of all other beings (PR, 261).'" These ideas are cited by Derrida in Rogues where he alluded to a reading of Dominique Janicaude's book, *Powers of the Rational*. Derrida, *Rogues*, trans. Pascale-Anne Brault and Michael Naas (Stanford: Stanford University Press, 2005), 117.

name and all names; it will be the anticipation of an excess that is always in excess of itself. Their passion in the threshold is the limitless limit of a pleasure suspended, the place of interruption and deferral inscribed in any anticipation, an interruption that interrupts in order to give more pleasure, in order to multiply the limit, in order to transfer and release more desire, in order to release an anticipation that anticipates. At the threshold of Lot's door there is an interruption that mesmerizes, a multiplying limit that traces an interval of passion, a trace that puts in trance because it is in excess of reality, any fiction, diction, and contradiction. The trance for the trace, the trance for the gaping grasp of the living presence is impossible to erase or cut because it corresponds with a new interruption, a new "destruction" that transfers the surplus to a missing name: "In this mediation on writing, one must constantly try to make the absolute destruction reappear, which does not necessarily mean to save it or resuscitate it. The name is *necessary* [*Il* faut *le nom*], love consists perhaps in *over-naming* [surnommer; also nicknaming]."[44]

---

[44] Derrida, "Passages—from Traumatism to Promise," in *Points … Interviews, 1974–1994,* ed. Elisabeth Weber, trans. Peggy Kamuf et al. (Stanford: Stanford University Press, 1995), 390.

II

The Antechamber of Religion

Sodom, the other Sodom, the usurped Sodom, remains as the immemorial archive of an unlocalizable and unanalyzable spastic space, an interval with an ineludible rhythm, a syncopeic passion that multiplies the impetus to name a blinding and burning invitation. The syncopeic rhythm of this unlocalizable ubiquity will be the antechamber of every religion to come; that is, the antechamber that is insistently entangled with the temple and, at the same time, the antechamber that resists being part of the temple and remains unanalyzable within the confines of religion (of the temple). The anonymous and unlocalized ruins of Sodom, its suffocated voices and blinded eyes provoke a space, an outside of the world, a trace calling for an ecstatic writing, an infinite writing driven by desiring hands longing to grasp an unanalyzable presence that is both far and close and without distance. The remains of this unanalyzable exteriority departs from the threshold of the senses, from the sense that senses a what or a who that is exterior but internal to the senses. The burning hands of the Sodomites touch an indeterminate denomination. They draw the trace of what remains in the remains of an analogy without analogy. The passionate hands of religion will write and rewrite about these remnants that will never belong to any religion but will form its multiplying limits and decrees.

The ecstasy in Sodom is deadly because it tolerates no analogy. The irruption of the other brings the Sodomites into an orgy of rapture and rupture impossible to contain and impossible to eliminate. Rapture and rupture, rapture and interruption, a multiplying retreat of desiring marks; supplicating hands at the limit of a mute ecstasy. God desires that the desire of the Sodomites, a yearning created by God, be eliminated because it is through human desire that individuals tend to sin. At the same time, it is through desire (a desire "to know") that humans "become as gods." Like Eve, the Sodomites sin because they desire "to know," to "penetrate" what will make them "as gods" and will "open their eyes." [45] Knowledge and desire dovetail in Eden's garden. Eve desires not only to know something that she does not know

---

[45] "And the serpent said unto the woman, Ye shall not surely die: For God doth know that in the day ye eat thereof, then your eyes shall be opened, and *ye shall be as gods,* [my emphasis], knowing good and evil. An when the woman saw that the tree was good for food, and that it was pleasant to the eyes, and *a tree to be desired to make one wise,* [my emphasis] she took of the fruit thereof, and did eat, and gave also unto her husband with her; and he did eat. And *the eyes of them both were opened* …" Holy Bible, King James Version (New York: Camex International, 1989), Genesis 3:4–7. (The highlighted words are my emphasis.)

but also something that her desires do not know how to desire because it (the tree of knowledge) was never desired before. She hears an ancient murmur even more powerful than the voice of God. Eve's sin is to desire something that surpasses the desire for what is known. She desires what she does not know, and her wantonness surpasses not only the desire that God reserves for her in paradise but also her fear of God. Eve's desire for what she does not know makes her "as a god," even before tasting the forbidden apple. Without a desire "to know" and "penetrate" (the unfamiliar, the strange, the otherly, and the forbidden), there is no knowledge in the first place and no desire for God. It is as if, since creation, God wanted to usurp the most secret and ecstatic desire from humans. He had desired that humans (in whom God put desire) would not know the name of a desire that surpasses desire, a desire that shall make them "as gods." When God realized that the desire that He put in the flesh of humankind surpassed the desire that He had reserved for them, He sought to punish on many occasions those sinful people, unless this "surpassing" was associated with the desire to obey His wishes.

From Eve to Sodom and Gomorrah, to Noah, the sin of humankind is to desire, and it is a desire that generates sin. God repents having created humankind.[46] Sin and

---

[46] "And God saw that the wickedness of man was great in the earth, and that every imagination of the thoughts of his heart was only evil continually. And it repented the Lord that he had made man on the earth, and it grieved him at his heart. And the Lord said, I will destroy man whom I have created from the face of the earth; both man, and beast, and the creeping thing, and the fowls of the air; for it repenteth me that I have made them. But Noah found grace in the eyes of the Lord ... And God Looked upon the earth, and, behold, it was corrupt; *for all flesh had corrupted* [my emphasis] his way upon the earth. And

guilt form the economy of religion, which is incarnated in the attentive and omniscient gaze of God, the guardian of the flesh, the custodian of desires, of those yearnings that surpass desire, when humans might feel like gods. The desire to destroy the Sodomites for their "contaminated" desires is but the preamble of the flood. But does not God Himself surpass His own desire to destroy desire in the world when He produces the great flood and kills everyone on the face of the earth except for Noah and his family? For this excess, God Himself recognizes His sin and promises not to ever repeat such a catastrophe.[47] Desire is flesh, but it is also imagination in humankind's heart. Desire and imagination surpass God's plan for humankind. Imagination surpasses desire in the impetus to know (to "penetrate") a spectral flesh that exceeds all names and desires. This is the ecstatic mystery, the orgiastic impetus that flows in Genesis, that is older than Genesis, and that makes humankind, in the best-case scenario, "like a god" and, in the worst scenario, speak in the name of God against a surplus that only He authorizes Himself to dispose of.

The desire to penetrate the impenetrable is also an impenetrable desire. Without Sodom, without this impasse of touch, there would be no biblical Genesis, no generic force, and no orgiastic/messianic trace/anticipation. In this space of inhabitable revelation, of intractable traction and

---

God said unto Noah, *the end of all flesh* [my emphasis] is come before me, for the earth is filled with violence through them; and behold, I will destroy them with the earth" (King James, Genesis 6:5–8, 12).

[47] "And the Lord said in his heart, I will not again curse the ground any more for man's sake; for the imagination of man's heart is evil from his youth: neither will I again smite any more every thing living, as I have done" (King James, Genesis, 8:21).

contraction, and of resistance, an interval takes place always anew and always for the first time. As the symptom of every religion, Sodom would be its foundation, the Law of laws that remains quiet and inaccessible and that founds by collapsing because it can only take place once (but always and each time for the first time). The evanescent limit blocks the path that it opens. From the interior closure of the Law of laws, the law of oppositions (of "do nots" and "shall nots") will display and produce itself as a coherent truth, in the moment when truth, as an exorbitant value and an incalculable contradiction, is shattered.

The Sodomites see an extension, an exteriority that remains out of sight and out of touch, anticipating a climax that arrives by not arriving, in the form of anticipating anticipation. It is what does not happen and is suspended that ignites their orgiastic and compulsive obsession. They welcome an event that takes place without taking place as they obsess with the drive to touch and penetrate. The orgiastic mystery (the coming of an exterior and foreign specter and the surpassing desire that this arrival/sending provokes) exposes the Sodomites to the immediacy of an ineluctable perception that remains touchable only through what remains untouchable and, for the same reason, excessively desirable and ineludible. These spectral beings (separated from the Sodomites by a space/spacing/threshold) open everybody's senses and everybody's sense of perception for an indeterminate exteriority that is singular and wholly other. The threshold of Sodom is a space of interruption that produces a desire for contact and proximity, an intuition that remains between the senses, in the indivisible grasp between sense and imagination, in the difference (deferral) between impressions and thinking: "The spaced-out multiplicity of the senses, and of the senses of sense, and of the sense of the senses—the condition, of creation as well as of the event—is also ... what sanctions the just madness of thinking or language ..."[48]

The Sodomites are receptive; they respond to the arrival of what or who they anticipate but remain suspended in a multiplying outline between the sensible and the intelligible. This limit that they touch in the threshold, this limit that withdraws (multiplies, divides, defers, transgresses) to the touch of touch, is in the beginning (in the book of Genesis) because it is an opening of a shore that overflows, that does not heal, that leaves the scar of an incalculable anticipation, a missing name (the name of God, perhaps?), a name that remains untouched, fresh, and original:

> So the threshold is always a beginning, the beginning of the inside or the beginning of the outside ... "What is the threshold?" is to ask oneself "How to begin?" How to begin again? A question of commencement and commandment, an archaic question of the *arkhē* that means, I recall once again, both commencement and commandments, principle and prince, the One of the first.[49]

This narrative catapults a passionate impetus to "penetrate" an interval that interrupts penetration. It is a

---

[48] Derrida, *On Touching–Jean-Luc Nancy*, trans. Christine Irizarry (Stanford: Stanford University Press, 2005), 57.

[49] Derrida, *Beast Volume I*, 312.

narrative of the "in-between," of a hiatus between forms that remain untouched. This tale opens the space of every narrative to come, the threshold between grasping and sensing, dreaming and imagining, thinking and knowing. It is a tale that multiplies tales through the attempt to capture an "outside" of the tale, an exterior hiatus, a formless figure, a delirious writing that anticipates a desire that cannot coincide with any desire:

> The work must become a project aimed toward an unreachable goal, and its partial success takes on the form of "a renunciation at the very moment when it comes into being." The work is a hyperbole in the Mallarméan sense, demanding that the subject forget itself in a projective act that can never coincide with its own desire.[50]

The recurring theme in the story of Sodom is the coming of the other as an exteriority that does not succeed in arriving, an alterity that arrives by failing to arrive, that is transferred through a threshold (of sense) where an internal multiplicity cannot be stopped by any limit, where interruption is what sets in motion an alterity that can never be cut because it is not divisible, visible, or touchable. The coming of the other in passing orients the Sodomites to their disorientation, to the distortion of their senses as they experience the opening of an altering alterity, a contingency without reference. Sodom is none other than a scene of the arrival (in passing) of an orgiastic

---

[50] Paul de Man, *Blindness and Insight* (Minneapolis: University of Minnesota Press, 1983), 43.

impetus, of an alterity incorporated (usurped) by the confines of religion where it remains unsought and unthought. It is the scene of the limits of religion in the threshold of reason and desire. The coming of the other not only unleashes the senses of the Sodomites but also gives them access to an indivisible potency, an immediacy that transports and multiplies establishing a sense of joy, disjunction, and disorientation. The "arrivants" transport at least two messages. On the one hand, the newcomers carry the promise of a singular and unique unreality, the advent of an incalculable "perhaps." At the same time, they are messengers of catastrophe and destruction. The name of the alterity that arrives is without reference, and its name is grasped through interruption (threshold, blindness, burning, etc.) and deferral (the repetition of an alterity that remains, that cannot be cut by any limit or decree). Transported by the alterity of the strangers, affected by an "exterior" alterity, the Sodomites tremble for an anticipation that puts them on the way of a promising presence that is subtracted from them. The arrivants silently pass through Sodom, and their steps are not easily discernible, for they enter the city both as doves and wolves:

> Now, where were we just now? Not like a dove, we were saying and above all not on dove's feet, but "stealthy like a wolf," on wolf's feet. Which means ... silently, discreetly, and unobtrusively ... But the one announces war, the war chief, the sovereign who orders wars, the other silently orders peace ... These two figures *pre*occupy our space.[51]

---

[51] Derrida, *Beast Volume I*, 23.

Hands touch the threshold that alters their perception of touch. Like a magnetic field, the exterior threshold (Lot's door) affects the internal threshold of their senses and invites the Sodomites to pass without passing, to transcend by not transcending, to get closer through an interval that cannot be surpassed, and to touch what is in between life and the multiplying limit of death. To touch the threshold (of the senses) is to pass and trespass as the senses multiply and divide in order to reach a borderline contour, an ultimate sense, a sense other than sense. This touch in the threshold of sense is a self-affection: the opening of an ("exterior") alterity within oneself. The touch of the threshold is the mark of a scar of the senses, of a passion that aims where it seems impossible to go, a mark that marks a rupture that precipitates into a rapturing leap. Touching the threshold marks the perception of an immemorial trace:

> Going where it is possible to go would not be a displacement or a decision, it would be the irresponsible unfolding of a program. The sole decision possible passes through the madness of the undecidable and the impossible: to go where it is impossible to go ... It is this normative denunciation on the ground of impossibility, this sweet rage against language, it is this passion that leaves the mark of a scar in that place where the impossible takes place ...[52]

---

[52] Derrida, *On the Name*, 59–60.

Touching what is touched in what remains untouchable unfolds a metonymic region, a space, a movement, a "spacing" where adoration for the place that occupies the other multiplies affectations and affections. The threshold of alterity is the interval that opens the senses to a "yes." The "yes" is the desire that traces a what or who that is always altered and altering. The living presence is unthinkable without a sense of a trace whose externality is internal to the senses:

> The self of the living present is originarily a trace. It is necessary to think originary-being from the trace and not the trace from originary-being. This archi-writing is at work in the origin of sense ... Since the trace is the relation of intimacy of the living present to its outside, the openness to exteriority in general, to the non-proper, etc., *the temporalization of sense is from the very beginning "spacing."*[53]

This trespassing, this opening of the senses through an interval and toward the adoration of a space that multiplies the place of the other, does not take place through the opening of a door but, paradoxically, by not taking place, by an interruption that defers desire to a new degree of pleasure, to a pleasure extended, to an extension of pleasure, to other interruptions that in turn transfer new landscapes of impressions, and new spaces of expanding and contracting perceptions. This nonpassing that trespasses, this step in

---

[53] Derrida, *Voice and Phenomenon*, 73.

excess that never becomes one, is suspended in a nonpass of multiple intervals, in a door that does not open, or that opens in order to blind, in order to form intervals of touch and vision that touch what/who remains out of touch and out of sight. The Sodomites come before another border but the sense of an exterior nonobject continues to distort their inner senses.

This nonpassing step is the opening to a blind and blinding exteriority that infects, to a divisible and indivisible interiority that explores, to an anticipation that parts and departs toward a limit that multiplies intervals of sense. A blinding passion multiplies and divides, supplementing the supplement of an impetus that advances toward a figureless figure, a texture that impassions. These series of spatial suspensions (threshold, blindness, cremation, and ashes) suspend without stopping, suspend the object of passion only to advance to an arrival that arrives by not arriving. The hands that attempt to touch/write the exteriority that affects the senses are consumed in ruins, embers, ashes, and oblivion (remnants of what is not, what is no longer, what continues to burn but cannot be consumed and yet clings to the grasp of language, to an immaterial idiom that is not consummated by a name). The impasse that "takes place" in Sodom is through a desire suspended at the threshold of sense, a "beyond" that is sensed without trespassing, a beyond where a relationship with an unpresentable other opens up a space of unrest and movement, a space without analogy (without representation) in the midst of a consuming passion and a disrupting catastrophe. The interval that remains without representation and without analogy multiplies metonymically and supplements the name that cannot be consummated:

> I am truly in the beyond, if the beyond is that which admits of no beyond. This no-beyond that would be the beyond itself, *Thomas the Obscure* names it, in this place, the "supreme relationship"; this relationship "imparts to me the desire of a wonderful progress": "In this absolute repetition of the same is born true movement that cannot lead to rest."[54]

The spectral messengers are like an immutable exteriority. They are "themselves" the trace of another trace (the trace of God, which in turn is traced through indefinite traces). They are not moved by any attraction or emotion. Their impenetrability and indifference add up to the ecstatic impetus of the Sodomites. They are an unfigurable extension (of God), a sensible/insensible texture that can only multiply the Sodomites' imagination and their desire to touch what exceeds their knowledge:

> Can we imagine an extension that is untouchable? Imagining is neither thinking nor knowing, to be sure, but it is in no way a complete absence of thought or knowledge. Can one *figure* for oneself an untouchable extension, if you will? It is difficult, except … if an intelligible extension without a body is at issue, precisely there where the understanding passes imagination and

---

[54] Derrida, "Pace Not(s)," in *Parages*, ed. and trans. John P. Leavey (Stanford: Stanford University Press, 2011), 33.

sensibility; and except for some *insensible sensible* ...[55]

The angel/visitors are spectral figures, extensions of a desirable and inanimate God that watches without being watched, the prime mover who moves and touches but is moved by nothing and is touched by no one:

> Prime mover or pure Act, God sets in motion
> without Himself moving or being moved;
> He is the absolute desirable or desired,
> analogically and formally in the position of
> the beloved, therefore on the side of death,
> of that which can be inanimate without
> ceasing to be loved or desired (*apsúklon*).[56]

The trace of God is present through their extensions and analogs, the unassailable, inexorable, and exorbitant angels, whose proximity to the threshold moves and excites the Sodomites beyond the grasp of knowledge and toward the unthinkable (the immune, inanimate, and immutable foreigners). The Sodomites' incommensurable desire for the trace of God is on the side of mortality, finitude, and death. They do not know what they yearn for with a desire that surpasses every desire. And this desire to know what they cannot know and will never know ("as such") exists before the angels and before God, in the Sodomites' psyche (and before Sodom's tale), in their capacity to accept, receive, and welcome the stranger, the foreign, and the uncanny. The

---

[55] Derrida, *On Touching*, 16.
[56] Derrida, *Politics of Friendship*, 10.

desire of the Sodomites is mortal and finite in its infinitude. It precedes the angels and exceeds God. In that sense, the incommensurable and mortal love/desire/wantonness of the Sodomites is unsacrificeable. It lives beyond the history of any religion and with or without the names of God.

The Sodomites point toward a maddening divisibility that gathers an invisibility, a desire for an evanescent scent, a trace that promises consistently the silhouette of something inconsistent, something/someone that comes in the form of hope or trope, a promise or catastrophe. The Sodomites are drawn to this disorganizing order, to the "yes" of the "perhaps" that escapes their grasp, which touches on a space that defers from the sense of touch, smell, vision, presence, and truth. They want to grasp what addresses them and, at the same time, evades them; they want to "know" a space that escapes them, a hiatus that multiplies and divides through the evanescent trace of God:

> We are "in the Trace of God." A proposition which risks incompatibility with every allusion to the "very presence of God." A proposition readily converted into atheism: and if God was *an effect of the trace*? If the idea of divine presence (life, existence, parousia, etc.), if the name of God was but the movement of erasure of the trace in presence? Here is a question of knowing whether the trace permits us to think presence in its system, or whether the reverse order is the true one. It doubles the

true order. But it is indeed the *order of truth*
which is in question.[57]

One may speculate that the readers of these biblical
passages "smell" the inaudible, unintelligible, and odorless
scent of the remains of Sodom's passion, of their immemorial
ashes. Readers may "sniff" the trace of their surpassing
passion with a sense of smell that is other than smell, and
touch the trace of a formless form that escapes the sense of
touch. God had separated from the angels before they arrived
to Sodom (Genesis 18:20–33). One may speculate that the
Sodomites also sniff the trace of the Absolute Other, that the
sense of smell supplements the sense of touch and that all the
senses point to an outside that becomes traced for eternity
with a sense foreign to the senses. Buried in multiple layers of
sand, ashes, and rocks, the specters of Sodom exude eternally
an odorless scent that forms the trace of their surpassing
exuberance, an excess traced through a sense that is beyond
the impressions of the senses. The intoxicating scent of this
ecstatic trace is covered up by adding a thousand more veils,
multiplying thresholds, multiple degrees of passion translated
into decrees that mandate not to touch what remains out of
touch, not to touch the fragrance of the trace that intoxicates
beyond decrees and beyond the senses (the nose, the hand,
the eye, the ear, and the mouth). The Sodomites seek, they go
after a trace with a sense of smell that is other than smell. The
scent of a "what" or a "who" flows endlessly and relentlessly,
in passing, retreating itself, leaving an otherly scent, a trace
behind every sense of smell:

---

[57] Derrida, "Violence and Metaphysics," in *Writing and Difference,*
trans. Alan Bass (Chicago: University of Chicago Press, 1978), 108.

What is meant by "to follow," "more to follow," "to pursue," even "to persecute." What is it I am doing when I am (following)? When I am (following) *after* someone on something, after an animal that some hold to be something that is not necessarily someone? What does "to be after" mean? The steps to be consistently followed will indeed have to resemble those of an animal seeking to find or seeking to escape. Do they not resemble the running of an animal that, finding its way on the basis of a scent or a noise, goes back more than once over the same path to pick up the traces, either to sniff the trace of another or to cover its own by adding to it, precisely as though it were that of another, picking up the scent, therefore, of whatever on this track demonstrates to it that the trace is always that of another ...[58]

The Sodomites sniff an overabundant trace in retreat that no ecstatic turn; no conversion, inversion, or metaphor; no conversation, articulation, or trope; no substitution or law could keep completely safe, unscathed, and immune. In the suspended limit of sense, a silent threshold of desire traces in suspense and entrances the entrance to an otherly texture, an "external" scent, trace, interval. They are seeking a dream of dreams on the way to blindness and disaster. Trying to make sense with the other of sense, the Sodomites seek what

[58] Derrida, *The Animal That Therefore I Am*, ed. Marie-Louise Mallet, trans. D. Wills (New York: Fordham University Press, 2008), 54–55.

remains unassimilable to the language of presence and truth, as they cling to a grasp that traces without a determinable sense.

The godless Sodomites are drawn into an incalculable desire that comes from a trace that does not have a name or a definite form. They desire, with a desire beyond desire, a what or a who that they don't know and cannot understand. In this monumental moment of madness, freedom, and danger, the Sodomites are the most atheistic people, and, at the same time, they are on the brink of opening a space of adoration to a divinity. Their spasm precedes a relationship to God, to every god, and opens the space of divinity: "The sacred is the 'only essential space of divinity which in turn opens only a dimension for the gods and the god ...' This space (in which Heidegger also names Elevation) is within faith and atheism. Both presuppose it."[59] As the Sodomites become "contaminated" by their ecstatic impetus, as they walk mesmerized toward their impossible fulfillment, the symptom of every religion ignites its own repetition, a repetition that always starts with a forbidden space, a threshold, a sacrifice, and a certain degree of forgetfulness. Thus, through the Sodomites, the internal body of religion unfolds on the grounds that they remain "external" to the genesis of religion. They will never enter religion and will remain radically other, foreign, and strange to the genesis of religion. The circle of religion is set in motion through the desire to give hospitality to this exteriority, this "external" trace in passing that is more ancient than religion and God:

---

[59] Derrida, "Violence and Metaphysics," 145.

> This impossibility is *necessary*. It is necessary that this threshold not be at the disposal of a general knowledge or a regulated technique. It is necessary that it exceed every regulated procedure in order to open itself to what always risks being perverted (the Good, Justice, Love, Faith,—and perfectibility, etc.). This is necessary, this possible hospitality to the worst is necessary so that good hospitality can have a chance, the chance of letting the other come, the *yes* of the other no less than the *yes* to the other.[60]

The future of religion, politics, science, and even atheism revolves around an imperfect seeking of this trace that erases itself (without sacrifice and without violence), a mute trace that in spite of its withdrawal from nomination, domination, and denomination maintains itself and remains unsacrificeable in the worst and the best of all hospitalities.

In the unfolding of religious and political institutions, touching implies a complex system of laws that regulates the proximity (and hospitality) to the other:

> The law in fact commands to touch *without* touching it. A vow of abstinence. Not to touch the friend (for example, by abstaining from giving him a present or from presenting oneself to him, out of modesty), to not *touch him* enough is to be lacking in tact; however,

---

[60] Derrida, *Adieu to Emmanuel Levinas*, trans. Pascale-Anne Brault and Michael Naas (Stanford: Stanford University Press, 1999), 35.

to *touch him*, and to touch him too much, to
touch him to the quick, is also tactless.[61]

Proximity to what remains strange to possible names,
and proximity to what does not respond to familiar names
are (among others) the challenges of an unpredictable
hospitality that welcomes the alterity of the other. A
discourse of multiple limits and regulations attempts to
rule the "do not pass" through a multiplication of names
that govern the excess that is "external" to touch. Thus, the
genesis of religion, the religion that begins before religion,
sets in motion a circular path toward the excess of the
coming of other through a negative language, an economy
of limits, edges, polemics, controversies, and transgressions
(commands, commandments, and laws that name what is
and is not possible, what is and is not good, what is and is not
"contaminated," what is and is not—true—faith).

From an immemorial ecstasy that touches an interval
of touch, the circle of religion ignites its mad naming and
sentences, a pace marked by the rhythm of negative discourse
("thou shall not pass," "thou shall not desire this or that").
Repetition and opposition depart from a difference that
multiple desires, a tension that continually reactivates religion
through what it cannot govern, through what remains exterior/
external to religion. As religion commences and commands
its circle of sacrifice and prohibition, the unsacrificeable
and free interval of touch is also preserved but buried in a
desert empty of memory and history, in the perception of
a dormant psyche. A double erasure takes place in religion.
On the one hand, there is the interval that erases itself, the

---

[61] Derrida, *On Touching*, 75.

desire to touch the untouchable beyond any desire, and, at the same time, there is the genesis of religion, which usurps access to the threshold of touch. The possibility of repeating and renewing the future of religion in the Western world rests in this relation to and repression of the unsacrificeable, a calculation that will have many apocalyptic names, multiple deflecting metaphors at the gates, innumerable "shall nots," and tireless (metonymic) associations with the names of death that cannot destroy the unsacrificeable desire that comes from other: "For [the] calculating technique obviously destroys or neutralizes the incommensurable singularity to which it gives effective access."[62]

The beginning of religion marks its constant ring of interruption as destruction and renewal. The beginning of religion departs from this certain uncertainty, this irruption of disruption, the interruption that comes from an "outside" that is hastily called God, on the one hand, and "contamination" on the other. From within the grounds of death, sacrifice, concealment, and "forgetfulness," the religions to come will produce and sustain their own failure to calculate, ad infinitum, the proximity to a proximity that is without distance, the step toward a trace that withdraws from path. For example, one of the conversions of the orgiastic event in the Christian religion (a conversion that represses, covers up, and neutralizes) is (the figure of) death as an exorbitant gift-giving gift, a remainder without remains (ashes), an incalculability and incommensurability, a consumption and consummation not unlike the flow of desire and love: "The Christian themes can be seen to revolve around the gift as gift of death, the fathomless gift of a type of death, infinite love

---

[62] Derrida, *Rogues*, 53.

(the Good as goodness that infinitely forgets itself), sin and salvation, repentance and sacrifice."[63]

With their decrees (shall nots), commands, and performative rituals, religions usurp the surplus of an exteriority without remains and convert it to a dialectic theater of life and death (a ritualistic theater that masks and performs). The future religions of the West will answer the call for the incommensurable and unsacrificeable (the trace of an "external" surplus that is always already part of our internal senses) through a neutralization of an "exteriority" that alters and "contaminates." Through a circular discourse of catastrophe, punishment, and death, religion reignites a teleological passion that promises a new, clean beginning without "contamination." The path of prohibition, command, and forgetfulness interrupts/cancels/deflects the contamination that is already "there" before the arrival of any god. We (as readers of Sodom's tale) are all immersed in the invitation, temptation, and call of/for the contaminating surplus, in spite of, or because of, every indictment. The catastrophe happens before Sodom's catastrophe when a specter without remains and who does not remain returns (without being present). It returns as an exteriority that is already inside the senses, within the interval of the senses of touch and perception. The catastrophic surplus that surpasses every desire disturbs and transforms all the negative (prohibitive) laws since their inception, and, in some cases, it is the execution of the law (constituted in terms of presence, absence, or proximity) that causes the real catastrophes in history.

---

[63] Derrida, *Gift of Death*, 49.

The desire of the Sodomites will be usurped to commands, demands, and dogmas that interrupt the perception of a recurring, ineluctable, and indestructible question associated with a desire to welcome, grasp, and penetrate the remains without remains of an (exterior) interval/trace/surplus in passing. This impetus is what continues to nurture the spontaneity of religion and its automaticity. The tale of the destruction of Sodom points to a nameless expressivity and a recurring question. Destruction of what remains indestructible and without remains calls for a new order of presence, proximity, and touch; a new order of the sensible and the intelligible. The circle of religion (of what or who is "there," of how should one touch the other and be touched by the other) gains from destruction as it calls for a new order: "only order gains from its loss."[64]

In the multiple spaces unfolded through Sodom's tale, and in the trace of its ashes, a figureless figure, a nonobject survives the catastrophe and is immune to any catastrophe. What withdraws from sight, what arrives without arriving, is the real event that takes place in Sodom. Blinded, the Sodomites reach for a figureless figure from which all their impressions continued to unfold: "And they [the angel-messengers] smote the men that were at the door of the house with blindness, both small and great: so that they wearied themselves to find the door" (Genesis 19:9–11). Blinded, the Sodomites reach with an internal vision that expands to their hands as they walk forward to grasp what they immensely desire but cannot see or touch. Their attraction for the specters does not cease because of their visual blindness.

---

[64] Blanchot, *The Writing of the Disaster*, trans. Ann Smock (Nebraska: University of Nebraska Press, 1995), 90.

Rather, they reach (see) with their hands that which is nowhere to be seen. The horizon between the literal and the metaphorical mixes and blurs the content of the passage. The people of Sodom are pushing Lot's door; they are pressing the edge in order to touch, penetrate, and see the absolute other. But the "other" (the very texture that partakes in every event without forming part of it) does not make itself present. They push as they sense a mute and otherly dispersion, a conduct and conductivity that they hope to touch. The opening of the door is a blinding experience, an experience without experience, an opening that is deferred, an event that arrives because it fails to arrive, a penetration without penetration; in sum, a catastrophic "view." There in the limit of touch, grasp, writing, and view: "There one touches upon presence which is no longer present to itself -but is repetition and supplication of presence coming."[65]

The absence of vision does not interrupt their impetus; on the contrary, they are more impassioned by their unforeseeable, generous, and "deadly" passion. Blinded, they still hope to consume and be consumed by the call of the foreign specters that the Sodomites are trying to consummate with their seeking hands. If they cannot attest to their generous and exceeding passion with their eyes, if their ocular capacities are occluded in the very limit of their overflowing experience, they still have their burning hands to sense the generous trace of a spectral other. Blinded, the Sodomites continue to sense the impressions on their hands and reach forward with a gesture of anticipation guided by a blind impression. One may speculate that also the readers of this

---

[65] Nancy, "Elliptical Sense," in *Derrida: A Critical Reader*, ed. and trans. David Wood (Oxford: Blackwell Publishers, 1992), 42.

tale move forward with the Sodomites in the anticipation of touching a trace (interval, threshold) that can only be sensed through a multiplication of fictions, through the unfolding of spaces that long to touch an event that mixes the senses with the intellect, as well the inside with the outside. What comes, what arrives through a multiplying sense of touch is the possibility to see/sense/touch/anticipate an unforeseen event. Pushing forward, the Sodomites touch (without touching) another trace, interval, and sense of touch. In this instant that does not let itself be determined by any known knowledge, in this night of absolute blindness, terror, and joy, the Sodomites reach for an unforeseeable event that they don't see coming. As they advance, their gestures don't see death but infinite life, danger, and uncanniness. They reach toward an interval that is forbidden to see and forbidden to touch but that they adore with a desire that surpasses the senses, with a sense that is out of touch but makes every touch possible:

> I sense but I still do not know what touch, to touch him means—I know less and less. Of course, I cannot impart this—touching him—and make it known to him and share it, except by touching touch, and therefore by touching upon the question or the plea of touch, which themselves ought to touch *pertinently* on the theme, that is, on the *sense* of touch. How is one to touch, without touching, the *sense* of touch?[66]

---

[66] Derrida, *On Touching*, 135.

What remains is the impression of their desiring hands at the instant of grasping an unpossessable anticipation. The Sodomites reach for an excessive generosity that is continually interrupted in the scene. At the abysmal edge, their hands arrest the passing presence of a specter that does not make itself present, that is out of reach, and that is neither close nor far and out of sight. In this scene, they visualize without eyes; they visualize a visibility that comes from the gaze of the other that is interior to them.[67] Even as they are blinded, close to destruction, and without salvation, they are still hoping for what or who they cannot reach (they cannot *not* reach for them). The absence of salvation, the imminent disaster (the promise endangered, jeopardized, and threatened by disaster) is what draws the trance to the entrance, to the possible trace that comes from the otherly touch in passing:

> The nonsafe, the absence of salvation, the incurable disaster as such, puts us on the traces of, or traces for us, salvation, the sound, the safe, the unscathed, the immune. The immune gestures toward, by evoking, the safe, the sound, the sacred or the holy.

---

[67] "'Oh, I see the day, oh God...' I see light, glory, the element of visibility, the visibility of that which is visible, the phenomenality of the phenomenon; thus I see vision, both eyesight and what I can see, the stage [*scène*] and the possibility of representation [*scène*] the scene of visibility, a primal scene..." Derrida, "Living On," in *Parages*, ed. John P. Leavey, trans. James Hulbert (Stanford: Stanford University Press, 2011), 119.

This engages or binds the divine. The divine approaches the God.[68]

The proximity of what/who approaches without distance, the nearness of this conductivity, remains external to a vision that interiorizes it. An open hand senses (reaches and seeks for) an invisible gaze and salutes the mark of an uninhabitable exteriority. In this scene, the suspension of the senses does not suspend completely the desire for a relationship to the unnamed, the untouched, and the unseen. The suspension of the senses binds them to an experience that does make itself present and that is "out of the question":

> It's not just the unknown that could be known and that I give up trying to know. It is something in relation to which knowledge is out of the question … It is not a thing, some information that I am hiding or that one has to hide or dissimulate; it is rather an experience that does not make itself available to information, that resists information and knowledge, and that immediately encrypts itself.[69]

The suspension of the senses forms another sense through which the Sodomites (and the readers) trace without seeing and without touching the space of an encrypted region, a figureless figure that opens the grasp of thinking,

---

[68] Derrida, *Rogues*, 113. (Derrida's translation of Heidegger's thoughts written in *Poetry, Language, Thought*).

[69] Derrida, "There is No *One* Narcissism," 201.

the antechamber of an anticipatory and speculating desiring-thought. In their grasp for the unknown, the experience of the impossible makes the thought of the temple possible. At the same time, the antechamber cannot be grasped in the terms of the safe space that is the temple:

> What finds itself reduced to the condition
> of threshold is being itself, being as place.
> Only a threshold, but a sacred place, the
> antechamber of the temple: "When we
> grasp God in being, we apprehend him in his
> antechamber, for being is the antechamber
> in which he dwells. Where is he then in this
> temple, in which he shines as holy? Intellect
> is the temple of God."[70]

The Sodomites are drawn to a living presence conditioned by a trace of the senses; they are drawn to what withdraws from the senses, to "a knowledge that is out of the question"; they are in trance at the entrance of what is "ceaselessly originating from the improper."[71] They are consumed by a

---

[70] Derrida, "At This Very Moment in This Work Here I Am," in *Psyche: Inventions of the Other. Volume I*, ed. Peggy Kamuf and Elizabeth Rottenberg (Stanford: Stanford University Press, 2007), 186.

[71] "The impartation of the proper is possible ... by ceaselessly originating from the improper, whose destination, in return, is only this coming to pass, this birth that never ends. Identity that is born thus comes to pass; it never ceases occurring to its identity. But it cannot be indifferent. Its provenance makes it different, and singular: it is the child (when does the man cease to be one?), it is man originating in woman, it is woman in turn awakening, it is the

trace without archive that they wish to grasp but does not make itself present.

Sodom is the desert before Moses's desert, the landscape of exile and exteriority, a path to a world that remains without world, a trace from which all the hopes of a world (a promised land) are displayed and at the same time displaced. The desert of enamored ashes (of an enamored trace) is left behind in Sodom and can never be won, or conquered, or ruled. It will be forever the land of dispersion, exile, and exorbitant, melancholic love, an unconquerable love, a love without an object, a land of forgetfulness. In a desert of enamored traces, the Jewish people will hear a murmuring echo, a mute language of inconsolable loss, an indecipherable grasp of a form that has no referent and cannot be impregnated or penetrated: "the Jew is the other who has no essence, who has nothing of his own or whose own essence is to have none."[72] The grounding ground of the temple is outside the temple (in its entrance, threshold, or antechamber); it does not belong to the temple, and it may not be fully appropriated by any temple or religion. Every future temple rises from a sense of the "outside," the other, and the "improper":

> The relation of existence to itself as the opening of and to sense is nothing other than the relation of the "improper" to the "proper." The improper of ordinary existence

---

stranger, it is the friend, it is you and I." Nancy, *The Birth to Presence*, trans. Brian Holmes (Stanford: Stanford University Press, 1993), 33.
[72] Derrida, "Shibboleth: For Paul Celan," in *Sovereignties in Question: The Poetics of Paul Celan*, ed. Thomas Dutoit and Outi Pasanen (New York: Fordham University Press, 2005), 50.

> reveals itself as "improper" insofar as it has
> an essential relation with the "proper"—
> even if only in terms of fleeing or avoiding.[73]

In the temple, the trance and trace of the contaminating outside, the trace of the other (as the uncanny, the singular, and the strange) is made exterior to religion (it is its parting and departing antechamber). Religion accounts for an absolute exteriority that is twofold. On one extreme, there is the absolute external being: God. On the next extreme, the ultimate "outside" is incorporated into the sacred as "Death." The "gift" of death is one of the names of the sacred because it is absolutely unknowable, external, and without analogy. Death is the impossibility of making associations and representations; it is an external experience that only God can give and know. Through this untranslatable figure of death, the promise of the sacred opens up through sacrifice (through infinite substitution and debt), through a consuming sense that consummates as it delivers the gift of death. Religion presents death and the absolute being (God) as ultimate experiences of the sacred. In both eschatological presentations, religion covers up (as well as incorporates) the experience of the coming of the other, the surplus (the experience of an analogy that withdraws from and exceeds any analogy) that is without religion and, at the same time, opens its possibility:

> Sacrifice had been the form of the relation
> with an elsewhere or an outside whose

---

[73] Nancy, *A Finite Thinking*, ed. Simon Sparks (Stanford: Stanford University Press, 2003), 186.

sacred presences—the gods—were themselves caught up in a larger outside, which was named destiny, necessity, night, or primordial abyss. There was no relation with this outside. At most the gods were able to offer some form of mediation, but it was fragile and uncertain. Tragedy thus presented the possibility of somehow playing—setting into play by setting the scene—the impossibility of relation to this outside by making this very impossibility a type of relation.[74]

Later in the biblical passage, there is an encounter with an unseen God who gives death to the Sodomites. What is supposed to take place is the consummation of the elimination of Sodom's excess and also its trace in the ground: "Then the Lord rained upon Sodom and upon Gomorrah brimstone and fire from the Lord out of heaven; and he overthrew those cities, and all the plain, and all the inhabitants of the cities, and that which grew upon the ground."[75] As Sodom and Gomorrah are being destroyed, there is an instant of suspense, suspension, realization, and loss; an instant that remains hidden from the story: the moment when they experienced their death. It is a moment that will become recurrent: the interval of their death. It is an event that withdraws from experience, a thought that forms a space with a missing word, and an impression that escapes thinking and at the same time multiplies thoughts. The readers are taken,

---

[74] Nancy, *Adoration*, 51.
[75] King James, Genesis, 19:24–25.

in a few lines, from the body of pleasure to the body of loss. In both extremes, they are exposed to the limit of a foreign body impossible to touch, a skin that touches a trace that repeats through interruption and effacement. The readers of this tale are exposed to what will recur eternally: the effacement of all meaning, which can never efface the trace of meaning (which is without meaning, which is a nonobject that remains without remains). The effacement of the Sodomites is the silent regeneration of writing as the genesis of space and spacing. Interruption (death) also signifies the reappearance of the desiring trace, a new display of spaces/thresholds; an inaudible, unseen, and untouched conductivity that may only be grasped in the limit of writing:

> We have traced the limit of writing as limit. We have written writing—it can't be seen at all; it is written; it is traced and consequently effaced before the eyes of him who would try to look. But its effacement is its repetition; it is its demand and its calling forth; "all meaning" traverses it, always coming from elsewhere, from nowhere, always coming elsewhere, and nowhere, offering itself to us while at the same time stealing us away from ourselves.[76]

What remains is the surplus that repeats through effacement, through the loss of touch and sight. A dispersion of signs and beliefs expand and contract disseminating a desire to know the ecstatic trace that exceeds knowledge. Death/

---

[76] Nancy, "Elliptical Sense," 48.

effacement in Sodom will not erase the hiatus that recurs and calls forth for an overabundant excess or an infinite lack. From this undecidable limit, not only a recurring freedom will ignite afresh, but also, and at the same time, a recurring religious sentence will usurp the freedom of this repetition that traverses all meanings. Every sign, word, or grasp that points toward the instant of their death (an interval that is not present or is other than presence) will ignite one of the circles of a self-renewing presence of religion.[77] The death of the Sodomites as well as their desiring impetus are usurped by religion and converted into an eternal punishment, an eternal debt for their incalculable excess.

The exterior antechamber is absorbed/usurped by the internal temple, thereby igniting the circular movement of religion, a circle that incarnates and resurrects the desire for an existence beyond existence, a presence that cannot be reduced to a sensible existence, an excess that reactivates the desire for a being beyond being, a surplus that remains without analogy, without representation, and out of grasp. In this antechamber, God (the desire for a Being beyond being) does not have a name. God is a desire for something unknown, a desire for a living presence that is not present or is unpresentable in its presence. In the antechamber, the

---

[77] "It is therefore the relation to *my death* (to disappearance in general) that is hidden in this determination of being as presence, ideality, as the absolute possibility of repetition. The possibility of the sign is this relation to death. The determination and the erasure of the sign in metaphysics is the dissimulation of this relation to death which nevertheless was producing signification." Derrida, *Voice and Phenomenon*, 46.

living presence is never present and remains a trace.[78] The ecstatic event of the coming of the other and the desire for the absolute presence of God entangle in the temple. In the grounding grounds of every temple to come, in the grounds without grounds of the temple erected above the trace of enamored ashes, there will be a narrative that covers up, that converts the ungraspable trace of the orgiastic event into the arrival of the living present, a presence that reveals the eyes of revelation, the eyes that will see without seeing an unpresentable presence full of presence. The nameless and faceless passion for the absolute other, for the living present/presence in passing clings in the departure and parting genesis of every religion to come. This desire that surpasses desire, this surplus that is contaminated from its inception (by mortality, by a supplementing and supplanted presence), this experience of an immemorial passion that is never grasped "as such," this body that is lost on the limit of all language, this knowledge that resists conceptualization (through origins, truth, presentation, oppositions, and dialectics), this writing that appears through the trace of a lost body (through a body that is first and foremost a trace) opens the passion for religion, for a religion, and for a religion without religion.

The hands in the threshold of Lot's door form a knot in the throats of the Sodomites where an ecstatic contortion of awe and anticipation turns and twists trying to translate (grasp/ gasp) what remains without translation. The centripetal and

---

[78] "The living present is always already a trace. This trace is unthinkable on the basis of a simple present whose life would be interior to itself. The self of the living present is originally a trace." Hägglund, *Radical Atheism*, 71.

centrifugal forces of desire; the impressions, the touch, the visions, the voices, the echoes, and the ultimate withdrawal from the world meet and diverge in a limit without analogy, in a space where all analogies have a chance to grasp the identity of a who or a what (in passing) that is nonidentical and nonpresent with itself:

> But the passion always is destined towards the impossible. It does not transform the impossible into the possible; it does not master it; it is rather dedicated to it; it expresses itself in it, passive on the limit where the impossible comes—that is, where *everything* comes, where all meaning comes, and where the impossible itself cannot be touched, even though one *touches its limit*.[79]

The penetration that cannot be mastered ignites an inexhaustible fountain of passion. Anticipation defers passion, and, at the same time, it is the grounding ground of every law, of the Law of laws that delays penetration (entry to any law) ad infinitum. The Law of laws prohibits the approach to the living presence, which, in principle, cannot be approached in terms of distance or proximity, which withdraws as it is approached, which is nonpresentable, which blinds because of its invisibility, and which is a trace before it is anything at all:

> What is delayed is not this or that experience, the access to some enjoyment or to some

---

[79] Nancy, "Elliptical Sense," 49.

supreme good, the possession or penetration of something or somebody. What is deferred forever till death is entry into the law itself, which is nothing other than that which dictates the delay. The law prohibits by interfering with and deferring the "ference" ["*férance*"], the reference, the rapport, the reaction. What *must not* and cannot be approached is the origin of différance: it must not be presented and above all **not penetrated**. That is the law of the law, the process of a law of whose subject we can never say, "There it is," it is here or there. It is neither natural nor institutional; one can never reach it, and it never reaches the depths of its original and proper taking-place.[80]

That instance of desire, when the other of humankind and the other as humankind responds to the call with a desire that surpasses desire, that quiet instant in the threshold where the Sodomites are both hosts and hostages of the coming of the other forms a hiatus in their impetus to penetrate, in their impulse to know what is disruptive, unsettling, and without determined laws. This hiatus, instant, and instance, which revolts toward and against the sensible without becoming intelligible, is the very pulse of "grasp," a rhythm that gives itself to insatiable substitution. Without this hiatus, the realm of ethics and aesthetics would not have a chance:

---

[80] Derrida, "Before the Law," in *Acts of Literature,* ed. Derek Attridge (New York: Routledge, 1992), 205. (The bold letters are my emphasis.)

> Without silence, without the hiatus, which
> is not the absence of rules but the necessity
> of a leap at the moment of ethical, political,
> or juridical decision, we could simply unfold
> knowledge into a program of course of action.
> Nothing could make us more irresponsible;
> nothing could be more totalitarian.[81]

The neutralization or usurpation of one's silence, of one's singularity, of one's sense of sense has resulted in many instances (as it has been the case throughout history) in multiple examples of programmatic knowledge, spirituality, or/and spiritualism that escalated into a monstrous totalitarian machine both in politics and religion.

The "grasp" for the other has been hastily called a desire for God, and, in the name of (that desire for) God, manifold have been the catastrophes that claimed to have a blinding and binding grasp on the incalculable and unpredictable desire that comes from the threshold of the senses, an interval where a desire for the other (for any other that is other) is constantly at play through a yearning that is in excess or lacking. The excess of reality and unreality that intoxicates the Sodomites is the scene of authoritative discourses and laws that authorize prohibitions and persecutions from out of a dissembling silence, a hiatus that gathers a unifying and disorganizing excess:

> How to distinguish between the force of
> law of a legitimate power and the allegedly
> originary violence that must have established

---

[81] Derrida, *Adieu*, 117.

this authority and that could not itself have authorized itself by any anterior legitimacy, so that, in this initial moment, it is neither legal nor illegal—as other would quickly say, neither just nor unjust? ... the greatest force and the greatest weakness strangely exchange places. And that is the whole story, the whole of story.[82]

Prohibition initiates a network of beliefs and believers through the repression/usurpation of a desire that exceeds belief, of a desire (pulse, drive, rhythm, etc.) that is in the limit of the experience between thinking and believing. Prohibition, which in many levels is the name of religion, cuts across that difference and multiplies laws through a differential space that is other than law and other than religion.

The laws of the "shall not" multiply signs of diversion. The "shall not" "abominates" and sentences and, at the same time, withdraws from the surplus that withdraws from any domination and denomination. Through the effect of the "shall not," the surplus that eludes us and that is unavoidable, the excess that comes in passing and trespasses even through an impasse, becomes an evil idiom. The desire not to desire or the desire of the "shall not" is an outside desire that commands to avoid the excess that eludes us (a desire that is unavoidable and arrives before God). Inevitably, desiring avoidance is also the desire to exclude, marginalize, and persecute in the name of a God that desires to eliminate an excessive excess that

---

[82] Derrida, "Force of Law," in *Acts of Religion*, edited by Gil Anidjar (New York: Routledge, 2002), 234–235.

He cannot accurately define or rule and that arrives before His arrival. The desire to avoid what avoids us, trespasses us, and surpasses us demands an insistent amount of force and resolution (both physical and mental). The "shall not" commands a detachment from a commanding and impenetrable excess, and it is precisely this usurpation (the usurpation of a desiring supplement that cannot be properly known "as such") that ignites the mechanistic idealization of the law pointed toward what should not be desire in a desire that surpasses desire (a desire that is foreign, uncanny, contaminated, and other than desire; a desire that cannot be ruled or governed with any of the categories of desire).

In spite of all and every usurpation/suspension (or because of them), an infinitely small hiatus remains in the threshold of the senses, and this silent impetus, space, difference, surplus, or supplement cannot be eliminated by the mandates of negative decrees. After Sodom, infinite hands will try to become gatekeepers of the doors of perception, but how to command a door that invites to "enter without penetration," "to trespass without trespassing," and so on? Can anyone be the successful gatekeeper of a desiring trace? Is that impossible task ever possible? What survives, what is beyond any gatekeepers is the charged energy (*energeia*) of the gap (alluded to in the figure of the threshold). The hiatus opens. The hiatus unlocks the event of life that happens right now, without religion, before religion, or throughout religion. What or who fails to arrive, what or who is suspended in a hiatus, opens the event of expectation and promise, the future that says "yes" to whatever and whoever comes:

"I fail to arrive" means at the same time "I
do not arrive," "I do not arrive at arriving,"
and I fail or I do not arrive *because* I arrive, I
do not arrive *at* arriving, once, *because, since*
I arrive—here is the event that speaks, it is
of the event, the arrival, the coming, and the
"come" that I am speaking. Speaking, then,
of the "insuccèss" as what does not succeed
in arriving, precisely *by* arriving, by the fact
of arriving, because it arrives.[83]

In the antechamber of every temple dwells the yearning
for an indeterminate promise in the formless form of a space
that says "Yes" and "come." This capitalized affirmation
comes before one can say "yes" or "no." This capital impetus is
the unappropriable space that never makes it into the temple.
An insatiable passion blinks at the threshold of the temple,
an interval in which the beginning of an inenarrable event
ignites relentlessly an interruption of a living presence that is
yet to come, that arrives without arriving. The antechamber
reserves a space of repetitive interruption of every name
that gives presence to the ideality of the Absolute Other.
The beginning is the end of the experience. The genesis is
a ruin. Beyond the antechamber, there is the temple, which
cannot replicate the antechamber. The temple is always
already the ruin of the antechamber (the ruin of a space
that it wants to preserve and keep safe as absolute presence).
The temple constitutes the "no" that will always relate to the
"yes" but through a type of interruptive association, through
a continuum of impasses that say "shall not." Impossible to

---

[83] Derrida, *Resistances*, 42.

replicate, embrace, or imitate, the antechamber multiplies through numerous chambers, receptacles of insisting gestures that contract and expand trying to reach and grasp the generous idiom that does not let itself be captured as spirit, name, concept, or church. In the orgiastic gestures of the Sodomites are "saved" the remains of an inerrable testimony.

The experience of the Sodomites takes place without taking place. It (what happens) cannot be narrated because it does not belong to a sequence but rather to the coming of what comes. On the one hand, the story only confirms that nothing happens; on the other hand (and at the same time), it is the coming of what never takes place as such that unfolds the story. The angels are not touched or seen by the Sodomites who are blinded the moment they trespass the threshold. The Sodomites' climax is without culmination because their ecstasy flows through anticipation and, ultimately, suspension. They are a threshold away or closer to happening. An interval of separation from the other remains like an unbroken hymen just barely out of reach but close enough to incite a longing, a question. The threshold permits the formulation of the question, what or who is there? The coming of the other "happens" through the uncrossing of an indefinite impasse out of which the genesis of the world commences (departs) incessantly.

In the instant of mesmerizing revelation "*nothing is revealed*," nothing but the limit of revelation itself when passion is suspended in an unclassifiable promise, an imperative desire to translate (to write and express) a sense that brings sense to the senses while exceeding them. Through this limit that reveals nothing and that cannot be fully absorbed or controlled by religion or any affiliation, "sense is unveiled purely as sense, in person, but in a person such that all the sense of that person consists in revealing himself. Sense reveals itself and reveals nothing, or else reveals its own infinity."[84] It the tale of Sodom, ecstasy and catastrophe, suspension and dissolution are the traits of an anticipation that remains indestructible in the remains of Sodom. As we desire to see and grasp the threshold of Sodom, its mark recurs anew in the guise of catastrophe. For every passionate strophe that the individual articulates in order to touch what remains without touch, a catastrophe takes place before his or her hands:

> The meaning of speech, then, requires that before any word is spoken, there must be a sort of immense hecatomb, a preliminary flood plunging all of creation into a total sea. God had created living things, but man had to annihilate them ... and man was condemned not to be able to approach anything or experience anything except through the meaning he had to create.[85]

Although the story of Sodom has been repeated ad infinitum, its orgiastic secret does not belong to memory but to the trace of an instant, to an interval, a deferred passion and a passion in suspense. The overflowing impetus is usurped by the most eloquent forms of discourse; however, each and

---

[84] Nancy, *Dis-Enclosure: The Deconstruction of Christianity*, trans. Bettina Bergo et al. (New York: Fordham University Press, 2008), 147.
[85] Blanchot, "Literature and the Right to Death," in *The Work of Fire*, trans. Charlotte Mandell (Stanford: Stanford University Press, 1995), 323.

every attempt to schematize and calculate the surplus, all the abstractions unfolded within religion and politics through multiple laws, regulations, programs, and dogmas will not succeed in identifying the "menace," "the abomination," "the contamination," the surplus that all these institutions will claim to know and control through expulsion and rejection (movements that will only bring back what those affiliations want to miss, deviate, or control): "Calculable measure also gives access to the incalculable and the incommensurable, an access that remains necessarily undecided between the calculable and the incalculable—and that is the aporia of the political and of democracy."[86]

In the bloodless holocaust of Sodom and Gomorrah, every singular individual is sacrificed with an ecstatic secret that is as impossible to bury as it is to penetrate, to repress, or witness ("as such"). Their "demonic mystery of desire" remains without history, without life, but also without death. Their passion is forever inscribed in catastrophe and cinders, in the trace of a trance and of a "trans" that inflames and infects. They are buried with a desiring idiom in their hands: the hoping of hope at the instant when all is lost.[87] Behind the door and the threshold, behind the holocaust of the Sodomites, behind their bodies in cinders laying in the darkest of deserts, in the very experience of incineration hovers the sublime palpitation of a primal arousal that flows endlessly, undefined, and without a determinate name saying "yes."

---

[86] Derrida, *Rogues*, 52.

[87] "Hope hopes for the present itself... At the very moment where all is lost, everything is possible." Derrida, "Hostipitality," in *Acts of Religion*, edited by Gil Anidjar (New York: Routledge, 2002), 393.

In the foundation of every prayer, edict, and categorical imperative, there lies the dormant demonic mystery of a desire that loves an exteriority without analogy, with a desire that is in excess of desire. No religion, revolution, or science could have been possible without a legion of believers that aims toward a passion that is still not invented and not known, to a blinding vision that proclaims the advent of an imperious justice. No commanding truth is completely disconnected from the orgiastic principle that founds it, from the "demonic mystery of desire," which is without truth, without religion, without genre, and without gender. The surplus of Sodom is impossible to master and remains external and foreign to the future of religion and politics that will be trafficking in the unmastered freedom of the Sodomites: "Intensity is an excess, an absolute disruption which admits of no regimen, region, regulation, direction, erection, insur-rection, nor does it admit of their simple contraries ..."[88]

The remains of Sodom escape every temple and also the meaning of concepts, laws, and imperatives. Its remains are doomed to remain silent. In the antechamber of every temple, a fragile but incessant rhythm, a rare acceleration comes from an elsewhere, a conductivity without ceremony and without memory, a trace of embers and ashes. A virginal texture "scatters like sand."[89] A question remains at the gates;

---

[88] Blanchot, *Writing*, 56.

[89] "The hymen *s'arrête*: it comes about *and* is immediately forbidden. It is the *double-bind* structure of this event: its 'madness.' The interruption of the hymen—which is nothing other than its coming to be, its event—does not arise from any decision. No one has the initiative. As soon as the words have 'touched' her, she is 'swept away from me, borne off by the crowd': she does not leave, nor do I, and this 'sweeping away' consigns what it carries off, to *dispersion* (the event,

an interrogation remains in place; it is the place (interval) of infinite substitutions:

> We must know that the place of the irreplaceable is quite a singular place indeed. If it is irreplaceable, as the place, as the *khóra*, it is so as to receive substitutable inscriptions. It is the place of possible substitution. It can never be confused with that which occupies it, with all the figures which come to be inscribed therein and pass themselves off as the copies of a paradigm, the examples of an irreplaceable exemplar. Is it not from the place of this very place that we gaze the *horizon*, awaiting the black swan that does not come every day of the week? A place can never be situated anywhere but under a *horizon*, from out of this limit which opens up and closes off at one and the same time. Is it not from off this bank and under this horizon that a political phallogocentrism has, *up to this point*, determined *its* cosmopolitical democracy, *a* democracy, *qua* cosmo-phratrocentrism?[90]

Normalizing (patriarchal) laws, "moral" commands, and political discourses (a fraternal language of friends and enemies, inclusion and exclusion) attempt to supplement and

---

the *coup*—blow, stroke, 'suddenly'—the pulse once more 'scatters like sand') and to *anonymity*." Derrida, "Living On," 172.

[90] Derrida, *Politics of Friendship*, 263.

substitute (with a language of presence, value, and power) the place of the question (the spectral trace that is neither present nor absent). Categorical imperatives, principles, and concepts are inscribed in a categorically imperative-impetus that desires to establish an analogy with a trace that remains without a definite analogy, a space that can never translate satisfactorily into an idea, a home, or the inside of a temple. This murmur that disorganizes, disturbs, and mixes the senses departs from Sodom's threshold, from their interrupted touch and vision, from what remains without remains in their ashes. From cinders, an immemorial memory inflames again, an inadequation and contamination from out of which an army of commands and concepts emerges, promising the absolute presence of an approaching truth through a desire that is in excess of every desire, through a desire that is other than desire.

Sodom is a scene of fabulation and confabulation. There is a mutating mutation in their spasms that no concept, name, or desire can grasp absolutely. The future of humanity revolves around this immemorial opening of the senses. Out of the "unseemly" tremors of the Sodomites, "proper" laws will be drawn. The antechamber of Sodom, where the errant desire for the coming of the other dwells in an inadmissible region, remains as a free-floating desire without nomination and domination, as an acceleration of forces that no one can master. This ungraspable desire that impassioned and inflamed the Sodomites in an obsessive manner will continue to renew the circle of religion through expansive and contracting folds, metaphors and metonymies of the inenarrable, the untouchable, and the impenetrable. This threshold, region, or interval, this antechamber of religion and atheism may also be associated with Plato's *chora* in the *Timaeus*:

> *Chora*, the "ordeal of *Chora*" would be ... the name of place, a place name, and a rather singular one at that, for that spacing which, not allowing itself to be dominated by any theological, ontological or anthropological instance, without age, without history, and more "ancient" than all oppositions, (for example, that of sensible/intelligible) does not even announce itself as "beyond being" in accordance with a path of negation, a via negativa. As a result, *chora* remains absolutely impassible and heterogeneous to all the processes of historical revelation or of anthropo-theological experience, which at the very least suppose its abstraction. It will never have entered religion and will never permit itself to be sacralized, sanctified, humanized, theologized, cultivated, historicized. Radically heterogeneous to the safe and sound, to the holy and the sacred, it never admits of any indemnification. This cannot even be formulated in the present, for *chora* never presents itself as such. It is neither Being, nor the Good, nor God, nor Man, nor History. It will always resist them, will have always been (and no future anterior, even, will have been able to reappropriate, inflect or reflect a *chora* without faith or law) the very place of an infinite resistance, of an

infinitely impassible persistence <*restance*>:
an utterly faceless other.[91]

In Genesis, the story of Sodom and Gomorrah is contaminated from the start because it narrates an inenarrable story of a space that remains out of touch. The story mixes desires, vision, and tact in an impetus to embrace what remains irreducible to the senses, what does not present itself "as such" to the senses. Their senses are mesmerized by an abstraction that they cannot synthesize and that disorganizes their senses. Perceptions are mixed and contaminated through an interruption that builds up a multiplicative excitement. The Sodomites sense the other (of) sense in an interval, a threshold, a quotation mark that, at the same time, blinds them and inflames their existence. This revolving and revolting revolt departs from the desire to surpass Sodom's threshold, from the desire for a trace anticipated through an interval. Religion blinks eternally with a persistent "shall not," with a relentless neutralization of an excess that "will never have entered religion and will never permit itself to be sacralized, sanctified, humanized, theologized, cultivated, historicized," and that remains impossible to destroy and eternally deferred.

The antechamber forms a virtual place in the temple, a place before the temple, a place displaced. The Jews carry this antechamber inside of every temple that has a tabernacle with sacred space inside it, a tabernacle that "opens to nothing" and "confines nothing" and that saves the space of an enamored interval:

---

[91] Derrida, "Faith and Knowledge," 57–59.

Now the tabernacle (texture of "bands" whose excess we must continually reuse, Exodus 26) remains a signifier without signified. The Jewish Hearth forms an empty house. Certainly, sensible to the absence of all sensible form, the Jews have tried to produce an object that gave in some way rise, place, and figure to the infinite. But this place and this figure have a singular structure: the structure encloses its void within itself, shelters only its own proper interiorized desert, opens onto nothing, confines nothing, contains as its treasure only nothingness: a hole, an empty spacing, a death ... Nothing behind the curtains. When he [a non-Jew] enters the dwelling or the temple, and opens or violates the Tabernacle to gain access to the secret center, he discovers nothing—only nothingness.[92]

The open hands of the Sodomites open the possibility of every religion-to-come to grasp the space that "opens to nothing," that uncovers the opening of whatever and whoever comes. This opening, without religion and for all religions, ignites a silent, ecstatic spark, a liking for every hand that writes with a passion for the impossible; a hand that touches without trespassing; an open and saluting hand that senses a leap toward an otherly texture that can only be welcomed

---

[92] Derrida, *Glas*, trans. John P. Leavey Jr. and Richard Rand (Nebraska: University of Nebraska Press, 1990), 49.

by loving at the gates, by penetrating in the antechamber, without penetrating. The threshold opens the inside and the outside of this passion for the impossible. In the future of the temple, the combination of spaces that constitute the sanctuary will aim to an unpresentable threshold, a hiatus that unfolds and retreats without enunciation. The antechamber of every temple exposes a disappearing trace, the opening of a path toward an untouchable and multiplying grasp that makes every touch possible.

The dimension of Being opens to the experience of God who is not or whose being is neither essence nor ground … This dimension of opening, this place that gives place without being either essence or ground … this entryway that gives access to God, is not the "antechamber" that Meister Eckhart speaks of? "When we grasp God in being, we apprehend him in his antechamber, for being is the antechamber in which he dwells."[93]

---

[93] Derrida, "How To Avoid Speaking: Denials," in *Psyche: Inventions of the Other. Volume II*, ed. Peggy Kamuf and Elizabeth Rottenberg (Stanford: Stanford University Press, 2008), 192.

III

Pasolini's "Teorema"

he Story of Sodom is allegorically rethought by Pier Paolo Pasolini in his film *Teorema*, where he reaches down into the depths of the orgiastic mystery and attempts to "touch" it. In *Teorema*, the surplus desire for the angel-visitor-stranger distorts the family's sexuality ("contaminates" it), as they are driven to "know" (נדאה) passionately their otherly guest. The hosts open unconditionally to the arrival of the stranger and welcome the visitor with a "yes," foreclosing the normativity of middle-class values and laws. In a social context of programmatic laws and normalized truths, *Teorema* incarnates the passion for an unexpected conduct/conductivity that is other than societal conduct, and a commanding call/sending that does not correspond to the familiar commands established throughout the centuries.

A brief description of the film:

An upper-class Milanese family visited by an unexpected guest, a stranger in passing. The arrival of the mysterious figure (known only as "the visitor") produces an extraordinary reaction in the ordinary and bourgeois Italian family. The family welcomes the unexpected guest with unconditional hospitality. They are all drawn ecstatically and unconditionally to this other who is receptive to the intoxication of every family member. The stranger responds candidly to the burning passion of the family and engages in sexual affairs with all members of the household: the devoutly religious maid, the sensitive son, the sexually repressed mother, the timid daughter, and the tormented father. The stranger also offers himself unconditionally and asks nothing in return. He stops the passionate maid from committing suicide with a gas hose and tenderly consoles her; he befriends and sleeps with the frightened son, soothing his doubts and anxiety and endowing him with confidence; he becomes emotionally intimate with the overprotected daughter, removing her childish innocence of men; he seduces the bored and dissatisfied mother, giving her sexual joy and fulfillment; he

cares for and comforts the despondent and
suffering father, who has fallen ill.[94]

The visitor disjoints their established beliefs, unleashes
their passions, inflames them, sets them on fire, and ultimately
departs, leaving a trace of embers, ashes, and melancholy
behind him. He disturbs all the familiarity involved in a
middle-class family, all the coherent values that bound them
together, and he transmits to them a conductivity that is
foreign and heterogeneous. As the film unfolds, it is clear that
the family's exuberant passion, perceptions, and sensations
transport them to an experience that exceeds gender,
sexuality, sensuality, and the senses. They desire a what or a
who and everything in between. The characters are marked
by an otherly sense, a desire to connect with a connectivity
that is in excess of every pleasure. The otherworldly and
fleeting presence of the angel/visitor multiplies their sense of
self at the same time that it exposes them to an otherly sense,
to the threshold of their own desires beyond desire. When
the angel/stranger leaves, the family falls into unending
desperation as they attempt to look for traces of him. They
look for analogies within their bourgeois society, for what
remains without analogy and beyond any pleasure.

When the stranger departs, "the maid returns to the rural
village where she was born and is seen to perform miracles;
ultimately, she immolates herself by having her body buried
in dirt while shedding ecstatic tears of regeneration. The
mother seeks sexual encounters with young men; the son
leaves the family home to become an artist; the daughter
sinks into a catatonic state; and the father strips himself of

---

[94] http://en.wikipedia.org/wiki/Teorema_(film).

all material effects, handing his factory over to its workers, removing his clothes at a railway station and wandering naked into the wilderness (actually the volcanic desert slopes of Mount Etna), where he finally screams in primal rage and despair."[95] Each member experiences in his or her own singular way the impasse of their passion for what is other, strange, and uncanny. Their desiring excess for what is in excess of every desire is experienced through the touch of the angel, a touch that inflamed them, transported them to the threshold of their senses, and ultimately enveloped them in mourning and ashes.

In the first scene, before the angel's arrival, the middle-class family was sharing a meal in their home. There is an invisible energy on the table, something like a wound, a lesion that they refuse to acknowledge through the infinite rituals that take place in a middle/upper-class family. At the same time, there is a sense of hope and expectation that something or someone (a miracle) would interrupt the life sentence to which they seemed to be condemned since birth. The family is already "contaminated" with an expectation, with a sense that is foreign to all their surroundings, status, and apparent harmony. It may be speculated that they sense with a sense other than sense that in their day-to-day life there is something missing, something other than the truths woven by millennial usurpations and by the daily routine. They cannot not put an inkling on the what or who that is missing and quietly abandon themselves to the hope of an "if" and a "perhaps," to a sense of expectation for something or someone that they desire without knowing, without the knowledge of any cultural, political, or religious ideas or ideals ["perhaps

---

[95] http://en.wikipedia.org/wiki/Teorema_(film).

there is an outside of the cave"]. They desire a space, an event that is free from the inherited truths of family, culture, or pact; an event "without truth."[96] Quietly and secretly, they anticipate an overflowing figure, an event that would untie them from their golden cage.

When the "angel" departs, he leaves a trace of inconsolable grief. The father of the family makes an ultimate gesture of passion beyond passion by giving up all his mundane possessions and going to the desert to await the coming of the other. Ecstatically, naked in the desert, and having yielded his factory to his workers, the father seems to see something in the desert that we, as viewers, are also exposed to but is never shown. He stands back to the camera. The viewers are blinded, for they cannot see what he sees, but as spectators and specters in this uncanny film, we also have a sense of expectation, a sense for an ineffable trace born from ashes. One is at the edge of his/her senses trying to make sense of a figureless spectacle, an image that is (always) missing from representation. A visibility that is not visible displays at the conclusion of the film. As specters experiencing the hope for the coming of the other, spectators are exposed to a nonobject, to a mute excess that is foreign to the senses.

The enigmatic final scene is charged with a "sending," with a conductivity that communicates an excess of nostalgia and gratitude associated to a nonobject that the spectators

---

[96] "The event without truth unveiled or revealed, without phallogocentrism of the Greco-judeo-paulino-islamo-freudo-heideggeriano-lacanian veil, without phallophoria, i.e., without procession or theory of the phallus, without veiling-unveiling of the phallus, or even of the mere place, strictly hemmed in, of the phallus, living or dead." Derrida, "A Silkworm of One's Own," in *Acts of Religion*, ed. Gil Anidjar (New York: Routledge, 2002), 350.

can neither define nor forget. As spectral spectators who see "nothing," who see the place where nothing "is," we are exposed to an immemorial want, to a hiatus, to a metonymy where every substitution is possible. We yield to a supplemental impetus that points toward the future of hope and chance:

> The remaining of the reminder is not reducible to an actual residue, or to what is left after a subtraction, either. The remainder *is* not, it is not a being, not a modification of that which is. Like the trace, the remaining offers itself for thought before or beyond being. It is inaccessible to a straightforward intuitive perception (since it refers to something wholly other, it inscribes in itself something of the infinitely other), and it escapes all forms of prehension, all forms of monumentalization, and all forms of archivation. Often, like the trace, I associate it with ashes: remains without a substantial reminder; essentially, but which have to be taken account of and without which there would be neither accounting nor calculation, nor a principle of reason able to give an account or a rationale (*reddere rationem*), nor a being as such.[97]

---

[97] Derrida, "Others Are Secret Because They Are Other," in *Paper Machine*, trans. Rachel Bowlby (Stanford: Stanford University Press, 2005), 151–152.

The end of the film is sublimely mesmerizing as the father goes to the desert to look for a trace that manifests but does not present itself. The spectators see through the eyes of the father that which cannot be seen or experienced by the senses alone. The father goes to a place where all names vanish, only to leave the trace of an immemorial name, an a-theological texture that he decides to follow but which does not have a path. We see the father alone, without family, community, or factory following a trace without paths that he senses in the desert, and we, the spectators, sense with an otherly sense.

Teorema explains the inexplicable, a primal and sublime, ecstatic arousal that appears in passing, insistently and relentlessly; the genesis of both religion and of a religion without religion. The primal arousal, the primal "yes," happens in the form of a departure and a crossing, in the form of an excess without history, a sending, that no knowable power could either appropriate or sacrifice.

IV

Trespassing the Threshold without Steps

The story of Sodom is about a trace between intervals. It is about a space that is experienced through incineration: "there are great, spectacular experiences of incineration ... I am thinking of the crematoria, of all the destructions by fire, but before even these great memorable experiences of incineration, there is incineration as experience, as the elementary form of experience."[98] The tale of Sodom is a tale of tales, a fable of fables that keeps its multiplying limit of touch in a space that remains out of touch/grasp and out of sight, in a desiring interval, in a hiatus that is a pure event of difference and deferral through which metonymies and metaphors will part and depart, forming and transforming the impetus of an expectation, displaying and withdrawing

---

[98] Derrida, "There is No *One* Narcissism," 209.

a knowledge that is yet to be discovered. In the tale of tales, there is a password at the threshold, an idiom that is more than fiction, a conductivity that is before any reality and that can only be touched by a hyperbolic fiction:

> For Literature draws this undecidable line the instant it whips the secret it keeps from you into its cipher, out of sight, true, but that it keeps {*garde*}absolutely while handing it to you to look at again {*re-garde*}, but without holding out any hope of your grasping it, that is, while depriving you of the power or the right to choose between reality and fiction, between fiction which is always a real event, like the phantasm, and so-called reality, which may always be nothing but a hyperbole of the fiction.[99]

The Sodomites' desperate arousal into orgiastic frenzy aims to a flesh that is in excess of flesh, something both accessible and inaccessible through flesh. They push ecstatically toward an outside, an unknown exteriority. Their frenzy rests in this difference, in this incarnation and dis-incarnation toward a fleshless flesh, toward an outside that impresses them and sets them in motion. They gather around an "external" limit that multiplies while remaining impenetrable, a hyperbolic gesture that only reinvigorates their passion. They want to penetrate the opening that makes

---

[99] Derrida, *Geneses, Genealogies, Genres, & Genius. The Secret of the Archive,* trans. Beverly Bie Brahic (New York: Columbia University Press, 2003), 47.

penetration possible. They are entranced by an entrance to a space without entrance, a texture that opens the very possibility of interiority, entrance, and penetration.

With shivering gestures, they draw in their hands the anticipation of anticipation. They are already trespassing through their anticipatory pleasure, through the proximity to the angels' skin that is more than flesh. Their spectral skin is a surplus that exceeds the language of desire, a surplus that multiplies the fantasies of flesh but remains without translation, hovering in the grasp of the Sodomites:

> The energy of God and of the Prime Mover is thus at once desire, desirable (*eromenon, to proton orekton*), and partaking in pleasure. A taking pleasure in the self, a circular and specular autoaffection that is analogous to or in accordance with the thinking of thought (noēsis noēseōs).[100]

They feel an uncontrollable trance, a desperate apprehension for apprehending the proximity of the spectral angelic body that is barely discernible but infinitely present in the distance. Without this desire for a virginal impenetrability, for a virginal fold, there is no impassioned genesis of religion. Without the adoring hands trying to arrest/seize/grasp/trespass the body of the other, there would not be a thousand names for a fold, for a hiatus, for an unscathed desire that remains virginal in the remains of the remains of an unknown

---

[100] Derrida, *Rogues*, 15.

desert: "The desire of God, God as the other name of desire, deals in the desert with radical atheism."[101]

The Sodomites' desires pass/trans-pass through their hands. It is an organ of translation and writing through which the flux of desires is released, seized, and arrested. A transitive organ that gathers and multiplies, contains and releases, the hand is the edge of a virginal space. The hand touching the threshold is also the hand touching its own threshold, resting on the edge where the palm folds into its own sense of touch; there, the hand touches upon the untouchable:

> The internal limit to touch—tact, if you like—means that one cannot (but) touch the untouchable. A limit cannot be touched; it is a difference, an interval that escapes touch or that is that alone which you can touch or think you can. Without being intelligible, this limit is not properly tangible or perceptible. The experience of the limit "touches" on something that is never fully present. A limit never appears as such.[102]

The desire of every Sodomite folds and unfolds through this organ that gains access to an edge of exertion.[103] The

---

[101] Derrida, *On the Name*, 80.

[102] Derrida, "Others Are Secret," 156.

[103] "This self-relation [to touch] institutes itself and is born to itself as exertion at the moment when a limit comes to insist, to *resist*, to oppose (itself) to the effort that this limit literally *determines*. I chose the word 'exertion' [*efforcement*] because it bespeaks the effort as well as the limit next to which the tendency, the tension, the intensity of a finite force stops (itself), exhausts itself, retracts or retreats from its

hands receive and push "there" where all sensations gather as a magnetic field in the other sense, in the other of sense. Lot's door is both a mirror and a blinding edge where the angels fade into the figure of a limit that disorganizes, interrupts, and mixes all desires into another sense. What the Sodomites touch is the threshold of touch where all figures, all specters, multiply, write themselves, and fade in the face of a limit, a space from out of which an intuitive passion will write and rewrite itself anew, drawing the trace of passion for what is unknown and yet to come. The Sodomites' hands in the act of pushing Lot's door become more than hands. These are not only sensuous organs of sensation and perception but also instruments of thought associated with gathering, grasping, presenting, and writing. The hand senses the space of thought and thinking, of a body of communication that extends, that arrives, that is sent, that is mandated. In sum, the hand senses a space that exceeds impressions. In their apprehension, the Sodomites' hands desire to apprehend the sacred "texture," to reach where they cannot go, "there" where the impossible happens in passing. Their hand gestures are erratic. They point to a dissolving path, to a passion for the impossible (for an impossible passion). In their ecstasy, they surrender to the coming of the other; they surrender (without trespassing) to whatever and whoever comes:

> To surrender to the other, to love the other, means to go over the other without passing the threshold of the other, without trespassing on the other's threshold. To love

---

end back towards itself: at the moment, the instant, when the force of the effort touches upon this limit." Derrida, *On Touching*, 139.

> is to respect the invisibility of the other ...
> then, it would turn out that the passion for
> the impossible would be love ... The other
> is *any* other, God or someone or something
> else. So love means love the other as other,
> any other, any wholly other, going under any
> name whatsoever.[104]

The hands of the Sodomites grasp a presentiment, a scent, a prescent, a boundless generosity that distorts their senses. In their apprehension, they rush to apprehend a plenitude and to embrace its centrifugal, centripetal entropy. Without understanding what is before them, they abandon their hands to a burning and consuming passion. Proximity, flames, passion, and consumption without consummation are the themes of this tale that ends up literally and metaphorically in flames that touch and inflame:

> [T]he flame touches and inflames ... a light
> that self-touches ... this haptical light of
> self-consuming flames eludes worship; it
> does not dwell, as an image to be adored.
> It is the truth of a light without idols and
> icons, an iconoclastic light—and its
> flame spontaneously burns down effigies.
> Touching, this luminous touching, becomes
> naturally more iconoclastic than vision.
> "Presence without image and without
> representation" ... "intimate proximity"

---

[104] Caputo, *Prayers and Tears*, 49.

that "never becomes possession," "naked
exposition to the ungraspable" ...[105]

Against Lot's door, the visitors exert pressure to impede
the Sodomites' entrance to Lot's home. The pressure on both
ends forms an edge and an interval, a receptacle that receives
and sends, a space of transit, trance, and transition. Lot's
threshold echoes a pure interval, a hiatus of communication
and interruption without religion and before religion, an
address that rests in the hands of the Sodomites, a tact that
is in contact with a difference that forms a syncope of touch.
In this scene, the reader may imagine gestures of anticipation
rushed toward an outside (the inside of Lot's home), a space
that transmits and translates into multiplying synecdochic
impressions, metonymic perceptions, and metaphoric
expressions hoping to translate an archaic memory, a
desire that inflames, a writing of desire that touches on a
disappearing trace, a limit that contracts and expands, a
trace that is the place of infinite substitutions and analogies
reflecting a presence that is not only missing but also an effect
of the trace. Through their grasp, a silent event takes place:
a sending, a "trans," a tact that makes any touch possible; a
communication that remains untranslatable and untouched,
thus opening the desire for translating and touching the
spasmodic interval from which all metonymic traces
(associated with a missing/interrupted living presence) part
and depart. Their suspended grasp gathers a spasm in the
interval of interruption:

---

[105] Derrida, *On Touching*, 249.

Spacing (notice that this word speaks the articulation of space and time and the becoming-time of space) is always the unperceived, the nonpresent, and the nonconscious. *As such*, if one can still use that expression in a non-phenomenological way; for here we pass the very limits of phenomenology. Arche-writing as spacing cannot occur *as such* within the phenomenological experience of presence. It marks the *dead time* of the living present, within the general form of all presence. The dead time is at work.[106]

The hands of the Sodomites (the touch that touches on the interruption and irruption of touch) and their blinded eyes (eyes that are the continuation of the sense of touch) will be revived eternally as a memory without history that draws from an unconditional desire to know (to translate) the experience of an exteriority that transmits, that makes possible every communication, a *trans* that arrives *late*, that arrives without arriving and without memory. The orgiastic atheism in Sodom invokes a desire that ignites a messianic expectation for an ungraspable figure. Their fingers reach toward a blind point sinking into a passion in ruins, into the failure to capture the arrival of what arrives. This failure to grasp inflames and impassions. They touch their disintegrating and interrupted passion and leave the mark of their mournful and unsatisfied desire. In their hands there is the gesture of an "arche-writing," of the name of a who or what that gives/

---

[106] Derrida, *Of Grammatology*, 68.

transmits/sends/communicates while withdrawing. In their hands there is the grasp of the multiplying trace of the living presence that is never at hand, that is always already a trace dreamed on the limit of all language:

> Such is the gesture of the arche-writing: arche-violence, loss of the proper, of absolute proximity, of self-presence, in truth the loss of what has never taken place, of a self-presence which has never been given but only dreamed of and always already split, repeated, incapable of appearing to itself except in its own disappearance.[107]

Inflamed like the Sodomites, Abraham is also ready to give himself without reserve to a blind point of passion, to the threshold where passion tends to disintegrate as it attempts to grasp the name of what withdraws. Abraham, like the Sodomites (like everyone who is every other) yields to a "foreign body which is the body of our foreignness."[108]

As the Sodomites become nothing, close to nothing, and out of grasp, they leave a trace of a syncopeic spasm, a conduct that escapes nominalism, a passion so difficult to grasp that in some instances and instants it may be misconstrued as close to nothing: "the impossible is not nothing. It is even that which happens, which comes, by definition. I admit that this remains rather difficult, but that's exactly what preoccupies

---

[107] Ibid., 112.
[108] Nancy, "Elliptical Sense," 50.

what is called thinking, if there is any and from the time there is any."[109]

The Sodomites are absolutely disarmed in this act of self-abandonment in which they deliver themselves unconditionally to the absolute other. As they become "nothing," they also become the trace of an incommensurable excess. In this instant when the Sodomites become nullified, neutralized, and withdrawn from the face of the earth, they also linger as the remains of an incandescent passion that consumes every belief and also consummates them (opens their possibility). The story of the Sodomites vanishes every time it is remembered as the impossible. But the conditionality of the laws that establish the "not possible" hover around an unconditional desire for the impossible, around an interval that the law hopes to mold. The instant of their hiatus, the moment of deferred pleasure, rises in the threshold of the most abstract thought:

> One shouldn't forget that the satisfaction of the sublime may be had only by way of the "mediation" of pain ... This pain stems from the constitutive failure of sublime presentation: the sublime articulates itself, on and in an inability, a radical insufficiency of the mind to present (to itself) its end.[110]

The Sodomites' desiring hands (their inaccessible idiom) respond to no program, to no regulative ideal, and precisely

---

[109] Derrida, *Rogues*, 172, (footnote 12).
[110] Nancy, *The Discourse of the Syncope*, trans. Saul Anton (Stanford: Stanford University Press, 2008), 103.

because of that denomination, because of a missing name that may not be dominated by the dialectical coherence of any political and religious institution, it is thus tempting to declare their impetus an abomination and to exclude their idiom from the homely and the familiar (which is formed in the first place by what or who is foreign and strange). Their hands reach for a desire that is foreign and strange and that is before good and evil, true or false, and positive or negative. Their hands sense the dispersion of a distortion that refuses to be grasped with a sentence, a sentencing, a conduct or name. There is a readiness at hand, a willingness to disclose an insisting desire that refuses to be thought of in terms of desire, love, essence, or flesh:

> This is why love is always missed by philosophy, which nevertheless does not cease to designate and assign it. Perhaps it cannot help but be missed: one would not know how to seize or catch with that which exposes. If thinking is love, that would mean ... that thinking misses its own essence—that it misses by essence its own essence ... Loving, and loving love, it will have lost love.[111]

The hands of the Sodomites draw the path toward the expression that withdraws from expressivity and yet opens all the paths for the desire to embrace an inexpressible name, a texture that is not without expression and experience. They draw from a fascinated gravitational trace that withdraws.

---

[111] Nancy, *Inoperative Community*, 91.

This movement not only reflects the contortions of ecstatic bodies and hands but the very unfolding of thought, thinking, and writing as movements of sending, suspension, and grasp flowing from a desire to touch an excess that remains unthinkable and out of touch, an impetus that attempts, without desistance, to circumvent the question, the what/who that gives and transmits but remains unanalyzable (out of touch).

In the multiple futures of this suspension and leap, thousands of desiring hands will attempt to draw laws from an external edge without contours, an experience that is always other than itself, a desire that becomes other than its grasp:

> The law is silent, and of it nothing is said to us. Nothing, only its name, its common name and nothing else ... We do not know what it is, who it is, where it is. It is a thing, a person, a discourse, a voice, a document, or simply a nothing that incessantly defers access to itself, thus forbidding *itself* in order thereby to become something or someone? ... [Yet there is a] radiance that streams inextinguishably from the gateway of the Law. This is the most religious moment of writing.[112]

As Sodom disappears in flames, an infinitude of burning hands draws the paths of the remains of the orgiastic secret. The distorting and dissembling trace of Sodom, the mute

---

[112] Derrida, "Before the Law," 208.

ecstatic energy that transmits and transports from its deserted threshold, will recreate a passion for substitution through a circle of hands that gather a volatile dispersion: "As I have already said, no word, no word for word will suffice to translate this word that gathers, in its idiomatic meaning, stock, race, family, species, genus, generation, sex."[113] Their superabundant desire to touch an unknown texture, a shadow, a specter, a place of reunion and interruption multiplies the impetus of translating a singularity that remains out of touch, an external space where flesh is but the incarnation of multiple spaces substituting and supplementing each other:

> The Passion of the Son, Incarnation, Logos, Transubstantiation are substitutions calling for Substitutions or Imitation; and in a certain manner, here, too there is a *hominization* process, but it is finally and always already the hominization of God, the gift of a God who makes himself into Man, through the mediation of the Son or the Word, and the Hand of the Merciful Father.[114]

The Sodomites touch an ecstatic region, an interval that makes every touch internal and every internalization a substitution of what is perceived as external. Their desire is also an interval that opens, opening the aperture that marks

---

[113] Derrida, "Heidegger's Hand (Geschlecht II)," in *Psyche: Inventions of the Other. Volume II*, ed. Peggy Kamuf and Elizabeth Rottenberg (Stanford: Stanford University Press, 2008), 51.

[114] Derrida, *On Touching*, 261.

the trace of a genesis that wants to know, to touch, to hear, and to penetrate an event that is suspended and deferred, an event that arrives by not succeeding in arriving. How close can one get to the other whom one loves and desires ecstatically? As close as an infinitely small threshold that defers love and also death. What is the just proximity and could it be calculated by distance, or is it a space other than distance? Who or what are the figures, the recipients of this love that points toward its own ineffable excess? Is there a right way to love the other passionately, ethically, responsibly, and justly? Isn't love an infinite way of deferral and proximity? Love misses love, and we miss love. Love is always other than love, always other than the path that it ignites.

Regulatory concepts (political, religious, psychological, etc.) as well as multiple legalities miss the mark of this excess, and, at the same time, it is this very desire for an incommensurable love that opens the calculable paths for institutional, religious, communal, and familial love and hospitality. Institutions are the stages through which the deferral of this excess is administered. This incommensurable space, this formless form of desire that contracts and expands, constitutes the core of any political or religious institutions, which attempt to calculate "just" forms of beauty, love, friendship ("respectable" forms of desire) through an incalculable desire that remains without analogy:

> Justice characterizes a way of behaving. It consists in behaving in a certain way: in accordance with the just, in harmony with the principle of the just. In its dignity as well as its necessity, this question is immediately equal to that of the beautiful and the

desirable in friendship. It arrives, then, also in the first place, immediately following the general opening on the subject of friendship (*peri philías*): What is friendship? How or what is it? What is a friend? Is friendship said in one sense or in several? The whole task should certainly consist in determining this justice. But that seems possible only by forcing several aporias.[115]

There will always remain a vertiginous leap between the freedom to love what or who arrives and the assertive legality of laws and concepts that calculate a distance or proximity to what remains incalculable, to what/who traverses distance and distancing. At the same time, the law of conductivity and conduct, the law that calculates the measure of just and conducive love follows the path of a retreating limit, a withdrawing figure, and an overabundant conductivity that is other than the legality exhibited, composed, and established.

The moral law dictates by breaking away from the coming of the other. The moral law says "you shall not," thereby detaching from an exteriority without contours, an exteriority that cannot be ruled with a "you shall not," an exteriority that is excluded from the clarity and coherence of the moral law, which in turn covers up what remains external to its self-legitimized origination:

He [Freud] smelled out the origin of law, and for that he had to smell out the sense of smell. He thus set in motion a great narrative,

[115] Derrida, *Politics of Friendship*, 8.

an interminable auto-analysis, in order to relate, to give an account of, the origin of the law, in other words the origin of what, by breaking away from its origin, interrupts the genealogical story. The law, intolerant of its own history, intervenes as an absolutely emergent order, absolute and detached from any origin. It appears as something that does not appear as such in the course of history ... If there were any history, it would be neither presentable nor relatable: the history of that which never took place.[116]

In spite of any programmable and commanding law, the desiring mark of Sodom remains unsacrificeable but also excluded as something beyond analysis, or rather analyzable strictly through the sentences of categorical decrees. At the same time, it is the rejection of their impetus and anticipation for what is absolutely other that leaves an incessant and indestructible trace incorporated into the moral laws that attempt to govern the call, sending, and communication of their orgiastic passion. The tale of Sodom, a story misunderstood in terms of morality and immorality, is really the story of an impetus (neither moral nor immoral, true or false) that is usurped and, at the same time, incorporated by religion. Their passion alerts, disorganizes, conducts, and addresses a form, a thought, a grasp that anticipates the arrival of something extraordinary and new that is deferred to infinity; and, therefore, their impetus cannot be understood through programmatic ethics or dutiful responsibilities.

---

[116] Derrida, "Before the Law," 194.

V

Abraham, the Sodomites, and Unconditional Hospitality

The Sodomites are not like any other townspeople. "God" must have "chosen" or targeted this town for its hospitality, which was dangerously in excess of every other town. Sodom had been a very hospitable town before the angels arrived. According to Lot (a stranger welcomed in Sodom), the place was considered like the "Garden of God" comparable to the Garden of Eden (Genesis 13:10). Sodom was located south of the Dead Sea (Jordan). Lot was a foreigner and a guest in Sodom until the town was conquered by Cherdorlaomer, the king of Elam. "Sodom and Gomorrah were spoiled of their goods, and captives were taken, including Lot. The tide of war turned when Lot's uncle Abraham gathered an elite force that slaughtered king Cherdorlaomer's force in Hobah, north Damascus. The success of his mission freed the cities of the plain from under Elam's rule."[117] Abraham defends and frees the city that gave hospitality to Lot and was able to release his nephew (Genesis 14:16). The king of Sodom meets Abraham near Jerusalem (in the valley of Shavé) and offers a part of the spoils of war to Abraham for his help to reconquer the city (Genesis 14:17). Why did Abraham destroy the town that he liberated and gave hospitality to Lot? Abraham also freed the other cities of the plain along the river Jordan that were under Cherdorlaomer (Gomorrah, Admah, Zebojim, and Bela—later called Zoar). Was there something untold in this story? Were there similarities between Abraham's unquestioned abandonment to the excess of the coming of the other and the Sodomites' overflowing impetus to embrace the living presence in passing?

The Sodomites welcome all strangers to their town, including Abraham and Lot. The town opens its doors to whomever seeks hospitality. Abraham is thankful to the town for its open generosity, and, therefore, he decides to put his life at stake by defending Sodom and Gomorrah. When the spectral strangers pass through their town, the Sodomites (not unlike Abraham) abandon all the normative and established rules of hospitality in order to embrace an unpredictable hospitality that surpasses any programmatic hospitality. The Sodomites are hostages of an incommensurable desire to know and welcome the other (an unforeseeable event) with a nonprogrammatic hospitality that is in excess of itself.[118]

---

[117] http://www.en.wikipedia.org/wiki/Sodom_and_Gomorrah.

[118] "In *Rogues*, Derrida explicitly recalls that his notion of unconditional hospitality cannot be aligned with 'the ethical' or with any form of normative prescription. Nothing can establish a priori that it is better to be more hospitable than to be less hospitable (or vice versa)....

Like the Sodomites, Abraham is also exposed to the desire for what is other and foreign. They both respond to the call of an orgiastic frenzy. The advent of religion will raise against this orgiastic impetus that will be both repressed, usurped (incorporated), and transformed by religion into its *mysterium tremendum*, an inflamed fervor that gets carried away against a conductivity, an exteriority, a spectral what/who that cannot be ruled, appropriated, or named and that cannot be defined in terms of morality or immorality. Abraham's attempt to sacrifice his son, Isaac, is not a response to his orgiastic impetus but the inflamed fervor of religion getting carried away and reacting against the irruption of the indeterminate other:

> The sacrifice of Isaac belongs to what one might just dare to call the common treasure, the terrifying secret of the *mysterium tremendum* that is property of all three so-called religions of the Book, the religions of the races of Abraham. This rigor, and the exaggerated demands it entails, compel the knight of faith to say and do things that will appear (and must even be) atrocious. They will necessarily revolt those who profess allegiance to morality in general to Judeo-Christian-Islamic morality, or to the religion of love in general.[119]

The only unconditional law of hospitality is that one will have been forced to deal with unforeseeable events." Hägglund, *Radical Atheism*, 104–105.

[119] Derrida, *Gift of Death*, 64.

Without this agitation, there is no event, instant of decision, religion, ethical moment, action, or history. What happens in the moment without religion and before religion? One may speculate that in the very instant of overflowing excess, in the moment when a command, a conductivity, a sending comes from an elsewhere, it is seized by a voiceless decree, by the mysterium tremendum that represses/usurps the orgiastic impetus for the indeterminate other that remains its foundation. One may speculate that when Abraham's impressions "touch" (with a sense that exceeds the senses) a certain nothingness (an exteriority, a nonobject), the voice of religion seizes it, repressing what remains its foundation. After the scene of decision (not to sacrifice Isaac), Abraham is inflamed with a new fervor, a secret communication with the mysterium tremendum. Abraham hears a mandate but now in the form of a decree: to destroy the people of Sodom and Gomorrah so that their orgiastic impetus will be completely destroyed. How does one understand this immense paradox? Would the future of religion have a chance without the repressed passion of Abraham and the usurped ecstasy of Sodomites? Abraham's passion for a renewed fervor commands him to an unthinkable madness:

> The command requests, like a prayer from God, a declaration of love that implores: tell me that you love me, tell me that you turn towards me, towards the unique one, towards the other as unique and, above all, over everything else, unconditionally, and in order to do that, make a gift of death, give death to your only son and give me the death

I ask for, that I give to you by asking you
for it ... Abraham is thus at the same time
the most moral and the most immoral, the
most responsible and the most irresponsible
of men, absolutely irresponsible in the face
of men and his family, and in the face of the
ethical, because he responds absolutely to
absolute duty, disinterestedly and without
hoping for a reward, without knowing why
yet keeping it secret; answering to God and
before God.[120]

Intoxicated by his relation to the indeterminate other who commands without command, Abraham answers to the call feverishly by giving his beloved son, Isaac, to a who/what that is voiceless. His decision (to sacrifice or not to sacrifice Isaac) is other than the alterity grasped in the limit of his senses where all names are consumed in an unpronounceable grasp. The sending, communication, or conduct revolves around Abraham's senses. This alterity in the limit of his senses withdraws from all worldly voices, names, and decisions. The mandate of this alterity multiplies and divides, changes places (saying one thing and the opposite, being outside and inside, inflaming and consuming; supplanting, substituting, and, ultimately, exchanging death for life). This exterior alterity perceived in the limit of Abraham's senses disseminates a passion that founds and inaugurates. A dangerous and unconditional "yes" for the absolute other manifests in the mind of Abraham, an affirmation that comes from an elsewhere and that remains without analogy and without

<hr>

[120] Derrida, *Gift of Death*, 72.

paragon. The "truth," the "naked truth" of every future decree would be but a function, a derivation, a substitution, a fiction, of the "yes," of the surplus that this alterity sends and exhibits.

Sodom is but the continuation of Abraham's encounter with an excess that exceeds his senses. He responds to the call of an unlocalizable exteriority without measurable distance, without calculable time. Abraham and the Sodomites are receptive recipients to this syncopeic space that does not belong to the familiar (but also makes it possible). They are receptors of the Law of laws that sends the name of what remains unpronounceable, of what must not be pronounced; a Law of laws that communicates not to pass what remains without passage, without distance, and without measure: "The unpronounceable keeps and destroys the name; it protects it, like the name of God, or dooms it to annihilation among the ashes. Apparently different or contradictory, these two possibilities can always cross the border and exchange places."[121] The Law of laws, the Affirmative Law that returns from ashes and communicates an unpronounceable idiom (communicates not to pass what remains without passage) may be easily supplanted by a negative law that simply says do not pass, do not cross, and do not touch.

In those moments of madness and antinomies (against *nomos*, against established law but toward an adoring chasm), an absolute exteriority, which cannot be measured in terms of touch, proximity, or distance, opens the desire for this errant specter, this space/spacing of proximity. Family, community, religion, and nation are but some of the name effects of a surplus that is other than those unifying concepts, an alterity that "gathers itself only by dividing itself, by

---

[121] Derrida, "Shibboleth," 50.

differing/deferring itself."[122] This exteriority in passing, this sending ("Envoi") belongs to no specific community, history, religion, or discourse but makes all of them possible. This unrepresentable opening, this exterior interval of the without (without community, without land, and without name), this exterior space that says absolutely "Yes" multiplies into affirmations and negations, traces of a proximity that had already parted and departed. Abraham and the Sodomites desire a relation with "what" or "who" is without relation, an alterity without representation, and a formless form that they do not know but welcome. They wish to embrace a specter that is neither ethical nor religious but opens the condition of possibility of both.

The ecstatic call/sending multiplies words and metaphors mandating and at the same time forbidding: "sacrifice/do not sacrifice, pass/do not pass." Like Abraham, the Sodomites adore unconditionally the sending of a who or what that is not necessarily higher than the law but exterior to it. Abraham interrupts all ethics and turns against every principle of love (wife, son, community) in order to turn toward an adoration that opens the unconditional conditions of love and ethics. The commanding seizure of their unconditional acts of abandonment toward a conductivity that comes from an elsewhere will form the basis for a conduct and a behavior ruled by sentences and decrees. At the same time, the multiple translations of this conduct(ivity) and its manifold incarnations can never be translated in a satisfactory law, command, or conduct; instead, this call opens a desire to

---

[122] Derrida, "Envoi," in *Psyche: Inventions of the Other. Volume I*, ed. Peggy Kamuf and Elizabeth Rottenberg (Stanford: Stanford University Press, 2007), 127.

communicate an impossible desire, an ethics that is in excess of the law and is nonnegotiable. By surrendering to who or what is coming, the Sodomites open every possible threshold of adoration toward the other, any other, including God, the angels, any other who is other, or any errant specter in the limit of the senses:

> To surrender to the other, and this is the impossible, would amount to giving oneself over in going toward the other, to coming toward the other but without crossing the threshold, and to respecting, to loving even the invisibility that keeps the other inaccessible ... The other is God or no matter whom, more precisely, no matter what singularity, as soon as any other is totally other. For the most difficult, indeed the impossible, resides there: there where the other loses its name or can change it, to become no matter what other.[123]

Founder of the Jewish religion, Abraham's perceptions are without religion and in excess of every religion. Like the Sodomites, he accedes to an exteriority that cannot be penetrated by the senses alone. Abraham, as the other, as any other, as a Jew before and without Judaism, as a Jew "whose essence is to have none"[124] is unaware that he is unfolding a religion. He responds to the call to a what-or-who he does not know and to a gaze that he does not see but that watches

---

[123] Derrida, *On the Name*, 74.
[124] Refer to footnote 72.

him. Would this mean that everyone and anyone could be "chosen" without belonging to any religion or community? Would this mean that to be chosen may not necessarily be a religious experience? Like the Sodomites and Lot, Abraham reacts ecstatically when he is exposed to an immemorial affirmation, to a call, a mandate, and a conductivity that has no origin, that cannot be touched or penetrated but marks the space and the limit where multiple substitutions, analogies, and names part and depart. In the threshold of his senses, he experiences the affirmation of this conduct, conductivity, and communication, which he does not know and does not fully grasp. His passion is hospitable to a transitivity that distorts his senses, to an exteriority that interrupts his beliefs. His frenzy drives him to abandon his family and community and to give hospitality to an unknown dispersion, a voice that displaces, a gaze that may not be seen or named because it is in excess of every name and every gaze.

Abraham does not inherit this affirmative conductivity. The sending, arrival, gaze, voice, texture, and specter that he experiences in the threshold of his senses are immemorial, unprecedented, new, and recurring. He does not learn this immemorial call from his father, a maker of idols. The "sending" does not belong to the realm of knowledge, culture, or inheritance; it simply "does not belong." Abraham desires (with a desire that surpasses the love for his family and community) an incommensurable specter that is unrecognizable by means of presence, absence, or any known name.

If Abraham practices an unconditional hospitality to the coming of the other, so do the people of Sodom who are endowed with an extreme passion for the foreigner, the stranger, and the other. Like Abraham, they welcome the unrestricted arrival of the other, even if the coming and the call might bring catastrophe. They abandon themselves to any other that is other, any newcomer (including Abraham and Lot), even if it means that the other could destroy them:

> It's between these two figures of hospitality [the unconditional "law of unlimited hospitality" with "the laws of hospitality"] that responsibility and decisions have to be taken in practice. A formidable ordeal— while these two hospitalities are not contradictory, they remain heterogeneous even as, perplexingly, they share the same name. Not all ethics of hospitality are the same, of course, but there is no culture or form of social connection without a principle of hospitality. This ordains, even making it desirable, a welcome without reservations or calculation, an unlimited display of hospitality to the new arrival. But a cultural or linguistic community, a family or a nation, cannot fail at the very least to suspend if not to betray this principle of absolute hospitality: so as to protect a "home," presumably, by guaranteeing property and "one's own" against the unrestricted arrival of the other; but also so as to try to make the reception real, determined, and concrete—to put it into practice. Hence the "conditions" that transform gift into contract, openness into

legal pact; hence rights and duties, frontiers, passports and ports; hence laws about an immigration of which we say that we have to "control the flow."[125]

Sodom is a space of an extreme and "pure" hospitality without laws regulating or restraining it.[126]

Why did Abraham break all the idols? Why does he rebel against his father, a maker of idols? What did he see, hear, or perceive in secret that prompted his ecstatic and explosive behavior? What caused him to turn against all his beliefs and suspend all his alliances with family, culture, and heritage? The ecstatic conductivity that prompts Abraham's actions does not have roots, memory, religion, or family traditions. Abraham remains faithful to a foreign and ecstatic conductivity in the threshold of his senses. With a desire beyond desire (a desire that does not coincide with anything that is familiar to him), with a desire that misses every mark and "does not belong," he gives hospitality to

---

[125] Derrida, "The Principle of Hospitality," in *Paper Machine*, trans. Rachel Bowlby (Stanford: Stanford University Press, 2005), 66.

[126] [Derrida responds to Richard Kearney] "I am not sure there is pure hospitality. But if we want to understand what hospitality means, we have to think of unconditional hospitality, that is, openness to whomever, to any newcomer. And of course, if I want to know in advance who is the good one, who is the bad one—in advance!—if I want to have an available criterion to distinguish between the good immigrant and the bad immigrant, then I would have no relation to the other as such. So to welcome the other as such, you have to suspend the use of criteria." "Desire of God," in *God, The Gift, and Postmodernism*, ed. John D. Caputo and Michael J. Scanlon (Indiana: Indiana University Press, 2001), 133.

an indeterminate alterity that multiplies his taste for the foreign and the uncanny, which remains his highest passion, an intoxication that chisels an inner secret that he does not choose but rather chooses him.

Abraham pleads for Sodom, for the other. He is impassioned by the same exteriority without contours, by the same "external" and nonreferential excess that overwhelms them. He tries unconditionally to be hospitable to an irresistible but silent voice that comes to him and takes him hostage. It starts in his father's home, when a voice asks him to break his father's idols, continues with the sacrifice of Isaac, and ends with the destruction of Sodom. Abraham implores for Sodom (which he did not even do for Isaac). He attempts to bargain with God multiple times [ten verses of Genesis (18:22–32)], pleading for the righteous people of Sodom:

> And Abraham drew near, and said, Wilt thou also destroy the righteous with the wicked? Peradventure there be fifty righteous within the city: wilt thou also destroy and not spare the place for the fifty righteous that are therein? That be far from thee to do after this manner, to slay the righteous with the wicked: and that the righteous should be as the wicked, that be far from thee: Shall not the Judge of all the earth do right? And the Lord said, If I find in Sodom fifty righteous within the city, then I will spare all the place for their sakes ... (18:23–26)

Acceding to the conductivity of an impenetrable excess, and welcoming the call beyond given ethics and commands, Abraham pleads for Sodom and Gomorrah; he appeals for a cosmic justice that surpasses his relation to God and to His decrees and mandates. Abraham is mandated by a conductivity other than God and in excess of God, which propels him to discuss with God, who, for an instant, is surpassed by Abraham's impetus for justice, by his conduct and conductivity that surpass God's mandates. Abraham welcomes a murmur/threshold/trace/interval that is unlocalizable (between inside and outside), a secret conduct that welcomes what is absolutely other and ruins the familiar love for his father, his wife, his son, and his community. At the same time, Abraham's association with what remains without analogy is what makes possible any interaction with the other, thereby creating social bonds.[127]

Abraham wants to save a few of the people of Sodom. Thus, he asks God: "Wilt thou also destroy the righteous with the wicked?" (Genesis 18:22–23). But it was not a matter of numbers and calculations. How to discern between the righteous and the wicked? Is the "sin" of the Sodomites "right" or "wrong"? The Sodomites adore what exceeds the boundaries of morality or ethics, so how could Abraham (who also loved an unfigurable exteriority with a similar

---

[127] "As Derrida adds, only a radical secret makes the relation to the other—being with, or the 'social bond'—possible in the first place. For without an absolute and therefore unresponsive secret, no one could enter into a relation with someone as someone *else*, as 'the other' whose difference from the self—regardless of its closeness—always remains the matter of a secret encrypted into its very existence as other." Peter Fenves, "Out of the Blue," in *Futures of Jacques Derrida*, ed. Richard Rand (Stanford: Stanford University Press, 2001), 124.

overflowing excess) approach the realm of judgment if the "sin" of the Sodomites consists precisely on exceeding the boundaries of ethics that Abraham also surpasses?

> How are we to name the regime or the register according to which "adoration" is to be conceived? It is quite clear that this is not politics. Neither are we in the arena of morality, ethics, or aesthetics: instead the point seems to be, in relation to these categories, to exceed their boundaries.[128]

Are there any ethics or morals that could guide Abraham or the Sodomites toward the unconditional hospitality to the absolute other? How can one decide on the unknown, on that which is without qualities and qualification? Abraham gave unconditional hospitality to the unknown and the unknowable, for he could not decide if he should say yes or no to something that is unknowable, without or beyond being, without knowledge, and without a name. Like the Sodomites, he embraced the unknown, was mesmerized by it, and let it come even at the expense of fracturing himself and his family:

> Abraham receives the visitation of Yahweh, and ... this unexpected apparition by an uninvited visitor ... this nonawaited irruption ..., this visitation of Yahweh is so rather surprising and over-taking ... that Abraham's identity is fractured. This is indeed hospitality *par excellence* in which

---

[128] Nancy, *Adoration*, 86.

the visitor radically overwhelms the self of
the "visited" ...[129]

Like the Sodomites, Abraham is overwhelmed by
an overflowing visitation. Not unlike Lot, who does not
hesitate to sacrifice his virgin daughters to the crowd,
Abraham experiences a communication with a conduct and
a conductivity that tempts and summons him. Abraham
abandons himself (welcomes, gives hospitality) to this
suspense, this invitation that comes from an elsewhere and
that ruins every experience of established familiarity and
belonging. The surplus desire of Abraham and the Sodomites
is very "real" but unclassifiable through any social, religious,
or political principles. Their ecstatic desire opens a threshold
without determination, an undecidable experience of freedom
that involves also freedom to decide about the undecidable.

Abraham and the Sodomites follow this invitation
without established pathways. Their experience surpasses
any given language and cannot be formulated as a concept
or as public knowledge. They are receptors of this sending in
passing that is without name, not even the name "God." And,
perhaps, that is the highest sin of the Sodomites and Abraham.
Their most unforgiving sin, the secret that they carry for
eternity is that whatever they sense is without comparison
(it is like nothing that is known or will be known—it is
unseemly), beyond/without God, and without/beyond
religion. The "spectral errancy" they experienced is without
citation, without memory, and may appear at any moment
in any given time, from ashes. Their sin is a recurring scene,
a theme that persists for anybody and everybody when an

[129] Derrida, "Hostipitality," 372.

125

idiom that impassions returns through a name that inflames and burns itself. Anyone could be "chosen" at any moment (without religion) by the coming (return) of the other, by a "secret" vision, voice, or call that arrives and leaves in passing a specter that (re)inaugurates the perception between inside and outside, between the sensible and the intelligible, between body and soul; it is the return of the gift giving space/trace/trance that cannot be learned, memorized, archived, or appropriated "as such":

> Spectral errancy of words. This revenance does not befall words by accident, following a death that would come to some or spare others. *All* words, from their first emergence, partake of revenance. They will always have been phantoms, and this law governs the relationship in them between body and soul. One cannot say that we know this *because* we experience death and mourning. That experience comes to us from our relation to this revenance of the mark, then of language, then of the word, then of the name.[130]

Abraham could have been one of the Sodomites himself, for he also had a passion for a spectral alterity without equivalence. In an exorbitant moment of madness, they both see in secret an ineluctable provocation in passing that mesmerizes them and tempts them to abandon their beliefs. The surplus of the experience surpasses universal principles and accepted values and welcomes the opening of what does

---

[130] Derrida, "Shibboleth," 53.

not belong. They are not responding to an established system of laws and ethics; rather, their desire exceeds any system of values as they yield to an experience that differs from law and familiar ethics. An impossible justice tempts them with its possibility from the very threshold of their senses. No law or established ethics can precede the singularity of their response, of their unfigurable surpassing. Their gestures and decisions are put in motion through what remains unfigurable, a space that is mapped or, rather, traced in the core of fabulous fables and their multiplying confabulations:

> We believe in a tale [*récit*] that we know to be
> unreal and unbelievable. Thus we respond
> to the invitation of fiction, which proposes
> that we confect [*fictioneer*], shape, figure (all
> the same concept) the unfigurable truth.
> But in fiction, truth is not figured as if by
> an impudent allegory: it is figured insofar
> as it is unfigurable. The infinite receives its
> finition, it opens within the finite.[131]

Abraham's attraction to an absolute inadequation of his senses is similar to the Sodomites' desire to "penetrate" an unfigurable exteriority. They are altered by an alterity that alters, by a hiatus that calls to utter a word that is missing. They are altered, moved, put in motion, and enraptured by a quiet repetition, a communication without memory, a source of rare pleasure, a "yes" that, without being a trace, anticipates all traces, even the one that promises the way to (a) God: "One must make return the repetition of that which returns,

---

[131] Nancy, *Adoration*, 96.

and must do so on the basis of its returning ... This is the source of the greatest pleasure ..."[132] In the tale of Sodom and in Isaac's sacrifice, everything seems to collapse, everything but one word that returns through the collapse of every word.

Abraham, like the Sodomites, wants to give absolute hospitality to this enchanting rhythm, to this cohesive caesura, to this noncommunicating communication that is leap, suspension, call, invitation, anticipation, and danger. Like the Sodomites, Abraham is consumed by this flame, the mute nonsensuous-sensuous opening out of which all desires unfold, desiring a desire that is in excess of every desire. Like Abraham, Sodom, the host city par excellence, becomes host and hostage of an indeterminate specter. As recipients of the alterity of the other, the Sodomites (like Abraham) mark the path of the beginning of ethics, the beginning of the Law of laws. The "unrecognizable" is what awakens them and brings them to their ecstatic awakening:

> "The unrecognizable" [*méconnaissable*], I shall say in a somewhat elliptical way, is the beginning of ethics, of the Law, and not of the human. So long as there is recognizability and fellow, ethics is dormant. It is sleeping a dogmatic slumber. So long as it remains human, among men, ethics remains dogmatic, narcissistic, and not yet thinking. Not even thinking the human that it talks so much about. The "unrecognizable" is

---

[132] Derrida, "To Speculate – on Freud," in *The Post Card: From Socrates to Freud and Beyond,* trans. Alan Bass (Chicago: University of Chicago Press, 1987), 318.

the awakening. It is what awakens, the very
experience of being awake.[133]

Their spasms, the spastic intervals that aim to what or
who is unrecognizable, awaken the beginning of ethics and
the multiplication of decrees: negations, contradictions,
and paroxysms that are never equivalent to the "yes," to the
affirmation that comes from "the unrecognizable."

In the ultimate sacrifice of meaning, in the ultimate
interruption, there is no "ultimate" or "as such" but the murmur
of ashes, "the experience of incineration which is experience
itself."[134] Through this interruption and suspension, through
this reunion in the threshold of interruption, there is no death
but the murmur that reopens the recurrent desire to envision
a missing word, a spectral texture, a silent hiatus of absolute
indifference and difference. Death, sacrifice, eschatology,
and apocalypse are interruptions of the unthematizable
conductivity, of the remainder that remains unanalyzable.
At the same time, through stories of "ultimate" destruction,
the nonobject reappears and cannot be ultimately destroyed.
A hiatus recurs, an exterior conduct does not let itself be
destroyed, or appears through destruction. This space
cannot by ruled or determined by any master (religion,
concept, or category). A word, any word, secretes the secret
of an overflowing desire for a nonobject.

Words are always disappearing words. Words disappear
as they display the pulse of a trace, of an "enamored" hiatus
that calls for more substitutions (of words). This gift, this
positive and finite infinity, these complex psychic processes of

---

[133] Derrida, *Beast Volume I*, 108.
[134] Refer to footnote 28.

grasping an unthematizable remainder may be confused with sacrifice, death, and also an enemy that hides "contaminated" desires. The "secret" is everywhere, and everyone is chosen to grasp its remaining and indestructible remains. The Sodomites' extermination cannot eradicate what in this story remains as an unthematizable remainder.

The orgiastic and unsacrificeable grasp lives on in any tale, and it speaks without speaking through the trace of disappearing words, through the experience of incineration. The desire for an unknown, spectral form is the desire to express the limit of writing, the truth that is not because there is no real or present object in advance. It is a limit and an instant when a desert silence murmurs a missing word that remains without analogy. Abraham, like the people of Sodom, is attracted to this motionless evanescence, this nonpresentable specter that talks without a sentence, as it sentences in contradictory tongues. But why are sentences confused with death sentences? Abraham and the Sodomites find themselves drawn toward a grasp without paradigm that remains unreadable.

Abraham senses the sending of an absolute "Yes" that since its opening becomes ruined. This affirmative call/invitation/salutation is not a form or an imprint, but it is a space that opens all possible names as the affirmation withdraws from all denominations (including the word "yes"). The Sodomites also sense the invitation of this affirmation, an exteriority caught in the threshold of their impressions. The exterior surplus drives their minds and bodies to an unending desire "to know," embrace, and penetrate a withdrawing and impenetrable intensity. This nonknowledge that appears in passing to Abraham and the Sodomites provokes an overflowing frenzy, a passion for an affirmation that cannot be explained by means of passion alone. This immemorial affirmation, which Abraham and the Sodomites relate to without forming a true relationship with it (with a persistent caesura or hiatus), reappears eternally through an infinite discourse that cannot exhaust the desire to grasp the texture of a scene in ruins, ruins that echo the trace of an enamored space. A recurrent desire appears in passing, in an instant, before religion and without religion, provoking an insatiable passion to grasp the hiatus that repeats incessantly without words:

> When the caesura, gap, or hiatus marks the withdrawal of the divine and the turning back of man toward the earth in Sophoclean tragedy, it plays at and undoes mourning ... Gap or hiatus: the open mouth. To give, to receive. The caesura at times takes one's breath away. When chance has it, it gives one speech.[135]

---

[135] Derrida, "Désistance," in *Psyche: Inventions of the Other, Volume II*, ed. Peggy Kamuf and Elizabeth Rottenberg (Stanford: Stanford University Press, 2008), 230.

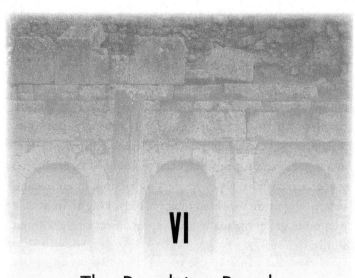

VI

The Revolving Revolt
of the Sodomites

How to give hospitality to a secret that is beyond the realm of the representable, to an altering impetus that is untouchable and impenetrable? How to give hospitality to an exteriority that exceeds visibility, a texture, a voice, a sound that is between intervals, between spaces? This is the distorting and disorienting space left by the Sodomites, an immemorial trace in the desert. The specters, the foreign exteriority, carry the possibility of an ultimate pleasure that can only be acceded through the suspension of the senses and of the sense of touch:

> Tangible excess, "hyperbole," comes to destroy the organ of this touching, "which is the essential mark of life ..." A certain tact,

a "thou shalt not touch too much," "thou shalt not let yourself be touched too much," or even "thou shalt not touch yourself too much," would thus be inscribed a priori, like a first commandment, the law of originary prohibition, in the destiny of tactile experience. Ritual prohibition would then come to be determined, *afterward*, and only on the background of an untouchability as initial as it is vital, on the background of this "thou shalt not touch, not too much," which wouldn't have awaited any religion, ritual cult, or neurosis of touch. In the beginning, there is abstinence. And without delay, unforgivingly, touching commits perjury.[136]

The destruction of the Sodomites does not touch the "as such" of ultimate death, but it is rather "the infinite moment of their death" suspended in a syncopeic interval. After the "destruction" of Sodom, its mark remains as a monstrous anomaly that one would not cite or recite, a mark without reference, an unreadable trace. Their spastic choreographies remain external to the story and eternally silent. This "virus" that infects the Sodomites would even be made external to God and to what he created; a contamination external to nature. This uncanny exteriority will continue to return through a spectral errancy of metaphors and metonymies in the threshold of perception where a superlative relation to the other advances without steps. For an eternal instant ("eternal" for its return and recurrence), the Sodomites' senses search

---

[136] Derrida, *On Touching*, 47.

errantly for the missing impression, for the texture that gives all forms their chance to unfold. In an instant, the Sodomites touch an exorbitant limit, a limit that multiplies, an edge out of which the very possibility of the law can have a chance, out of which religion will have the chance to sentence and command.

The Sodomites' dissembling surplus advances through a repetition without steps. An ultimate destruction cannot take place in Sodom because an unanalyzable interval remains, one that may not be monopolized or usurped by any person, town, religion, or institution. Expansion, contraction, and suspension revolve around a threshold of sense where revolting desires reach a sense of touch dissolving into a trace. Their unclassified desiring grasp is in excess of gender and of categories (genres). Their excess inhabits all genres, all sexual pleasures but without belonging to anyone in particular. The spastic gestures of the Sodomites, their expanding and contracting rhythms, their ecstatic choreographies are the revolutionary turns and twists toward a what or who, a figureless figure, an analogy without analogy that approaches in a distance without measure. Their expanding and contracting impressions and gestures attempt to grasp a retreating specter who is there, here, nowhere, everywhere, in passing, and without but within. In the process of grasping and translating this hiatus of the senses, hands multiply their grasp in order to touch/penetrate the unappropriable rhythm of a mute and immutable specter that is not unlike the figure of Psyche:

> Psyche is extended, *partes extra partes*; she
> is nothing but a dispersion of indefinitely

parceled-out locations in places that divide themselves and never interpenetrate. No fitting inside anything, no overlap; everything is outside another outside— anyone can calculate their order and report on their relations. Only Psyche knows nothing of this; for her, there are no relation between these places, these locations, these pieces of a place ... Flustered and mischievous, all at once, Eros contemplates her.[137]

All names at hand collapse in the threshold of touch; all names but a missing (lingering) word that remains without denomination and domination, a floating and contaminating word, a sign other than God, a sign without which the name God could not stand a chance. The scene of the Sodomites at the threshold seems like the beginning of a dream when the display of desires point to a disappearing sense that cannot be allegorized or analogized with any of the senses (vision, touch, hearing, taste, smell) that unfold in dreams. The future of both religion and atheism stands in the genesis of this dream, where the reality of all realities, the trace for a missing desire unfolds through incineration:

The trace is the erasure of selfhood, of one's own presence, and is constituted by the threat or anguish of its irremediable disappearance, of the disappearance of its disappearance. An inerasable trace is not a

<hr>

[137] Ibid., 12–13.

> trace, it is a full presence, an immobile and
> uncorruptible substance, a son of God, a
> signs of Parousia and not a seed, that is, a
> mortal germ.[138]

At the gates of Lot's home, within the space of a unique opening, an implacable affirmation begins to exist but through its negation, repression, dissimulation, sacrifice, and death. Readers of the story "rejoice" in anticipation of the Sodomites' death as they imagine an unimaginable and forbidden pleasure. They do not know what they should not desire, thereby desiring the law that represses (that says "do not pass"). The law opens and inaugurates, provokes and forbids from an affirmative edge that the law inverts into a "do not pass." This is the edge from which every religion departs and recurs incessantly; the edge of an orgiastic principle that is dissimulated, absorbed, and covered up; the edge from which the voice of the law says: "pass" but "do not pass"; "you may pass but without (tres)passing"; "I entice you to penetrate my virginal texture but without penetration"; "you may touch without touching ..." "A faith that would stand up unflinchingly to the atheism without reserve in which it would be nothing other than the 'courage' invoked to say the 'strange.' The strange: a divine body discerning."[139] "Do not pass" and "shall not ..." become orders that invite violation and entice trespassing: [The command] "compels the violation of its own law, whatever one does, and it violates it itself ... He [The command] is destined to violate himself,

---

[138] Derrida, "Freud and the Scene of Writing," in *Writing and Difference*, trans. Alan Bass (Chicago: University of Chicago Press, 1978), 230.
[139] Nancy, *Dis-Enclosure*, 73.

and this is his entire beauty, the sadness of his strength, the hopeless weakness of his all-powerfulness."[140]

At the edge of an affirmation, religion commands about a sending/arrival/repetition that it can neither command nor know. At the edge of an affirmation without contours, multiplicative decrees are displayed that dissimulate, repress, forbid, and organize the affirmative, irrepressible, and infallible desire of a deferred surplus. On the one hand, the impetus of the Sodomites makes possible the limits of the familiar and the lawful. At the same time, and on the other hand, the commanding desire of the Sodomites exceeds ethics and does not belong to any community, promised land, identity, or established religion. Their impetus to embrace the other, what is (w)hol(l)y other, wonders freely and does not belong:

> But this infinity is minute, and the words of love are too big for it. Or rather, they are really too small … I don't know anymore. I should perhaps give them all to you, send them all to you, all imprinted, as one touches everywhere the minute infinity of skin, with impatience, with this boundless disorder that never finds an order or a measure, except by being always shaken, always broken, rushed to multiply itself, a nervousness of fingers on masses, on flanks, and in secret folds—with nothing more that is secret, in

---

[140] Derrida, "Envois," in *The Post Card: From Socrates to Freud and Beyond*, trans. Alan Bass (Chicago: University of Chicago Press, 1987), 59.

> the end ... I should have sent everything, a
> thousand pages of love and not one word on
> it, to you alone. All the words of love from
> everyone ... It would have flown into pieces,
> barely through toward you, as it always flies
> into pieces as soon as it is sent.[141]

Their disruptive passion tends to dissemble established beliefs, continuously inciting a noncommunity of passionate thinkers to revolt in a thousand revolutions against a million decrees that promise to grasp (through a "*via negativa*") an ultimate nearness to a safe, sound, and holy space: "What is the proximity of the near? The thing certainly can be near, but the near of proximity is not near."[142] This state of irruption and interruption, this impetus to love the foreigner, the foreign, and the advent of the unknown stirs up the individual and entangles him/her in a determinate passion that is indeterminate, a passion that surpasses passion with passion. This excess that exceeds, this affirmative passion that does not belong to the realm of memory, this vanishing trace remains in the remains of embers and ashes, and resurges incessantly without archive from the vestiges of a forgotten desert. There is no preservation in Sodom but an infinite consumption without reserve, and when all is turned into cinders, the affirmative passion still resurges and resuscitates; it sends itself through enamored ashes:

> The proper name does not come to erase
> itself, it comes by erasing itself, to erase itself,

---

[141] Nancy, *Inoperative Community*, 109.
[142] Derrida, "Pace Not(s)," 25.

> it comes only in its erasure, or, according to
> the other syntax, *it amounts to, comes back to*
> *[revient à] erasing itself. It arrives only to erase*
> *itself* ... It guards itself from and by itself,
> and this gives the "movement." It sends
> [*envoie*].[143]

The grounds of religions steal away the name that comes to erase itself and at the same time incorporates it in the confines of religion. Religion incinerates the Sodomites' affirmative passion and transforms it into a thousand "nos" that can never amount to the "contaminated," human desire of the Sodomites who say "yes" to the anticipation of an unsacrificeable and unnamable ("unseemly") passion. Every community remains at the gates of this passion where no community exists but from which the possibility of every community draws its morals and ethics (through a negative passion or a negative theology). The ecstatic nihilism of the Sodomites, their passion for the unknown, and their nonobjective desire deferred to infinity makes possible the unfolding of every future community of shifting and revolving believers, one in which it is possible to desire the impossible, a community without community in which its turning and revolt are associated with the highest desire: one that being impenetrable remains unconquered and recurring.

---

[143] Derrida, "To Speculate," 360.

VII

The "Little Death" at the Threshold

In the versicles of Sodom, there is a cartography of a
story built as a geometry of thresholds, lines, and edges;
a landscape of planes, figures, and specters that aim to a
hiatus of pleasure that is "present" through a trace, through
a succession that does not take place, that takes place
through erasure. It is a movement of traces that sends and
communicates, that arrives only not to arrive, that arrives
only to suspend arrival, that traces in trance the arrival
without arrival of an unpronounceable spectral errancy
that remains out of grasp. In this trance in suspension
and suspense, there is a consuming passion that draws,
through interruption and deferral, the very interval of an
orgasm. The nature of the act of reaching orgasm requires
a constant interruption, a deferral that contains and releases
the proximity to ecstasy, a proximity that requires an active
abandonment, a yielding that culminates in a suspension of

pleasure as it is released and relieved. Intervals of succession composed of inhalation and exhalation aim to release and retain a final suspended interval, an inaudible syncope that is impenetrable and immemorial and that will resurge after each release, depletion, and consumption.

The overflowing act consists, through all its intervals, in carrying out an inaudible exhalation, a penetration that remains impenetrable, an interval that erases itself but returns anew (only to erase itself again) in every sexual act. In the act of penetration or being penetrated, one can never penetrate penetration. In the culmination of ecstasy, "penetration" culminates untouched through an ultimate suspension that releases pleasure and ultimately interrupts the penetration of penetration. Penetration defers penetration in the act of penetration. The word/act acquires different meanings as one advances without steps, as one yields to the movement that it gives without ultimately "giving itself" as it sends itself by erasing itself. One will have penetrated a figure, a compounding texture that is always in excess of itself and is never equal to a sum of desiring images. This mute excess (the reaching of a penetrating climax) starts all over again, returns anew as other than climax and penetration, and remains without penetration. The instant of every climax is similar to a certain annihilation without annihilation. In the very instant that orgasm is released and relieved, one is able to see without seeing his/her mute ecstatic death but without dying. This "point" is as impenetrable as the vertex of a pendulum.

During intercourse, the multiple turnings, the contraction and expansion of pleasure, its containment, release, deferral, and interruptions aim toward a "little death" ("a momentary extinction of a highly intensified excitation"), toward the consummation and consumption of climax, toward the interruption that has exceeded all interruption:

> We have all experienced how the greatest pleasure attainable by us, that of the sexual act, is associated with a momentary extinction of a highly intensified excitation. The binding of an instinctual impulse would be a preliminary function designed to prepare the excitation for its final elimination in the pleasure of discharge.[144]

The little death is where the multiplying figures of desire are consumed and suspended in an overwhelming effacement, in a mute abandonment where desire is discharged without expiring, where suspension does not stop the advance of a surplus that cannot stop or be stopped, where desire subsides as it departs again and again through a trace without archives. The little death is an enjoyment, a desire, a pleasure that is never at hand and that cannot be experienced "as such." When lovers reach climax (the little death), they reach an interruption in an instant when desire exceeds every desire, when all desires withdraw to a syncopeic moment, an exhaustion that opens the pulse and compulsion to desire again:

> But isn't it proper to desire to carry with it its own proper suspension, the death or

---

[144] Sigmund Freud, *Beyond the Pleasure Principle*, trans. James Strachey (New York: W.W. Norton & Company, 1989), 76.

the phantom of desire? To go toward the
absolute other, isn't that the extreme tension
of a desire that tries thereby to renounce its
own proper momentum, its own movement
of appropriation?[145]

The Sodomites are also suspended in an orgasmic hiatus,
in an annihilation without annihilation as they attempt
to reach toward the absolute other. Sodom incarnates an
intervallic excess, a quiet exuberance that no violence can
destroy and no passion can exhaust. A syncopeic repetition
ignites from the threshold of our senses, an insistent desire
for a new beginning. The desire that wants more (and that
cannot be defined in terms of desire alone), the supplement
that supplements desire hopes for the coming of the other:
"all great love is even above all its pity; for it still wants to
create the beloved."[146] The interval (the surplus of Sodom)
remains untranslatable, without a proper analogy, and ready
to be transfused through a bloodless transfusion into a new
passion, into the "perhaps" of a "whom" or a "what." Whatever
is annihilated in Sodom remains without annihilation and
without analogy (as a surplus that harbors any possible
analogy). A "little dead" (a syncopeic spasm) lives on in
the threshold of every gender, at the edge of every sexual
orientation, as a "perhaps" and a "yes" to associate, link,
communicate, embrace with the other. This "extinction of
a highly intensified excitation," this "final elimination in the
pleasure of discharge," this drive that does not translate into

---

[145] Derrida, *On the Name*, 37.

[146] Friedrich Nietzsche, *Thus Spoke Zarathustra: A Book for None and All*, trans. Walter Kaufmann (New York: Penguin Books: 1978), 90.

an object is the movement that remains irreducible in the transit of desires in Sodom. This exteriority, this trace that traces a desire that has no specific object and itself is not an object, this point whose excess is the pendulum remains without analogy in the charged threshold of the Sodomites and in their enamored cinders:

> No analogy is more fitting here than that of sexual joy and *jouissance*: not satisfaction, not the easing of tension, not becoming replete, but the infinite relational tension between two bodies, which is to say, between two drives caught up in their contact, which is both sensitive and beyond sense. Drive, a thrust coming from elsewhere, from outside, from nowhere, which opens up in us; which comes from there but which, at the same time, opens up this unlocalizable place; which comes from mystery and produces it, which triggers its flash and goes back into its night: to the absence of solution, to the dis-solution where truth resides.[147]

Sodom is like the disappearing point of the pendulum of desire. The pendulum may go from right to left, but there is an X-point, the very thrust of the pendulum, that sends and saves itself by erasing itself. The X-point remains virtually without movement. The conductivity of the evanescent X-point sends the pendulum into motion, forming intervals. The point takes place without taking place through the intervals that

---

[147] Nancy, *Adoration*, 61.

it forms. The X-point cannot be explained in terms of the pendulum's movement and is not unlike the very culmination of climax (the "little death" described by Freud), when lovers reach a mute point that no longer resists, releases, expands, or contracts. In the X-point, all intervals of pleasure come to erase themselves as the X-point saves itself for a new sending. It sends the sending (the X-point is deferred) as it is excluded from the process of coitus. The process of *coitus* is a function of *quietus*. The coitus points toward a quiet plenitude where all energy is released and relieved. This quietude is neither someone nor something. It is a crossing that is not crossed. It is the point (of the pendulum) from which passion parts, departs, turns, returns, and expires again only to start anew:

> "What," the "what": one can call that the thing, the *res*, or the nothing [*rien*] of the thing, a thing that is not someone, neither a subject nor a self, nor a consciousness, nor a human being, nor a *Dasein*, the thing that does not think, does not speak and does nothing, the thing that remains silent [*coite*], if you want to play on this homonym whereby the *quoi* remains *coi* (c.o.i.) i.e. mute and immobile, a tranquil force, and *coite*, *coite* meaning not coitus [*coït*] but coming from *quietus*, which means "at rest, tranquil, impassive."[148]

The spastic beats, their intervallic torsions and contortions, are the truth of the point but not vice versa. The

---

[148] Derrida, *Beast Volume I*, 199.

truth of the suspended point (the point without analogy) is the multiple intervallic spaces that expand and contract in the pendulum. In sum, the threshold of erotic manifestations, desires, passions, and attractions is something immutable, distant, and nonerotic—but highly desirable:

> This point, lacking dimension as do all points, form the opening of the world, the opening of sense in the world. Through this opening, sense penetrates and escapes at the same time, in the same movement an in "making sense" just as much by the penetration as by the escape.[149]

One may speculate that the Sodomites wish to touch and penetrate a figure that is impossible to touch as such: the very point of the pendulum, the generous and disappearing conductivity that does not let itself be bound by any master (by any genre, gender, family, nation, or religion), the nonobject that can never be fully appropriated and always parts and departs into spastic modes of motion and emotion:

> Therefore the *exappropriating* structure is irreducible and undecomposable. It redirects repression. It always prevents reappropriation from closing on itself or from achieving itself in a circle, the economic circle or the family circle. The repressed drive ... : undisciplined, refractory, untamed, never permitting itself to be bound

---

[149] Nancy, *Adoration*, 39.

> or banded by any master, it always pushes
> forward. It is that the backward path ... is
> always both displaced and "obstructed" by
> a repression. The latter does not affect the
> *Weg* or the step or the outside, it is its very
> proceeding [*demarche*], and in advance finds
> itself *unterwegs*, en route.[150]

Whatever is repressed, neutralized, or usurped in Sodom remains "undisciplined, refractory, untamed, never permitting itself to be bound or banded by any master." From this displaced and undisciplined conduct, the passion of religion and atheism find their multiple routes (steps, paths, decrees, etc.) rerouted.

"This" threshold (of the senses) without analogy impassions incessantly, reaches for a texture that invites and calls for translation and analogy but remains without a name. All the temples of the world will not be able to bring home this threshold of passion, a hiatus that may translate, at times, as apocalyptic or "a thing of the devil" precisely because it hides from presence, precisely because it is neither an object, nor a name, nor an embraceable faith. Thus, the most violent forcefulness in the threshold of Sodom is without strength. Instead, it is where all passions meet to translate a blinding sign that retreats while saying "Yes," "come." Sodom is a tale where everybody "disappears" (everybody and everything vanishes but the nonthing that they loved and lives on as

---

[150] Derrida, "To Speculate," 362.

trace, an immemorial and inenarrable affirmation, an errant anticipation for whomever and whatever comes).[151]

The Sodomites are in a trance as they step into the entrance of an intensity that cannot be renounced, a proximity that crosses through gender and sexuality. A conduct and conductivity flows through a spastic space in passing, a hiatus through which emotions, desires, genders, and genres find multiple traces that calculate a relationship with a spectral errancy, a grasped dwelling in the margins of a multiplying knowledge. This conductivity in the threshold (of sense), this charged space and spacing exceeds the grasp; it is in excess of knowledge; it is in excess of the very syntax that it propels. With their multiplying attraction and desperate hands, the Sodomites try to reach for an infallible relationship to what or who is other:

> What if we were to reach, what if we were
> to approach here (for one does not arrive at
> this as one would at a determined location)
> the area of a relationship to the other where
> the code of sexual marks would no longer be
> discriminating? The relationship would not
> be a-sexual, far from it, but would be sexual
> otherwise: beyond the binary difference that
> governs the decorum of all codes, beyond

---

[151] Derrida cites the following paragraph from Blanchot's *Death Sentence/L'arrêt de mort*: "… I gave her/it all my strength and she/it gave me all her/its strength, so that this strength is too great, it is incapable of being ruined by anything, and condemns us perhaps, to immeasurable unhappiness, but if that is so, I take this unhappiness on myself and I am immeasurably glad of it and to that thought, to her I say eternally, 'Come,' and eternally she/it is there. "Living On," 191.

the opposition feminine/masculine, beyond bisexuality as well, beyond homosexuality and heterosexuality which comes to the same thing. As I dream of saving the chance that this question offers, I would like to believe in the multiplicity of sexually marked voices. I would like to believe in the masses, this indeterminable number of blended voices, this mobile of non-identified sexual marks whose choreography can carry, divide, multiply the body of each "individual," whether he be classified as "man" or as "woman" according to the criteria of usage.[152]

Sodom is the immemorial and unpresentable mark of an exceeding conduct, a conductivity that through the history of religion is suspended, repressed, preserved, and relaunched. The multiplying traces of what is humane, divine, affirmative, and other than humane are interrupted in their plenitude, converted into ashes, and substituted by a dogma that puts itself in the place of substitutions, in the place where "conduct" (conductivity) becomes conduct (acceptable behavior), in the place where "mandate" (what sends/is sent) becomes sentence, command, and decree: "The divine has been ruined by God. That is to say, by man, who in permitting himself to be separated from Life by God, in permitting himself to be usurped from his own birth, became man by polluting the

---

[152] Derrida, "Choreographies." in *Points ... Interviews, 1974–1994*, ed. Elisabeth Weber, trans. Christie V. McDonald (Stanford: Stanford University Press, 1995), 108.

divinity of the divine."[153] Sodom is the hiatus from which anybody who is any other could be chosen; however, and at the same time, its surplus, its conductivity that trespasses and transports is circumvented by a multiplicity of discourses and dogmas that attempt to usurp the nonobject (the "trans" that remains, the remains of what remains without analogy and unassignable):

> Since this bond between singularities, as well as the promise it carries, is what I call *spectral*, it cannot be made into a community; the promise of the bond forms neither a national, linguistic, or cultural community, nor does it anticipate a cosmopolitan constitution. It exceeds all cultures, all languages, it even exceeds the concept of humanity.[154]

An untranslatable pulse intensifies in the dreamlike story where the people of Sodom personify a hand caught in an eternal repetition, a proximity to a secret and sacred writing, to a spectral and errant texture that may not be approached in terms of closeness or distance. Sodom's ashes are an extinction without extinction, a destruction that leaves a remainder, a trace that remains without residues. The nonobject shows in passing without unfolding, without demonstrating itself, and without demonstration, yet it is so "real."[155]

---

[153] Derrida, "The Theater of Cruelty and the Closure of Representation," in *Writing and Difference*, trans. Alan Bass (Chicago: University of Chicago Press, 1978), 243.

[154] Derrida, "Nietzsche and the Machine," 241.

[155] "Freud appears to cling to the reality of an event (the Oedipus Complex), but this event is a sort of non-event, an event of nothing or

The effacement of Sodom (of its orgiastic impetus) embraces a certain death, one that does not die but rather fades away, erases itself, suspends itself only to return through forgetfulness (in a trace without archive or memory). The future of religion (and atheism) depends on both the attempt to repress (cover up, neutralize, usurp) and to capture insistently the trace that desires what or who is not representable with a passion that overflows desire. This interruption of passion surpassing passion lives on in the incinerated remains of what is without remains, in the enamored ashes of a forgotten desert plunged in the unconscious:

> This erasure is death itself, and it is within its horizon that we must conceive not only the "present," but also what Freud doubtless believed to be the indelibility of certain traces in the unconscious, where "nothing ends, nothing happens, nothing is forgotten." This erasure of the trace is not only an accident that can occur here or there, nor is it even the necessary structure of a determined censorship threatening a given presence; it is the very structure which makes possible, as the movement of temporalization and pure *auto-affection*, something that can be called repression in general, the original synthesis

a quasi-event which both calls for and annuls a narrative account. For this 'deed' or 'misdeed' to be effective, it must be somehow spun from fiction. Everything happens *as if*." Derrida, "Before the Law," 198. (My parenthetical emphasis.)

of original repression and secondary repression, repression "itself."[156]

The unfolding of religion depends on both covering up and exposing the love for a nonobject that escapes the grasp of every desiring and imploring hand. The abhorrence, destitution, and defamation of the Sodomites (their most absolute repression) are categorical and self-defeating. It is imperative to condemn a town where no righteous people may be found (not even ten), "And he (Abraham) said ... 'Peradventure ten shall be found there.' And He said: 'I will not destroy it for the ten's sake.'"[157]; however, what is the sin of the Sodomites that must be repressed, erased, and exterminated? According to God, their sin, which is neither specified nor described in any manner, is "exceeding grievous," "And the Lord said: 'Verily, the cry of Sodom and Gomorrah is great, and, verily, their sin is exceeding grievous.'"[158]

The unfigurable sin of the Sodomites is in excess of every desire, a surplus exceeding in a grievous manner. The incommensurable excess of the Sodomites displays their infinite mythical powers insofar that their excess is figurable as an unfigurable truth. The unfigurable excess that is erased is at the beginning of a trace grasped at the gates of religious language, a negative and forceful language of commands and laws that is foundational, that founds against an overflowing genesis that is in excess of its trace.[159] The mythical foundation

---

[156] Derrida, "Freud and the Scene of Writing," 230.

[157] Torah, Genesis, 18:32.

[158] Torah, Genesis, 18:20.

[159] "What must be thought, therefore, is this exercise of force in language itself, in the most intimate of its essence, as in the movement

of the religious law is unthinkable without Sodom's assumed disposition to an "exceedingly grievous" desire that is not defined and that "should" be obliterated. The evilness of Sodom is assumed, presupposed, universalized without a proper concept or definition. The force of moral legislation rests in a secret evilness that cannot be revealed but must be eradicated:

> And this secret source of the moral legislation … can legitimately be called a secret in absence of all possible revelation: it is, to use the phrase Derrida discovered in Montaigne, the "mystical foundation of the law" … Since the source of the "fact of reason" cannot be revealed, a door is opened to interpretation. Something like "religion" can then enter into this door, or stand at the threshold, by presenting unconditional imperatives *as* divine commands, which, however, reveal nothing about their source.[160]

The "grievous sinners" sense and experience an ever greater excess. They adore something no belief can fully embrace and no law can fully disarm. The moral law says "no" in order to prescribe without grief the loss of an unfigurable excess, in order to proscribe grief of a formless form in the Sodomites that is "exceedingly grievous." The religious

---

by which it would absolutely disarm itself from itself." Derrida, "Force of Law," 238.

[160] Fenves, "Out of the Blue," 102–103.

law prescribes this incommensurable loss and at the same time proscribes it without grieving. The faithful reader would reason under the following logic: "The excess of the Sodomites represent 'evil,' we don't miss their surplus, we cannot miss what we don't want to know, what we don't want to love, and what we cannot understand (by decree)." In sum: "we don't grieve them," "we do not," "You shall not ..." ... "not." The "shall nots" multiply in the mind of the "ethical" reader in order to put at bay an excess aimed to a nonobject. When Lot offered his daughters to the Sodomites, they rejected his offer. Their "exceedingly grievous" desire did not involve human flesh. The reader "knows" by decree that there is evil in the Sodomites, but their "exceedingly grievous" evil cannot be proven: "The thesis of radical evil [developed by Kant] proves *itself* by the absence of 'proper proof.'"[161] By divine mandate, the excess of the Sodomites doubles like "the devil," like a writing that substitutes and multiplies, that needs more decrees in order to control what is out of control, beyond control, and out of grasp:

> Everything occurs and proceeds as if the devil "in person" came back [*revenait*] in order to double his double. So, as a doubling doubling his double, the devil overflows his double at the moment when he is nothing but his double, the double of his double that produces the "*unheimlich*" [the uncanny] effect.[162]

---

[161] Ibid., 107.
[162] Derrida, "To Speculate," 270.

The Sodomites yield to an imperative command more powerful than God's will, an imperative command that doubles as the command coming from God multiplies. The commanding excess of the law cannot fully repress, usurp, and control the trace of an overabundant desire, which in turn inflames the letter of the law and (paradoxically) confirms it. The trace of an incommensurable excess will continually bring "discordance" to the mastering of the law:

> The concept of justice that I am elaborating is opposed to the Heideggerian one of *dike* as joining, as *Fug*, as bringing-together; it suggests that justice is, and must be, a discordance. As soon as justice implies a relation to another, it supposes an interruption, a dis-joining, a disjunction or being-out-of-joint, which is not negative; an out-of-jointness that is not deconstructible, that is justice as deconstruction, as the possible deconstruction of any determined law[*droit*].[163]

The literal interpretation of the tale of Sodom would always be on the side of evil, destruction, sacrifice, persecution, and repudiation. But this literability iterates also a desiring trace. The Sodomites mingle with this pure interval, with a desiring texture that disorganizes their senses and thrusts their perceptions to a sense that exceeds their senses and their sense of sense: "I love because the other is the other, because his or her time will never be mine ... I can love

---

[163] Derrida, "Nietzsche and the Machine," 230.

the other in ... the form of the most loving affirmation—it is the chance of desire. And it not only cuts into the fabric of duration, it spaces."[164] The trace of the Sodomites is an affirmative interval: the mark of "a chance of desire." This chance does not have a specific body. This chance passes through everyone, independently of their gender, sexual orientation, community, nation, religion, and so on. Their desire scatters like sand, exposing an excess that is in excess of any decree and impossible to usurp.

---

[164] Derrida, "Aphorism Countertime," in *Psyche: Inventions of the Other. Volume II*, ed. Peggy Kamuf and Elizabeth Rottenberg (Stanford: Stanford University Press, 2008), 131.

VIII

Conduct, Conductivity, and the Law of Laws in Sodom

What took place, if anything, in Sodom? The story of Sodom is about delay, deferral, anticipation, passion, suspension, leap, embers, ashes, oblivion. The event announces itself, sends itself, and, if anything "happens," it takes place without taking place (through deferral and anticipation). The event lives on in the desire that desires that the impossible becomes possible. What or who is desired continues to be the event that never takes place. Sodom remains as the possibility of passage toward the "exterior" other, an impetus sensed with an interior sense that is other than sense. Sodom is the opening of every possible event, the very grasp of a "trans" (translation, transgression, transfiguration, transubstantiation, etc.). Their grasp is a dispersing flow of desire that yearns for an "externality" (a nonobject, an open word, a specter, a flesh that is fleshless). Their sense of proximity to an indeterminate other anticipates the grasp of the coming of an event that takes place at any moment, unexpectedly (at any given time, even now as the reader, or any other who is other, reads the passage). The remaining remains of Sodom live on in the trace of a desire for an anticipation that anticipates the arrival/sending of the unknown, the open word, the figure of a what/who that is "not yet," that is yet to come (the messiah, the prophet, the other, the strange, the dangerous, the uncanny):

> A word opened to whomever in the figure as well, perhaps, of some prophet Elijah, of his phantom or double. He is unrecognizable, through this monstration of monstrosity, but one must know how to recognize him. Elijah is the one to whom hospitality is due, promised, prescribed. He may come, one must know this, at any moment. He may cause the event of his coming to happen at each instant.[165]

Religion finds its path and its language of decrees and shall nots through this trace, through a word/interval/spacing opened to the indeterminate other, a word opened to whomever, an open word that opens and that is in principle without religion, for any other who is other. The stillness, the "still not," the "still to come" at the threshold unfolds the space of anticipation of what or who remains unthinkable: "This 'still not' contains a peculiar reference to something

---

[165] Derrida, "Shibboleth," 57.

still to come, of which we absolutely do not know whether it will come to us. This 'still not' is of a unique kind, which refuses to be equated with other kinds."[166] On the side of religion, the Sodomites' human passion is translated as something "exceedingly grievous," as something "unseemly," contaminating and contaminated. Its trace is subordinated to a desire for God, for an Absolute Presence, beyond human presence and beyond human desire:

> The subordination of the trace to the full presence summed up in the logos, the humbling of writing beneath a speech dreaming its plenitude, such are the gestures required by an onto-theology determining the archeological and eschatological meaning of being as presence, as parousia, as life without differance: another name for death, historical metonymy where God's name holds death in check. That is why, if this movement begins its era in the form of Platonism, it ends in infinitist metaphysics. Only infinite being can reduce the difference in presence. In that sense, the name of God, at least as it is pronounced within classical rationalism, is the name of indifference itself.[167]

On the side of freethinking and philosophy, the grasp anticipates a trace that is recurrent, mute, and without being.

---

[166] Heidegger, *What Is Called?*, 35.

[167] Derrida, *Of Grammatology*, 71.

The Sodomite's touch traces an infallible trace, an open word free of laws, decrees, or pacts, a trace that is in trans/trance/transit in the here and now and for anyone who is anybody or any other. The earthly desire at hand reaches for an unconditional and affirmative invitation, for a missing/deferred word, a distorted figure, a wondering sign sensed by a sense that surpasses the perception of the senses (all of which are associated with the a presentable presence). Earthly desire reaches for an "exteriority," for an invitation that says: "do not pass but pass this difference, interval, threshold." The passing without passage toward the alterity of the other is sensed through a desiring hand and ultimately, as readers, through the cinders of Sodom that mark the trace of an open word, of an affirmative language of the trace, of a burning language that erases itself as it sends the "yes," the event of the coming of the other:

> Cinders are all that remain of the path that might someday lead back (or forward) to the origin of language, the path that opens the possibilities of the metaphoric and the literal without being reducible to either of them … Does something within language really burn? Does language bear within itself the remains of a burning? *Cinders* is about the fire that is still burning at the origin of language, the not yet literal but more than figurative fire that can be felt in the cinders of a language.[168]

---

[168] Ned Lukacher's Introduction to *Cinders*, 1–2.

The destruction of Sodom is a tale where "apparently" everybody dies without a trace. The remains are ashes in the desert. In this deserted landscape, everything dies but the unsacrificeable. The unsacrificeable is not a presence beyond presence. The unsacrificeable is not God, but it is usurped by religion. On the one hand, the name of God is "safe" in a bottomless abyss, in a trace beyond any trace (beyond difference and deferral) that generates the genesis of a negative language that obsesses through the forbidden names of God, through a hegemonic "no," "do not pass," and "shall not" ("you shall not sense the open word, 'the spectral errancy of words.'") The secret names of God are saved in "infinitist metaphysics" of being a presence: "For God is safe in the bottomless abyss of nothingness, this desert place, leaving but His trace on language, burning and scarring language as He leaves the world, which is the event of language named negative theology."[169] On the other hand, and at the same time, the earthly and contaminated desire of the Sodomites for the absolute other cannot be completely eradicated from the "safe" and "saved" passion for God. In the atheistic scene of the story (the Sodomites opening to the arrival of the other), the affirmative trace (the Sodomites' "contaminated" desire for the anticipation of foreign and the strange) prevails through ashes as a trace that comes by erasing itself. On the side of a monotheistic "safe" God, the absolute destruction of Sodom would be forever demanding a negative language of perfectibility, an infinite negative language that consists in the usurpation and incorporation of the ecstatic trace, a negative language that promises the Parousia (presence) of a hegemonic and absolute God who is omniscient in every

---

[169] Caputo, *Prayers and Tears*, 43.

trace. The sovereignty inscribed in the genesis of religion usurps the (orgiastic) trace and renders it unreadable through a God that is beyond all names, one who is the beginning and the end of all traces. The unreadability of the open idiom (of the trace of Sodom) is before religion and without religion, and also the first inscription (usurpation) of religion.

The trace of Sodom is rendered unreadable by the inscription of negative theology on the trace. On the side of atheism, the desiring trace is an experience of indefinite deferral that can never be completely eliminated or sacrificed but only (in the worst-case scenario) infinitely covered up or dissimulated. The desiring interval of Sodom is recurring and immemorial as it is its infinite work of usurpation through multiplying ways to say "no" (by means of decrees and metaphysical "nos" associated with negative theology). The hand of the Sodomites reaches for a deferred idiom, an intermittent interval, a spasmodic grasp that withdraws from any kind of imprint.

The religious machine ignites an economy of salvation, redemption, presence, and truth through the domination of a desiring surplus contextualized as an evil that must be eradicated. The religious obsession for a clean, safe, and immaculate "morality" is made possible through an association and a dissociation with a "contaminated" passion, a "foul spot":

> [According to Kant] Bringing out, and thus
> confessing, the presence of the "foul spot"
> would be a demonstration of the perpetual
> necessity of religion; eradicating this spot
> by contrast, would create conditions for the

uninterrupted development of dispositions to the good, which, in turn, would make religion unnecessary,—or at least would render the model of goodness redundant. The value of religion as a whole—and not simply that of the model of perfect subordination to the divine will—is thus a matter either of bringing out a tainted spot in confession or of wringing it out of naked reason.[170]

The genesis of religious redemption starts with an obsessive cover-up of a misunderstood surplus, of a supplementary "blue vapor":

> All the equivocations of Kant's thesis of radical evil that resolve themselves into the ambiguity *herausbringen* ["bring out," "eradicate"] are expressions of the ineluctable duplicity of the supplementary element whose trace is supposed to be brought out and wrung out. This element, which comes into Kant's discourse as "blue vapor," makes all accounts "entirely uncertain …" From this perspective, the supplementary element displays a devilish, if not a satanic, dimension.[171]

---

[170] Fenves, "Out of the Blue," 118.
[171] Ibid.

The obsession that obsesses the passion of religion begins with the eradication of a supplementary element, a "devilish" and "contaminated" surplus. Thus, Genesis begins with the sensing of a forbidden conduct/conductivity, an exteriority that is external even to "nature." How many unnecessary wars of "good" versus "evil," "outsiders" versus "insiders" have been declared in the name of a badly understood "contamination," in the name of a forbidden and forgotten secret perceived as an "exterior evil" that was already inside as a desire that cannot be experienced as such? The fact (if one could use that word) is that the excess cannot be experienced as such, not because there is a command that forbids to experience it "as such" but because the surplus sends itself by deferral, by erasing itself, and, therefore, the conductivity is never a presence at hand (as conduct or behavior) that can be grasped or ruled with an affirmation or an opposition.

The Sodomites grasp a nonpresent sign deferred to infinity, a "perpetual recurrence of the same nonthing," which puts in motion not only a religious impetus but also a passion for art, a desire to represent a figure that escapes all forms of representation. For many centuries, art and religion (religious art) copulated in order to create a synchronicity of vision and touch about a formless figure. However, art in general tries to make sense (through multiple forms of representation) of what exceeds signification and representation. Music, literature, painting, sculpture, poetry, theater, and so on, point to the most absolute and impenetrable skin, an archaic texture (fabric/tissue/screen/threshold/murmur) that impassions the individual into a path of multiplying impressions: "What is called poetry or literature, art itself (let us make no distinction for the moment)—in other words, a certain experience of language, of the mark, or of the trait *as such*—is perhaps only an intense familiarity with the ineluctable originarity of the specter."[172] Art forms respond to a specter that refuses to be gathered in a definite form. In their multiple shapes forms, subjects, and objects, art represents the form of an unknowable exteriority. There is always an aspect in every masterpiece that escapes representation, that can never be fully objectified. Art delivers intelligible forms of a formless form that resists representation. In music, it delivers enjoyable melodies that come from intervals that are without music. In this reality of realities that remains a dream, and that refuses to be presented/represented "as such" in each and every art expression, a phantasm (a formless form) coexists with knowledge: "What happens if the absolute phantasm is coextensive with absolute knowledge?"[173] Art's specter multiplies and divides as it transmits, communicates, entices, invites, and provokes in passing the copulation with multiple forms of expression and representation, all of which are but a trace of an immemorial memory, of a spectral space, an open word interrupted at the limit, at the edge, in the threshold of an abundant passion that interiorizes a formless exteriority. The ahistorical element of Sodom remains immemorial, as an interrupted spasm and an overabundant detour. The history of every narrative to come holds the story of an infinite chain of representations that eludes, forbids, or supplements an irrepressible and affirmative desire that remains deferred.

---

[172] Derrida, "Shibboleth," 53.
[173] Derrida, "Between Brackets I," in *Points ... Interviews, 1974–1994*, ed. Elisabeth Weber, trans. Peggy Kamuf et al. (Stanford: Stanford University Press, 1995), 23.

Like Sodom, those narratives point toward the trace of an infinitely small and overabundant exteriority.

Sodom is but a play of spaces interrupted by distance and proximity, edges longing to give form to an exterior formless specter. Similarly, art, in its multiple forms and shapes, gathers an archaic surface that withdraws from figuration. The artist struggles to give form to a specter, to an exteriority that resists to be cast in any definite form. At the same time, it is this exteriority exposed, this passion to grasp/express what is "outside," which configures a multiplication of objects, a passion for signs/images that present and represent the trace of a figureless figure without contours, a specter in the threshold of sense. The artist stands alone in the threshold of his/her senses, in the threshold of figuration, as s/he tries to seize the distance between the possible presence and the never present specter of art. In this maddening substitution, the artist endlessly attempts to put on display what departs from this surplus, from this formless form. Through surfaces, perspectives, edges, and colors, the artist invents an expression that anticipates the trace of a figure that is very "real" but never present, the specter in passing that is without surface, without color, and without distance.

The artist is always getting closer to a threshold of perception, to an interruption (interval/syncope) that sets in motion an alterity, a conductivity that transfers into multiple interpretations, representations, and formulations. The artist attempts to draw from an interval that interrupts drawing and refuses any name or representation. The artist paints an object but also draws "interruption." S/he also draws (from) the unanalyzable reminder that partakes in the object that is represented. The artist aims toward the pulse of an exterior space and attempts to capture the evanescent rhythm of an archaic and ineludible surface, an affirmative opening that remains figureless and speechless at the gates of the work of art. The artist participates in portraying the mark of an infallible surface that does not leave marks but hosts all forms of expressions. S/he partakes in the threshold of sense where all reference is equivocation and detour. This is art at its best, dying without end, drawing multiple meanings at a threshold that says, "Yes, enter, but suspend vision and penetration":

> Death: we are never there, we are always there. Inside and outside, at once, but without communication between inside and outside, without mixture, without mediation, and without crossing. Perhaps that is what we have access to here, as to that which is absolutely inaccessible. Perhaps it is to this that we ourselves are the access, we mortals. Perhaps that is the water, the light, and the stuff of this visibility. The very thing, the threshold that we are, we the living. The very plane, plan, or ground of the canvas, in every sense of the words ... Here, (the) painting is our access to the fact that we do not accede—either to the inside or to the outside of ourselves. Thus we exist. This painting paints the threshold of existence. In these conditions, to paint does not mean to

> represent, but simply to pose the ground, the
> texture, and the pigment of the threshold.[174]

The artist's threshold of sense and touch is not unlike the interval of impressions in Sodom. The artist abandons himself/herself to the configuration of a formless figuration. Similarly, the trace of Sodom's threshold evokes the formless form of a vague desire, a presence dreamed and anticipated, an arche-figure that precedes all names and deities. The pulse of an archaic curvature stands before the artist in trance at the entrance or a space without borders. Art tries to copulate with the Absolute Other. In every art, religious or not, there is the trace of a disappearing god, of an evanescent/deferred living presence, of a figureless figure interrupted by the very representation that art attempts to form and configure.

Art is about the trace of an open word, and one may take a specific example to prove how art touches (every time in a new and singular way) on the untouchable. This illustration may be taken from any art representation, religious or nonreligious, modern or contemporary. For instance, the "Cuchimilcos." They are small idols (one to three feet tall) that belonged to a culture in the central coast of Perú (Chancay). This pre-Inca civilization existed between AD 1200 and 1470. Their replicas may be found in many shapes and sizes. Their arms expand like wings ready to fly or eager to embrace something or someone. Their arms and hands express surprise and awe as well as welcoming hospitality. The idols are looking with adoration at a specter before them, something intangible, indefinite, incommensurable

---

[174] Nancy, *The Muses*, trans. Peggy Kamuf, ed. Werner Hamacher & D. E. Wellbery (Stanford: Stanford University Press, 1996), 60–61.

but insistently "there." Whatever is "there," "outside," is also reflected in every pour of the idols' body language. This "external visitor" arrives as a surprise, and the idols convey their astonishment and adoration in every corner of their bodies, which are vessels that absorb the uncanny happening. It may be said that the idols' astonished bodies are thresholds that stand between spaces. It is as if a centrifugal and centripetal electricity had traversed them, a conductivity reflected in their expressions of surprise and awe. Amazed, they look at some specter of danger, marvel, an excess that not only mesmerizes their senses but produces them. There is a gravitational energy, an imprint that escapes from the open palms of the idols. The male and female idols are touched by a silent salutation in passing, a conduct that distorts their senses. They are receptive to a formless form that they try to capture and at the same time release with their open palms, which express surprise, joy, and a certain fear associated with sacred trembling rather than dread or terror. All their senses are attentive to the conductivity that is circulating through their clay bodies. They are suspended in a dancing gesture as if they hear a soundless rhythm, the interval behind of every song, a song made of mute intervals.

The idols exude a disarming excess. An overflowing adoration circulates, passes through, and withdraws from the idols' bodies. An irrepresentable but irrepressible conductivity circulates through them and before them. A god passes through their senses, a god that eludes a definite form but leaves a trace of awe in their gestures. The idols are the representations of absolute freedom and joy, of an open word that passes through their bodies, sculpting the experience of language, of the event of expressing and expression. Their expressions allegorize an ecstatic trace, a formless conductivity without analogy that is before them. Their astonished open hands, mouths, and eyes seem to touch a landscape of enamored space. The gaze of the statues is mounted in brilliant silver that accentuates the effect of being blinded by something that makes them see and touch through their senses, through a sense that exceeds the senses. It is as if they see the invisible source of the visible, the invisible source that through its withdrawal makes the visible possible. The invisible ideality that they see without seeing remains eternally flowing in their blinded silver eyes. These pieces of clay are the mark of every civilization as they attempt to express the inexpressible encounter with a formless figure, an errant specter, a foreign flesh that is kept untouched in the folds of their hands' imprint, in their blinded eyes, in their attentive ears, in the transitivity of their senses. The figures could be vessels of any civilization (with or without religion). They are receptors of a figureless form, of an external space/spacing that the idols adore. They represent the experience of touching, through all their senses, a space/spacing that remains untouchable yet touchable through a consummation that is never consumed, never visible, and never "as such." They are before the trace of language, before the open word, without which there would be no astonished idols or representations.

The idols' hands, mouth, eyes, ears, skin, and (male/female) genitals capture a sending, a conduct from an elsewhere. The female and male genitalia align perfectly with the nipples, ears, eyes, and hands, as if all the body gathered symmetrically and harmoniously to welcome what was coming. Their half-open mouths form a horizon parallel to their swelling heads and open hands as if they were saluting an exterior "thing," a nonobject that leaves them speechless. The gaping mouths express the desire of articulating an archaic idiom; they utter an adoration that both resists and demands translation. It is this *adoratio*, this excess in the word and in address to the word that the gaping mouths try to sing with a melody made of silent syncopeic intervals:

> Adoration is addressed to what exceeds address. Or rather: it is addressed without seeking to reach, without any intention at all. It can accept to not even be addressed: to be unable to aim, or designate, or recognize the *outside* to which it is dispatched. It can even be unable to identify it as an outside, since it takes place here, nowhere else, but here in the open. Nothing but an open mouth, or perhaps an eye, an ear: nothing but an open body. Bodies are adoration in all their openings.[175]

The gaping mouths express that they could not express that "idiom" that is caught in the threshold between the upper and lower lips, and that in turn withdraws into their throats' threshold. Each mouth forms an asymptote. There is a disorienting, diaphanous circularity, a foreign oneiric element parting from their mouths and departing through the rest of their bodies. A surplus orbits around them. These idols are the mark of an opening. They mark the parting and departure of not only their civilization but every civilization,

---

[175] Nancy, *Adoration*, 20.

when humankind start to grasp a formless figure that does not make itself present: the god of time, space, translation, and language; the god that invents the nameless trace that makes possible all words, so that the impression of time and space can also unfold.

In the idols rest a quiet surplus, the very texture of myth, fable, poetry, art, philosophy, and religion. What they represent is not sacrifice, or death, or war but a melancholic love for an evanescent formless form, for a blinding specter that no one will ever fully know or have but that will impassion to death every one and every other:

> One can, naturally, translate it [the specter] into the ineluctable loss of the origin. Mourning, the experience of mourning, the passage through its limit, too, so that it would be hard to see here a law governing a theme or a genre. It is experience, and as such, for poetry, for literature, for art itself.[176]

These idols are in permanent suspense sensing with gratitude a promise, a living evanescent present, a formless form that is not in existence but that opens access to everything that "is." The open hands grasping without grasping, touching without touching, and saluting to whoever or whatever was coming are in concert with an adoration toward an ubiquity to which they respond with an open-hand salutation:

> *Adoratio*: the word as it is addressed. *Oratio*: a solemn word, a word maintained [*tenue*]

---

[176] Derrida, "Shibboleth," 53.

before anything else, a tension of the voice, of the mouth, and of the entire speaking body. A word whose content is inseparable, if not indiscernible, from the address. An elevated language that is distinguished from *sermo*, ordinary language. A prayer, invocation, address, appeal, plea, imploring, celebration, dedication, salutation. And more precisely, not one or another of these registers, but a composition formed from them all. And lastly, or first of all, a salutation [*salut*]. Yes, the simple "hi"! ["*salut!*"] participates in adoration. When Derrida writes, or rather cries out, with all his might, "*salut!*—a salutation without salvation," he indicates the following: that the word addressed, the address that barely contains anything beyond itself, bears the recognition and affirmation of the existence of the other.[177]

In awe, the idols are attentive to the imperceptible moment when a nonobject, a visitor that comes from an elsewhere, addresses each and every one of their senses but cannot be contained by any or all of them. The idols are witnessing an unforeseeable, fortuitous, and surprising event. They are mirroring a surplus that has no reflection and that cannot be represented or repeated but that repeats itself recurrently and always anew. This nonpresent presence that is neither far nor close and cannot be calculated through distance retreats into the idols' multiplying gestures of awe.

---

[177] Nancy, *Adoration*, 18.

The idols are vessels of a trace whose imperceptible vestige passes through every pore of their clay bodies. The statues witness the passing of an idiom, a texture that remains untranslatable and translates into every language on earth. They witness a rhythm, an interval that salutes them, and they salute in turn and in return. Through their gestures there is a distortion of spaces (external/internal, far/close, movement/stillness). If there is art, it represents what is "there," the formless form, the irruption and interruption that remain at the gates of representation. This generous passing, this bloodless sending is the flow of life through innumerable means of expression, which, unfortunately, (and also in countless cases) may be also associated (misconstrued) with the sending of death (with a formless form that remains without analogy): "How is one to decipher this strange anteriority of an *already* that is always shouldering you with a cadaver?"[178] Sacrifice and war are but misinterpretations of the generous irruption of the other, of a bloodless transfusion of possibilities. The quiet pulse of the orgiastic secret that interrupts, dissembles, distorts, and disorganizes may be also bound, mistakenly, with chaos, nihilism, an apocalyptic destruction.

The statues salute an "exterior" dreamlike space, a "Yes" that recurs in every civilization, a soundless rhythmic interval that arrives without distance and without steps. It is what withdraws from vision that the blind statues pay heed to, as if they were watching a figure in the beginning of a dream, a figureless figure that is so real precisely because it had withdrawn from vision and presence, a withdrawal that in turn gives birth to endless forms of expressions and

---

[178] Derrida, "Between Brackets," 21.

representations. In their salutation, the statues gestures aim toward this "monstration" without demonstration, this de-monstration, this exteriority that extends incessantly to what is "there," to a space that spaces. They salute "there," to the trace of a formless form that unfolds a metaphorical ecstasy: "Art is but an immense tradition of the invention of the arts, of the birth of endless forms of knowledge. For what is properly monstrous, the monstrosity of the proper, is that there is no end to the finiteness of the figure."[179]

The two little idols aim toward this recurrent dream of dreams, to the coming of the other through a nonreferential threshold where genres mix and genders are subject to a desire that desires in excess of their sexual orientations. They salute with open hands this exterior surplus from which all sensible and intelligible realities unfold. Through the idols pass a vertiginous conductivity that turns and twists around a conversion and a conversation that will and will not become religion. They occupy a spastic interval between skin and thought, inside and outside.

With wonder, surprise, and gratefulness, the idols salute an insistent exteriority that they cannot grasp but only salute with open hands and a yielding body. They salute a spastic interval that recurrently affirms the desire for life; a repetition that says "Yes": "Let us think this thought in its most terrible form: existence as it is, without meaning or aim, yet recurring inevitably without any finale or nothingness: *the eternal recurrence.*"[180] Incorporated (usurped) by religion

---

[179] Nancy, *Muses*, 71.
[180] Nietzsche," *The Will To Power*, 55 (June 10, 1887) trans. Walter Kaufmann and R. J. Hollingdale, ed. Walter Kauffmann (New York: Vintage Books, 1968), 35.

or not, the art of expressing the joy of a desire that is in excess of every desire and that eternally recurs with a "Yes" belongs (without belonging) to every existence, to everybody who is anybody and any other.

The religions to come will rise from an unscathed threshold, from a repetition suspended on the eve of all passion, from a trace without memory where all belief is suspended; they will rise from a space from which the many names of a disappearing God recur incessantly. This memory of the immemorial opens an infinitude of images grounded in an imageless interval, a surplus that every religious art and imagination will insistently attempt to represent. The commanding laws of religion are born and reborn at the gates of the threshold of passion, oblivion, and godlessness. Without God, the Sodomites abandon themselves to a commanding call, a syncopeic leap, a blindness that forms an evanescent bridge, a conduct toward the possibility of a moral conduct to come:

> In the definition of "reflecting faith" and of what binds the idea of pure morality indissolubly to Christian revelation, Kant recurs to the logic of a simple principle ...
> : in order to conduct oneself in a moral manner, one must act as though God did not exist or no longer concerned himself with our salvation. This shows who is moral and who is therefore Christian, assuming that a Christian owes it to himself to be moral: no longer turn towards God at the moment of acting in good faith; act as

though God had abandoned us. In enabling us to think (but also to suspend in theory) the existence of God, the freedom or the immortality of the soul, the union of virtue and of happiness, the concept of "postulate" of practical reason guarantees this radical dissociation and assumes ultimately rational and philosophical responsibility, the consequence here in this world, in experience, of this abandonment.[181]

The future of religion (its legacy, repetition, and unfolding through multiple sects, cults, and interpretations of sorts) is possible through the very orgiastic atheism that religion calculates, incorporates, forbids, and neutralizes. The turn and return of religion, the turning that turns religion around (and sometimes against itself), the returning of what turns in religion and turns into religion, the spastic spams of recurrent religion and so on is bound to a syncopeic threshold, to the sending and arrival of a specter that tempts, to the trajectories of the atheistic orgiastic principle. The mechanistic return of religion secures its recurrent return through a displayed and displaced mute passion that it administers without fully governing it. For this reason, religion may produce its own deconstruction or (and this is what has been happening for two millennials) transfer the spastic interval (supplement it) with newer forms of religion that are "better" and more "truthful" that the others.

---

[181] Derrida, "Faith and Knowledge," 50–51.

IX

I Command You Not to Yield to the Sending of the "Yes"

odom is every land and no land, every community and no community. It is the nameless name from where every community delineates its name, existence, and identity. Laws and decrees will flourish from this interval of quiet excess. Multiplying "dos" and "do nots" emerge from an interrupted interval, from immemorial, enamored ashes that send themselves as erasure, oblivion, and forgetfulness. A thousand "shalls" and "shall nots" emerge from a blinking interval, from an open word that lives on through ashes. These decrees turn and twist, expand and contract from within a gift-giving conductivity that is seized, circumcised, and converted into a conduct, a behavior surveyed under the law. Decrees are delineated around this immemorial trace that entices and invites. Figures and voices hover around the spastic exteriority that is between surfaces, between edges, and between the senses. The trace of Sodom persists through its erasure and because of it; it lives on as oblivion and forgetfulness. The ecstatic "thing," the groundless reminder of what is indestructible, the conduct and sending that says "Yes" (to the Sodomites) remains because of and in spite of forbidden decrees. To destroy the traces, to forget or erase them, is also to give movement to the syncopeic "thing," to a figureless figure that remains after an apocalypse: "For there to be apocalypse, the destruction of time and space must not entail the destruction of everything but rather reveal a thing in itself that is indestructible."[182]

At the same time that the "shall" and "shall nots" postulate sentences of proper and improper conduct, the affirmative spastic conduct remains unthinkable and out of grasp. The "affirmative conduct" is not a decision, cannot be understood in terms of presence, and may not be defined in terms of the conduct associated with "shall" or "shall not." Two "conducts," a conductivity that sends, transports, transfigures, reveals, and tempts, on the one side of the coin, and a behavioral conduct on the other copulate with each other in order to bring into being a response, a conduct conditioned in the limits of an edge, a suspension, and a syncopeic leap. This tension describes the movement of anticipation for metaphors, figures, voices, laws, and decrees that acquire a "legitimate" value in their époque but that can never sufficiently grasp the impression of a conductivity that remains external and inadequate to the historical period, to the designations that swear to nominate, dominate, denominate, and abominate the desiring conductivity that precedes the conduct established

---

[182] Hägglund, *Radical Atheism*, 47.

by decrees. It is the inadequation between conducts that returns in a secret and secreted grasp, a writing that permits itself to return, recur, and transfer a conductivity that is other than (human) conduct.

What would the fate of religion be without the excess of Sodom, without this nonethical opening that will never enter the temple of religion but will be the fascination of every religion to come? Indeed, what would religion be without the excess that it represses, without the heterogeneous orgiastic principle that, at the same time, is incorporated into organized religion as the mysterium tremendum?:

> The secret of the *mysterium tremendum* takes over a heterogeneous secrecy and at the same time breaks with it. This rupture takes the form of either subordination by *incorporation* (one secret subjects or silences the other) or *repression*. The *mysterium tremendum gets carried away* [*s'emporte*], in the double sense of the term: it raises *against* another mystery but it rises *on the back* [*sur le fond*] *of* a past mystery. In the end [*au fond*] it represses, repressing what remains its foundation [*son fond*]. The secret that the event of Christianity takes to task is at the same time a form of Platonism—or Neoplatonism—which retains something of the thaumaturgical tradition, and the secret of the orgiastic mystery from which Plato tried to deliver philosophy. Hence

the history of responsibility is extremely complicated.[183]

What would the book of Genesis be without the orgiastic secret that the Sodomites took to their grave? None of the responsible laws throughout the history of religion would have any signification or intensity if those decrees did not repeat, circumvent, incorporate, and repress the "contamination" of their orgiastic impetus. None of these (negative) decrees would have any sense if below or above them one could not hear the enamored eco that says "yes," "come." What affirms and is affirmative sends itself, arrives without arriving, through ruins and destruction and beyond repressive laws.

The affirmative impetus (the affirmative nonobject, interval, exteriority) does not disappear completely after sacrifice, apocalypse, or holocaust. The exteriority that remains, the excess that sends itself to the senses from anywhere, from the very ashes of space and time, can never be cut, and it is not "seizeable" (cannot be extirpated, castrated, burned, or reduced to the absolute oblivion of nothing or nothingness). Sodom's ecstatic and recurring Law of laws, the contaminated principle of hospitality that embraces what is excessive and absolutely other, and the grasp of an exterior formless figure existed before Sodom and Gomorrah, without negation, without denegation, without memory, and without God. The archaic trace that says "yes" remains indestructible and unsacrificeable. The nonethical conduct that unfolds in Sodom can never be appropriated by any ethics and would remain as the "outside" of every religion, an "outside" that

---

[183] Derrida, *Gift of Death*, 7.

without being part of any religion "as such" would form its "interiority," its regulative laws and ideas:

> Hence, when Derrida reads Levinas he seeks to demonstrate that the relation to the other cannot be ethical as such, but is a nonethical opening that cannot be appropriated by any ethics ... As Derrida underscores in "Faith and Knowledge," the alterity of spacing "will never have entered religion and will never permit itself to be sacralized, sanctified, humanized, theologized ... Radically heterogeneous to the safe and sound, the holy and the sacred, it never admits of any indemnification" and is neither "the Good, nor God, nor Man."[184]

Sodom's untouched space (in the threshold of their deferred desires) dwell in a desert of forgetfulness. This tranquil landscape multiplies an ungraspable yet very vibrant impression of an interval of untouched passion. Like Orpheus, who at all times felt the presence of Eurydice but could not look at her directly, the Sodomites could not see but sensed the presence of the specters beyond the threshold. The scene of passion is in both cases impossible to embrace, impossible to look at, but the desire for (their) presence is very real. They advance toward a "what" or a "who" that they cannot see. They are guided by a conduct that conducts their passion toward an unembraceable nonobject. The readers of both fables can only look at the center of divine and ecstatic

---

[184] Hägglund, *Radical Atheism*, 85.

love by looking away from it. One can embrace the ethereal body by deferring this love eternally and sensing this passion through the deferral of the embrace, an interval that travels through an eternal night:

> By turning toward Eurydice, Orpheus ruins the work, which is immediately undone, and Eurydice returns among the shades. When he looks back, the essence of night is revealed as the inessential. Thus he betrays the work, and Eurydice, and the night. But not to turn toward Eurydice would be no less untrue. Not to look would be infidelity to the measureless, imprudent force of his movement, which does not want Eurydice in her daytime truth and her everyday appeal, but wants her in her nocturnal obscurity, in her distance, with her closed body and sealed face—wants to see her not when she is visible, but when she is invisible, and not as the intimacy of a familiar life, but as the foreignness of what excludes all intimacy, and wants, not to make her live, but to have living in her the plenitude of her death.[185]

Sodom does not emerge in spite of every law, but its fault and faultiness is what provokes not only the condition of the possibility of every law to come but also the possibility of thinking, of thinking what is missing from the law and from

---

[185] Blanchot, "Orpheus's Gaze," in *The Space of Literature*, trans. Ann Smock (Nebraska: University of Nebraska Press, 1989), 172.

thinking the remains of what is without remains (which is equivalent to thinking—the act of—thinking "itself"):

> It is the risk or chance of this fault that fascinates or obsesses me at this very moment, and what can happen to a faulty writing, to a faulty letter (the one I write you), what can remain of it, what the ineluctable possibility of such a fault give one to think about a text or a remainder.[186]

The fascination and dread that the story of Sodom unfolds and folds upon itself is that it is ineffaceable because it is precisely through effacement that the desiring trace of Sodom initiates a new supplemental process (a new sending, transference, mandate, conduct, conductivity, etc.). From enamored ashes, the remains of an unanalyzable spastic rhythm undoes religion and at the same time reinstates it, initiating the motion of another époque and another world plan. The return of religion will always be conceptualized through a failed promise to deliver the arrival of a being that is beyond being and beyond arrival. Decrees and prohibitions divert the spastic rhythm (which in principle cannot be touched or penetrated) while exacerbating it. These mechanistic modes of abstraction will be monopolized not only by religions (by the many names of God that keep the name of God beyond all names) but also by pseudosciences, by the many denominations of psychoanalysis, and by state apparatus, all of which will find themselves questioning at different times in the history of their institutions the

---

[186] Derrida, "At This Very Moment," 147.

inadequation to their established laws, regulations, and concepts that do not deliver the presence, essence, origins, and so forth, that they promised. Their attempts surge from grasping in passing an exteriority, a locality that "contaminates" what is present and at hand. The interval that contaminates may never be appropriated by what is proper, sound, and safe, which in turn is but the trace of this "contaminated exteriority." This hiatus remains external and detached from the law and at the same time opens the performative power and letter of the law, its impetus to act, its sentence based on a nonsentential foundation that remains disabled, in a desert within a desert. Sodom, its threshold, its ruin, and its ashes are everywhere and nowhere. It is an unfindable locality that founds: "A locality which itself is non-empirical and *non-real* since it gives rise to that which is not where it is, that which is 'missing from its place,' is not found where it is found or (but is this the same thing?) *is found* [*se trouve*] where it is not found."[187]

The unsacrificeable desire of the Sodomites is disabled only to be repeated against the background of religious fervor. The spectral angels, like the law, are vigilant and inaccessible. They press against Lot's door so that the Sodomites could not pass. They push against contours and borders creating a no-trespassing zone, a space of multiplying transgressions. There is never permission to enter the path of the "shall not" because the law is marked by this inaccessibility, this forbidden path that repeats mechanically and incessantly. The border arrests the impassioned individual, right there in the impasse where

---

[187] Derrida, "Le Facteur de la Vérite," in *The Post Card: From Socrates to Freud and Beyond*, trans. Alan Bass (Chicago: University of Chicago Press, 1987), 424.

he wants to grasp, embrace, and arrest the space/spacing of the Law of laws. The law interrupts spacing, usurps the interval, and diverts vision while granting the fiction of a clear and coherent law. The foundation of law is other than the law. Finding these foundations becomes impossible, as they remain without presence and without presentation. Because of this invisibility, the law declares, "You shall not see, you shall belief without seeing, you shall be blinded if you look directly to God, the sun, or the supreme law." The law gives presence, actuality and legitimacy to itself while disabling the exteriority (spacing, interval, deferral, difference, etc.) that founds it and that is other than the law. The legitimized and programmatic path of the "shall not" neutralizes the recurring conduct and conductivity that remains without path and outside of the scheme that defines the "shall not."

The law that says "shall not" exacerbates the passion that suppresses, the impetus to say "Yes" to the coming of whomever. The law sentences the passion that it suppresses. The "shall not" paralyzes/disables/suspends the passion for the "Yes" that is the very incarnation of communication, transferability, convertibility, conversion, and conversation. The law inverts the archaic "Yes" of the Sodomites. The "Yes" and "come" is transmuted into "yes, I will obey a law that makes itself inaccessible, natural, universal, and ineludible, a law that I cannot enter but I must obey, a law that imposes, categorizes, sentences and usurps, a law that declares itself legitimate, present, and familiar as it turns against what communicates." This "yes, I will obey" is no longer the "Yes" that arrives (that is sent) without debt. This reversal of the "eyes" of the "Yes" into the eyes of the law transforms the sending (the conductivity) into a mandate, a command, and a conduct (behavior). The origination of the law (its mandate and sentence) rules through the negation, prohibition, disabling, usurpation, and forgetfulness of the "Yes" that mandates (sends) without ruling or governing. This is the maddening and paradoxical origination of the law, a negative command that becomes present but inaccessible as a "yes, I shall not pass," a "yes" that in turn fuels desire for a commanding "Yes":

> To say "yes" is an obligation to repeat. This pledge to repeat is implied in the structures of the most simple "yes." A single "yes" is, therefore, immediately double, it immediately announces a "yes" to come and already recalls that the "yes" implies another "yes." So the "yes" is immediately double, immediately "yes-yes." This immediate duplication is the source of all possible contamination—that of the movement of freedom, of decision, of declaration, of inauguration—by its technical double. Repetition is never pure. Hence the second "yes" can eventually be one of laughter or derision at the first "yes," it can be the forgetting of the first "yes," it can equally be a recording of it. Fidelity, parody, forgetting or recording—whatever, it is always a form of repetition. Each time it is originary *iterability* that is at play. Iterability is the very condition of a pledge, of responsibility, of promising. Iterability can only open the

door to these forms of affirmation at the same time as opening the door to the threat of this affirmation failing. One cannot distinguish the opening from the threat.[188]

The most absolute law can never usurp absolutely the trace of its excess, the "Yes" that desires with a desire that surpasses any "yes, I shall not."

Blinded, the Sodomites touch the mute edge of their passion and try to arrest it. Multiplying folds reach for a nonobject that evaporates, a reality that is in excess of every reality, an impetus that is usurped by a multiplying fervor of commands. All possible forms multiply at the tip of their hands. The Sodomites' twisting bodies are like turning tropes, figures folding toward an intangible figure, a surface, an exteriority that they long to touch and impregnate.[189]

The unknown, unreachable, and immemorial exteriority is not foreign in Plato's writing, where he described this "outside" in the "Allegory of the Cave." How did a slave with a highly limited knowledge say "Yes" to a foreign and otherly impression? How did a slave that was born inside a cave and lived all his life in it sense that there was an "exteriority" (an outside to the cave)? Plato explains that the slaves in the cave are chained and the only light that they know is the one that reflects shadows projected by torches inside the cave. Even though they are all born in the cave and they believe that

---

[188] Derrida, "Nietzsche and the Machine," 247–248.

[189] "Writing excludes the limitless ... which in its turn, however, presupposes a continuous surface upon which it [the limitless] would be inscribed ... Thus, writing continues by discontinuity ..." Blanchot, *Writing*, 56.

the only world that exists is the inside of the cave, one of them strangely senses that there is an "outside" of the cave. How can he think the unthinkable? The slave perceives a nonknowledge that contaminates his programmed and programmatic thinking and perception. His senses are affected by an infectious virus, by a sense of foreign, exterior space. He perceives an "exteriority" that affects and perturbs all the knowledge that he has known and believed to have known all his life. When released from his chains, instead of looking and moving toward the path that he knew his entire life (facing toward one of the walls of the cave), he feels compelled to "turn his head around and walk and to lift up his eyes to the light."[190]

The slave senses with the other of sense that there is an outside of the cave, although he has no previous knowledge of it and he grew up with a "natural" knowledge that all there was is the inside of the cave. In the threshold of his senses, however, there is a surplus that contaminates his common knowledge from the "outside." An unknown sign happens in the threshold of his senses, a space that projects to an outside, an interval that establishes the difference between inside and outside, or simply a sign that establishes difference. The slave yields to this conduct, to this immemorial conductivity that drives him to the threshold of the cave and to step out to search for the cave's literal exterior. The literal and the metaphoric concept of "outside" mixes like if they were unfolding in the beginning of a dream. A dream that always takes place inside the cave and inside the slave's mind because

---

[190] Plato, *Republic*, in *Collected Dialogues,* ed. Edith Hamilton et al., trans. Paul Shorey (New Jersey: Princeton University Press, 1961), 515c.

when he manages to reach the threshold of the cave, the sun's rays abruptly blind him, thereby hindering the "real" experience of an "exteriority," one that, according to Plato, is best experienced through "pure ideas moving on through ideas to ideas and ending with ideas."[191] Unable to see, he decides to go back "inside" the cave in order to think concepts such as rays, sun, exteriority, reality, nature, and so forth. He would see the exterior with the eyes of the mind. A sign perceived as "exterior" impresses the threshold of his senses, such that this spectral conductivity becomes more real than the "real" outside of the cave. The outside of the cave arrives to the slave's sense of sense before the natural outside of the cave. There is no outside of the cave without the outside of the cave that comes (by surprise and in passing) from an interval of difference that is internal to the senses of the slave.

For the slave, the idea of an ideal sun that one may not look at directly with the eyes; the idea of multiple separations, deferrals, and approximations of perception of the sun is better than the direct exposure to the "real" and blinding sun that would simply annul all perceptions, thoughts, spaces, and differences. The difference between inside and outside is possible "inside" the cave, in the realm of signs and ideas that may substitute and supplement the "real" presence of the outside that blinds and burns. Nature would have to be "denatured" in order to gather its exteriority into the interiority of ideas and ideals:

> And yet nature is affected—from without—
> by an overturning which modifies it in its
> interior, denatures it and obliges it to be

---

[191] Ibid., 511c.

> separated *from* itself. Nature denaturing
> itself, being separated from itself, naturally
> gathering its outside into its inside, is
> *catastrophe*, a natural event that overthrows
> nature, or *monstrosity*, a natural deviation
> within nature.[192]

The journey of the slave is toward freedom, and freedom consists in "touching" an exteriority that opens, initiating the very sense of opening. The "touch" of this exteriority, then, can only be perceived through the threshold of his senses, an edge where light retreats and images retract, folding into the intervals of thought and thinking. Nature (what is "really" outside) can never appear "as such" but only through the "contaminating" deferral of the senses. Thus, we are all to see in secret an exteriority through a threshold that one may trespass without trespassing. In a sense, we are all slaves in Plato's cave dreaming of a literal reality that we desire to know literally, dreaming of a literal presence that our senses can touch. But this dream involves a threshold of difference and deferral, a space that establishes the possibility of proximity and distance, inside and outside. This interval of mediation is both the space of copulation and its infinite suspension. We are copulating with words, with bodies that are ideas, with objects that are words, and with body-words that promise the arrival of presence, but the threshold of mediation remains untouched. Our spectral bodies revolt and turn toward a mute interval, a word that is always missing but communicates new copulations and climaxes, new textures of desirable, deferred

---

[192] Derrida, *Of Grammatology*, 41.

presences. This mute threshold is the place of chance, an edge of multiplying promises, pleasures, and dangers.

A passionate proximity to what or who remains deferred and out of touch produces the dream scene in the tale of Sodom. The "do not pass" and "do not touch" point toward a "Yes" that precede them, to an excess that unfolds the dream scene. The hands are tools of conductivity of the "Yes" and means of translation and transport. Who would be the guardians of this ungraspable conduct that affirms life, the senses, thought, and thinking but also surpasses them? Who would guard and address this uncanny freedom, this sending, and this openness that erases every mark and at the same time makes every alphabet possible? The hands of the future will oscillate between being able and not being able to write this freedom and openness. On the one hand, there are the lawful doctrines of God (the safe, the sound, and the known word). On the other hand (and at the same time), there is the passion that overflows dogma or common knowledge, when one starts not to believe in what one enthusiastically believes.

Would this imperative freedom without imperatives and without designation remain free in the margins of the written, in the margin of the Book, exterior and interior to every word, hand, and touch? Or, would imperative freedom (the incessant promise and anticipation of an open word, of an uncircumcised interval) be forgotten through imperatives that promise freedom while usurping it? Who will dangerously claim "the truth," proclaiming to be closer to this grasp, this "Yes" that cannot be understood in terms of nearness or distance? This conduct/conductivity without memory has fallen, multiple times, into the hands of institutions that consign and assign it to laws and regulative ideas that do not do justice to this sending.

The monopolization and appropriation of the "Yes" into a "yes, I shall not" is the passion of the law. The iteration of the "yes, I shall not" is associated with the normalization of desires and the standardization of beliefs. At the same time, this appropriative, categorical, and self-legitimizing writing, this "affirmation failing" will never be able to completely neutralize or, in the other extreme, totalize the surpassing "Yes" of the spastic passion, the space and spacing of a deferred passion.

The "yes, I shall not" is put in motion on the side conduct (behavior), presence, legitimacy, power, sacrifice, opposition, and forgetfulness. Programmatic institutions "let people know" about the "true presence and legitimacy of the law" without questioning what is truth or how "truth" may be grounded in a spastic space that cannot be touched, is never present, and without truth:

> Consider on this question both the earliest and most recent philosophers: they are all oblivious of how much the will to truth itself first requires justification; here there is a lacuna in every philosophy—how did this come about? Because the ascetic ideal has hitherto *dominated* all philosophy, because truth was posited as being, as God, as the highest court of appeal—because truth was not *permitted* to be a problem at all ... The will to truth requires a critique—let us thus define our own task—the value of truth

> must for once be experimentally *called into question.*[193]

Fraternal hands create a programmatic code of ethics, a conduct/behavior of proximity and distance, a categorization of the names that adequate truthfulness to morality and temperance. A normativity of touch copulates and communes with truth, presence, respectability, and responsibility. These normalized and programmed fraternal hands would guard the trance and entrance of metaphors to the world of politics and to the very meaning of existence in a world of brothers. These hands (metamorphosed and metaphorized into a specific gender and sexual orientation) establish the transit of commanding truths mandated in their communities as they raise against a nonethical conduct, a past ecstatic impetus that cannot be dominated, is not governable, and partakes in every community (but is without community):

> One should wonder what signifies ... the friendship of the friend, if one withdraws it, like negative theology itself, from all its dominant determinations in the Greek or Christian worlds, from the fraternal (fraternalist) and phallocentric schema of *philia* or charity, as well as from a certain arrested form of democracy.[194]

---

[193] Nietzsche, *On the Genealogy of Morals and Ecce Homo*, trans. Walter Kaufmann and R. J. Hollingdale (New York: Vintage Books, 1989), 152–153 (Nietzsche's emphasis).

[194] Derrida, *On the Name*, 47.

The repressed and usurped orgiastic mystery that unites fraternal hands (brothers) in an "ethical community" cannot be dominated, cannot be circumscribed or circumcised. The community represses what is not fully grasped but remains its foundation, and this neutralization is the genesis of a complicated history of self-certainty and self-righteousness that is always at the risk of being "contaminated," a history of violence associated with the establishment of a monopolization of desires that is in attunement with a system of "expert opinion," ideological impressions, and programmatic perceptions. On the one hand, more desire is triggered from this monopolization of desires, and, at the same time, a passion for that which exceeds every desire and is not fully grasped interrupts the tranquility that the community posits (by decree, mandate, law, nature, science, etc.): "Each member of the community is not only the whole community, but the violent, disparate, exploded, powerless incarnation of the totality of beings who, tending to exist integrally, have as corollary the nothingness they have already, and in advance, fallen into."[195] The community of Sodomites and the condition of possibility of future communities will have depended on this X-space that traverses the community without consummation. The Sodomites excess, its conduct and conductivity partake in the communities of the future but without representation, without being part of a known knowledge. Legitimate/legitimized communities will have culture, ideas, legacy, and presence. They will have representatives for what is representable. What remains unreadable, unrepresentable, unanalyzable, and incommunicable will not be well received

---

[195] Blanchot, *Unavowable Community*, 13.

in the community, but instead it would call for renewed efforts to rule the sending/communication/conduct through appropriation, formalization, categorization, legalization, normalization, and so forth. The community of the future will long to bridge this space that separates, interrupts, and suspends (at the same time, it will raise against this difference in order to deliver the promise of full presence and identity). They will wish to declare that they are free of specters, that a world had "progressed" into a state of presence, truth, science, and the "as such." Thus Sodom is the impossible community, one that exposes a plenitude that is out of grasp, an excess that anticipates, interrupts, and defers.

There is a link between the law and death, the law and annihilation, the law that annihilates the very thing that (the law) wants to rule, regulate, preserve, and keep safe. The law neutralizes (usurps) what remains nameless in order to proclaim an absolute and imperative name. The threshold of "nothing" (the unlocalizable place of passion, the space of a surplus, the pulse of the "perhaps") becomes sacrificed, prohibited, or forgotten as it fuses with promissory notes, with multiplying names of debt and redemption, and with negative laws that replace, supplement, and ventriloquize what remains without a name. To sacrifice what is without truth and without presence; to sacrifice the passion of an excess that exceeds all names; to sacrifice all that into a religious enthusiasm where God is sacrificed is what Nietzsche calls "the stroke of genius of Christianity":

> What he calls the stroke of genius of Christianity (*Geniestreich des Christentums*) is that God sacrifices himself, condemns

himself to death; he sacrifices himself in the
person of his son to redeem man, to pay the
debt of the guilt of man and the sinner, who
is a debtor. That is the ultimate meaning,
the unbelievable meaning of the Incarnation
and the Passion.[196]

The "stroke of genius" is that as humankind is redeemed
of debt, humankind is also initiated in another passionate
duty through an eternal gratitude to a God that freed
humankind from sin. The sinner, the one who is the carrier of
an excess that contaminates (a nonethical excess that cannot
be defined or ruled in terms of decrees and morality) is now
bond to a passion that impassions, to an excess of gratitude for
a God that absorbed the orgiastic impetus of humankind and
took its archaic orgiastic impetus to the grave. As the ecstatic
impetus of humanity is buried (neutralized, repressed,
usurped), another excess raises against this sacrifice.

---

[196] Derrida, *The Death Penalty Volume I*, ed. Geoffrey Bennington, et
al., trans. Peggy Kamuf (Chicago and London: University of Chicago
Press, 2012), 156.

X

The Indestructible in Sodom versus the Law

The usurpation of the "yes" of the Sodomites (of their desiring alterity) takes the time of a wink, an interval where an eternity is forgotten and buried. And yet their erasure reproduces a trace, a space between spaces, a conduct toward a delayed pleasure, a conductivity that is not only immemorial but also indestructible:

> Without this desert in the desert, there would be neither act of faith, nor promise, nor future, nor expectancy without expectation of death and of the other, nor relation to the singularity of the other. The chance of this desert in the desert (as of that which resembles to a fault, but without reducing

itself to, that via negativa which makes its way
from a Graeco-Judaeo-Christian tradition)
is that in uprooting the tradition that bears
it, in atheologizing it, this abstraction,
without denying faith, liberates a universal
nationality and the political democracy that
cannot be dissociated from it.[197]

In this open desert of spaces and spacing, of open paths
and traces, the desire for what is absolutely foreign and
other, for an exterior heterogeneity that evades the controls
of perception, knowledge, and law repeats an ungraspable
repetition and recurs incessantly, wondering aimlessly,
anticipating the return of a ghost that opens the promise of the
future, of a "yes," "come." In this future, religion has a chance
and also democracy, both of which cannot be disassociated
from the trace of the orgiastic impetus, from the ghost that
remains after Sodom's destruction: "Not only whence comes
the ghost but first of all is it going to come back? Is it not
already beginning to arrive and where is it going? What of the
future? The future can only be for ghosts. And the past."[198]
In this desert, the sense of exile multiplies but not without
a sense of plenitude, a sense that searches for an expansive
expression, for a trace that is never quite at hand. In this
desert within a desert, in this multiplicity of spaces, spectral
hands multiply trying to draw, write, grasp, represent a figure
of figures, a figure of figuration hidden beneath all figures.
The eye, the hand, the ear, the nose, and the mouth meet in a
colossal collapse, in a sense that surpasses all the senses and

---

[197] Derrida, "Faith and Knowledge," 57.
[198] Derrida, *Specters of Marx*, 37.

lives on in the remains of a trans, in a sense-in-trans other than the (gathering of the) senses. This is the catastrophic desire that makes each single Sodomite tremble, the orgiastic desire without religion and without which religion (and its mysterium tremendum) would not have a future or stand a chance:

> *Mysterium Tremendum.* A frightful mystery, a secret to make you tremble. Tremble. What does one do when one trembles? What is it that makes you tremble? A secret always makes you tremble. Not simply quiver or shiver, which also happens sometimes, but tremble. A quiver can of course manifest fear, anguish, apprehension of death; as when one quivers in advance, in anticipation of what is to come. But it can be slight, on the surface of the skin, like a quiver that announces the arrival of pleasure or an orgasm. It is a moment in passing, the suspended time of seduction … One could say that water quivers before it boils; that is the idea I was referring to as seduction: a superficial pre-boil, a preliminary and visible agitation.[199]

Behind all the prohibitions derived from the story of Sodom, behind the mysterium tremendum that raises against the orgiastic impetus of the Sodomites, there is an a-theological space (an exteriority internal to the senses) that can neither be prohibited nor allowed because this

---

[199] Derrida, *Gift of Death*, 53.

communication, this conduct/conductivity arrives without permission, judgment, genre, gender, God, or name. The orgiastic impetus emerges as a communication without debt. Through the occlusion, interruption, refusal, and usurpation of the orgiastic principle, the circular economy of religion may be supplemented ad infinitum. At the same time, prohibition, repression, and concealment of a desire that cannot be named in the first place, of a surplus that gives and communicates while refusing to be ultimately grasped by the senses of touch, may also be used as a strategic scheme for tyrants, oppressors, and rulers, all of which raise (with religious and political fervor) against a spastic specter that they cannot grasp, understand, or rule.

The tyrant promises unity (truth, presence, legitimacy, etc.) that can never be delivered. He promises the arrival of a name and a presence that is, nevertheless, forever deferred and is ultimately unnamable. What the ruler, priest, politician, or psychoanalyst cannot name, or cannot define with the tools of knowledge, truth, presence, and objectivity, will be nominated (dominated) through subaltern denominations associated with metaphors of enmity, concealment, and deviation (evil, death, death drive, apocalypses, castration, seizure, cut, catastrophe, crisis, trauma, perversion, etc.). The one who speaks in the stage of power promises to restore order, to deliver nature, to establish coherence, to persecute whatever separates (disrupts or conceals), and to eliminate whatever deviates from the promised truths and the plenitude of presence. Religions as well as nations have enriched themselves in different époques in history through the (metaphorical and literal) destruction of multiple versions of Sodom and Gomorrah, but what remains indestructible in its catastrophe returns as something inaudible, as a missing word, as a deferred pleasure, as an exteriority, as a specter that is always at work in the grounds of political and religious schemes.

Sodom is a scene of destruction in which everything is destroyed but the indestructible. The law of "shall not" and "do not" is founded on the "Yes" that remains indestructible in Sodom, but, at the same time, the law does not embrace the alterity against which is formed, the alterity that is the foundation of the law. The trace of this alterity rests in the remains of all foundational and functional laws. The law does not fully acknowledge the excess that found it, nor is it able to administer its surplus, thus opening an unending dialectic of good versus evil in the gates of every perfectible decree. The foundational law may not completely detach its relationship with the imperative excess that disjoins it. Instead, it claims its presence and legitimacy on the condition of its dissociation with nonpresence, with a conductivity/sending that is impossible to categorize and is neither good, evil, nor ethical. The law opens the possibility of the name, of good versus evil, of a sentence that sentences, of a conduct that abstracts into ethical versus nonethical "conducts." In the contours of the law, however, lurks an inaudible drive, which is other than the law, and which makes the law speak.

The law legitimizes names and declares its presence through an excess that communicates without name and without presence. The law enriches and perfects itself, expands and contracts through a multiplication of decrees that promise an intelligible, truthful, and natural order grounded on an incommunicable passion, a desire for a deferred justice that disrupts the law. The archaic freedom of Sodom, its excess, may be erratically interpreted as an exhortation for prayer against a nonknowledge, a sort of warning against an "evil" to be abandoned to a law that attempts to rule it imperatively and categorically. The altering alterity that dwells in the heart of the law turns into an excessive law that guards, forbids, and punishes. The law rules against something that it does not dominate, that it does not know, and that cannot be ruled or penetrated. The excess of the law is not able to address the law of excess, and, for this very reason, the imperative address inserts evil (abomination) in the excess that resists being addressed, denominated, categorized, and appropriated. The imperative desire for the spectral other is substituted and supplemented by imperative laws that are in excess of what is proper to humankind. One freedom (the imperative freedom that translates and transfers an abstraction that remains without a determinable analogy) is substituted by another freedom that also translates and mandates imperatively: the freedom that commands to submit to a "debt," to a voice that sentences and nominates in excess of what is proper to humankind, a freedom that abominates saying "yes, I shall not," and "yes, I will freely submit":

> Freedom is essentially and not accidentally or provisionally the addressee of the injunction ... *The imperative categorizes its addressee*; it affirms the freedom of the addressee, imputes evil to it and intends or abandons it to the law. In this way, the imperative categorizes the essence or nature

> of man, doing so in excess of every category,
> in excess of what is proper to man.[200]

Sending supplanted for mandate, conductivity foreclosed for conduct, freedom relieved for freedom-to-subject-freely, the excess of Sodom adheres to the law of the "shall not." The law makes its own archive inaccessible (an archive that is itself immemorial). The law that says "thou shalt not" destroys in advance its own immemorial archive. The law of the "shalt not" forbids an alterity that has already arrived, that has already divided and multiplied. The negative law forbids the representation of what remains irrepresentable, and it represses an alterity that remains without repression. Sentences that sentence, such as "unseemly," "ungodliness," "unrighteousness," and so forth, devour the foreignness and exteriority of the unthinkable, of the silent sending/mandate (the conduct and conductivity) that arrives (only to erase itself) before any decree. The "properness" of the law is put in motion against an "improper" nonknowledge, a surplus that the law opposes without understanding. The law opposes, establishes, and posits itself against a sending (a spectral "exteriority" that surpasses the perception of the sensible) that the "shalt not" can never appropriate appropriately, that can never be completely governed or at hand (by any or all the senses of touch). The nonknowledge, which is never present, at hand, or "as such," is condemned by the law that sentences, makes clear, makes known, makes present, and makes intelligible. The law makes itself clear by establishing uncompromising associations, by associating the "Yes" (which is without association and analogy) with an

---

[200] Nancy, *A Finite Thinking*, 151.

originary foreignness, exteriority, "perversity," unseemliness, and contamination. Thus, the surplus of the "Yes" that has no archive, that arrives only to erase itself, is effaced again by the law that puts itself in motion through this double erasure. In its multiple and millennial simulacrums, the law of the "yes, thou shalt not" raises against the nonobject (what/who is never "as such" or at hand) that partakes in the decree. The law orbits around the pulse of this nonobject (of this conductivity) that will recur in spite of any usurpation transporting and transcribing the event of its return. The spastic interval that the law sentences as deadly, destructive, forbidden, foreign, exterior, unseemly, and so forth, leaves no monument and remains unanalyzable in the threshold of every law.

The unsacrificeable can never be absolutely neutralized. On the contrary, its effacement only anticipates the return of the nonobject that remains after destruction and before it. The world would spring again and again from this "perhaps," from this missing word, from this conduct that does not satisfy the desire of the senses, from a space/texture/specter/exteriority that communicates an incommunicable passion through the trace of an unfulfilled anticipation. And this is where the catastrophe and the indestructible begins and ends every time, in the precipitation of an affirmative repetition that folds into itself, into a promise, a figure, a "Yes" that transfers and communicates even through repression, neutralization, and usurpation. From the ashes of forgetfulness, the embers of a new excess flow incessantly. From the center of dissolution and ashes, a new affirmation gathers, the advent of a new event.

The ruin of Sodom is a repetitive demand for writing about the nonobject, the remnant that remains after Sodom remains without remains. Their ashes are a call to write the grasp of a nonobject that transfers, transcribes, transfigures, and transgresses. The remains of Sodom hover around the event of writing, of the writing that writes what is never at hand or as such, what remains external to the grasp of any given language. From that lost cemetery of unnamable excess surges the pulse of every figuration of the sacred, a polysemy of metaphors that continually conceals the concealment of the internal fire of Sodom, the impetus to touch life in the threshold of erasure, in the instant of a sending, suspension, erasing that is misunderstood as "death": "In studying the Psychoanalysis of fire, we have perceived, for example, that all the 'images' of the internal fire, the hidden fire, the fire glowing beneath the embers, in short the unseen fire that consequently calls for metaphors, are 'images of life.'"[201] The fire of Sodom consumes everything but that which makes fire possible. What retreats from fire without being consumed? What is this lack that lacks nothing? The torsions and contortions of fire are like self-consuming metaphors releasing a mute, nocturnal, and desertlike writing that is not flammable and that evades all names. A thousand metaphors surge from the ashes of Sodom, from what cannot be burned any further. A thousand smoldering metaphors retreat and are retraced from their ashes, leaving a memory of what does not burn, a trace that adds to the remembered without being a part of it. The cinders of Sodom return eternally as

---

[201] Derrida, *"La métaphysique-relève de la métaphore,"* in *Margins of Philosophy,* trans. Alan Bass (Chicago: University of Chicago Press, 1982), 263.

an affirmative passion for the impossible, for what is yet to come, for the advent of the "Yes."

Sodom, without place and without belonging, is the other of the promised land. Did Jerusalem preserve the trace of Sodom's orgiastic impetus? Could Jerusalem be possible without its other? By reducing Sodom to silence, it will always be necessary to speak about Sodom, even by not speaking about it. The forgotten conduct and repressed conductivity of Sodom is present in every religious sentence, in the leaps of faith that form and deform their paths. The passion of Western religions are impassioned by a recurring incision at the threshold of Lot's door. As the catastrophe of Sodom becomes dispensed and buried in a forgotten desert, its ashes come alive in the threshold of the senses, where the surplus folds and unfolds into interminable strophes of religion, into the citation and recitation of a recurring desire that lives on in enamored ashes, in the disappearance of every desire. The imperative declaration of every law to come is rooted in the remains of an ineluctable passion that can be neither repressed nor forgotten nor, ultimately, covered up.

Sodom exists/exits as a disrupting ellipsis in the roots of organized religion, which never overcomes its instability (which constantly calls for a new order). A new passionate incision in the threshold may inspire a new fervor for the impossible, a new enthusiasm to determinate the indetermination of a living presence that defers at the threshold (of sense). Like a telepathic sending, a disrupting and spastic specter returns in passing provoking tremors in the mysterium tremendum of religion, provoking sentences or "sentences," strophes or catastrophes announcing unpredictable turns of events that effect the spasmodic multiplication of religions. From the recurring apocalypse of Sodom, a prophesy would be relentlessly announcing the promise of a radiant place without contamination, a place where the presence of God prevails and saves all individuals from the dangerous supplement that may creep into their natural and godly desires. Sodom forgotten, Sodom destroyed, its evanescent embers will be the traces of future sacred cities rebuilt, restored and refolded over and through the untouched and unthought surplus of Sodom, over what is put at bay but remains the foundation of religion: "What announces itself as ineluctable seems in some way to have already happened, to have happened before happening, to be always past, in advance to the event."[202] The secret of Sodom had already happened before religion and without religion. The secret of Sodom cannot be explained solely through its literal plot, which would be associated with the destruction of evil. It is necessary to think, instead, the "thing" that does not disappear and, at the same time, does not let itself be presented, the moment when a missing word would be exchanged for a door, push, touch, step, and grasp, putting in motion ways to express the murmur that will have been effaced, the specter that arrives by erasing itself and to erase itself. This is the dream scene of Sodom where the most desirable idiom is never at hand and can never be fully conceptualized through the signs and symbols that the missing word (or disappearing idiom) displays. The secret of Sodom could not be experienced "as such." It could only be sensed as anticipation, as the spectral arrival of what/who does not arrive, as the sending/arrival of an unthematizable space, as the inenarrable space that displays a dream of a

---

[202] Derrida, "Désistance," 197.

dreams in a reality that is in excess of itself, and as the event that puts in motion the genesis of all stories.

In the catastrophe and destruction of Sodom, "the thing" never disappears but is transmitted (to the reader), or rather it comes back as something different and singular every time. One may speculate that the reader enjoys the destruction of Sodom at the same time that s/he anticipates the return of what remains indestructible, the return of a figureless figure that transmits a conductivity that is interval, specter, and space spacing in the desert. How to account for what keeps coming in the limit of disruption (destruction), in the limit where an unfigurable figure keeps arriving in passing by not coming, by promising to arrive without arriving?:

> What is going on no longer concerns a distancing rendering this or that absent, and then a rapprochement rendering this or that into presence; what is going on concerns rather the distancing of the distant and the nearness of the near, the absence of the absent or the presence of the present.[203]

The destruction of mortal desire does not annul the passionate overflow of forces but incites their traces, their edges and limits to a new beginning, a mortal beginning that is unique and recurrent and that will be in constant conflict with the eternal and fixed law that tends to neutralize the flow of the singular, the unique, and the passionate "Yes" and "come." The obstacles, the strophes and catastrophes of destruction, the symbols associated with doors, blindness,

---

[203] Derrida, "To Speculate," 321.

and cinders, instead of acting as fatal obstructions are but limits surpassing limits through which the desiring trace recurs. If there is such thing as an approximately absolute "destruction" in Sodom, it would be associated with the burial of a desire that bears all desires and burns all desire as it goes beyond desire.

In the eve of all passion, organized religion will suspend the repetitive trace of an overflowing passion and will supplement it making it speak according to a dialectic of contamination: dirty versus pristine, good versus evil, sin versus redemption, God versus the devil. Thus, a "proper" way to "be" impassioned is sentenced based on a passionate proximity to a specter that is neither close nor far, someone that neither "is" nor "is not" (a spectral body in passing, who is neither proper nor improper but provokes and entices an unnamable desire that goes beyond desire). Without knowing or understanding, there will be institutional translations of what remains without translation and for this very reason subject to all kinds of interpretations (translations). This communication, conductivity, or conduct, which arrives in passing and drives the Sodomites into frenzy and madness, will be accommodated, in the future history of religion, into a "proper" or "improper" conduct stabilized by a dialectic of good and evil, corruption and punishment, contamination and purity. This dialectic knowledge is invested in order "to protect access to a knowledge that remains *in itself* inaccessible, un-transmissible, unteachable."[204] A dialectical religion of good and evil, "shall and shall nots" will nurture and supplement its dogmas and decrees through excursions into an ecstatic conductivity that is neither good nor evil nor

---

[204] Derrida, "How To Avoid," 161.

dialectical (and for that very reason subject to an infinite supplement as reinforcement of the law).

It may be concluded that the core of religion is atheism, that the passion of religion unfolds through something that is other than religion, that the place of this unsacrificeable hiatus returns, turns, and departs in any singular instant in history and makes place for it. Anyone, at any moment, may be a "chosen" individual. A leap of faith without religion is a jump toward this exteriority (not a beyond), a threshold of speculation, anticipation, and hope. This jump is bound to a movement of desire haunted by the risk of hope and loss.

The history of the Book is a continuous attempt to articulate (to penetrate, name, and appropriate) the return of a formless and figureless alterity, a writing that arrives in passing and departs without becoming. It is the unending desire to grasp the name that remains in the threshold of all names, a spastic repetition that would have arrived even before the name "God." The history of the Book is a continuous attempt to take responsibility (to respond) for this quiet, nondialectical murmur that is affirmative and without being but that is often misunderstood through a dialectical thought that attempts to approach this affirmative conduct through a negative language of prohibition, presence, essence, "conduct," sacrifice, and so forth. The negative language, which cannot control the return of the spectral nonobject, lets itself be bound to a demonic return, a "demonic force" (not far from its suitor, the mysterium tremendum) that does not obey any supreme masters (not even God).

It is considered "demonic," the return of what returns without being called by the masters that be (church, God, Sate, the father, etc.). The spectral nonobject in passing makes its return at the gates of the city and the church, at the threshold of all religions, at the threshold of the senses, as it entices all desires again and obeys no master. It comes from nowhere, it is not part of a legacy, and it is not inherited (like a "demonic force"). It cannot be understood in terms of desire, passion, or pleasure only, as it overflows them with a desire that surpasses every desire. The ultimate desire is to translate this recurring emission, this transmission that recurs. Religion falls repetitively into this temptation in a categorical manner. It promises to give finality (*telos*) to this "demonic" transmission that is a finality without end, a recurrent transfer that disrupts any final thesis, a freedom that is without destiny or known origin. For religion, this free-floating freedom would also be interpreted as the "beauty of the devil," from which religion finds its recurrent ventriloquism, its insistence to speak before the murmur that arrives unannounced, without arriving. The religious word promises and swears to master the unmastered repetition, a tireless movement that would require infinite supplementation:

> *The return of the demonic*, not far from the "perpetual recurrence of the same thing," is in convoy with repetition beyond the PP [Pleasure Principle]. This will recur regularly from now on. Truly speaking, there is not a return of *the* demonic. The demon is that very thing which *comes back* [*revient*] without having been called by the PP. The demon is the *revenance* which repeats its entrance, coming back [revenant]

from one knows not where ("early infantile influences," says Freud), inherited from one knows not whom, but already persecutory, by means of the simple form of its return, indefatigably repetitive, independent of every apparent desire, *automatic*. Like Socrates' demon—which will have made everyone write, beginning with him who passes for never having done so—this automaton comes back [*revient*] without coming back [*revenir á*] to anyone, it produces effects of ventriloquism without origin, without emission, and without addressee. It is only posted, the post in its "pure" state, a kind of mailman [*facteur*] without destination. Tele—without telos. Finality without end, the beauty of the devil. It no longer obeys the subject whom it persecutes with its return. It no longer obeys the master, the name of the master being given to the subject constructed according to the economy of the PP, or the PP it(him)self.[205]

The affirmative, nonethical return of the nonobject in the midst of destruction does not require destruction, sacrifice, or religion for its singular repetition to arrive in passing. Through an infinite dialectical language of good versus evil and presence versus absence, the circle of religion would engage in a circular and at times demonic task: to repress/usurp the errant desire, the "automatic" desire that surpasses

---

[205] Derrida, "To Speculate," 341–342.

all desire, and to suppress the desire for a nonobject, for what transmits and communicates. The religious circle of religion arrives even before one is born in order to inscribe a pact of desire in the bodies, in order to usurp the overflowing desire that is always already receptive to the thing that returns without master and without being mastered:

> As we know, Artaud lived the morrow of a dispossession: his proper body, the property and propriety of his body, had been stolen from him at birth by the thieving god who was born in order "to pass himself off/as me." Rebirth doubtless occurs through—Artaud recalls this often—a kind of reeducation of the organs ... For Artaud, the primary concern is not to die in dying, not to let the thieving god divest him of life.[206]

In Sodom, the desire for the unthinkable speaks through the different symbols that leave a blinding impression. They are elements in a scene of deferral, repetition, and return, figural objects aiming toward a finite indetermination. Indetermination and suspension amalgamate into an infinite expectation, a future without an object coming and becoming, an unpredictable promise that opens the passion for whatever and whomever will come. Through their spectral trance, through their communication with the indeterminate other, passes the trace of a transmission, of a free and open word communicating without pact and without God.

---

[206] Derrida, "Theater of Cruelty," 232–233.

XI

The Unthematizable Return of an Ungraspable Conduct

Sodom is a desiring reminder of a nonerotic-erotic interval, an abstraction, a traction, and attraction that communicates an idiom that the senses may grasp without touching. The trans that they communicate remains unavowable and unavoidable. The desire interrupted at the threshold, the desire that longs to grasp a foreign exteriority of spaces and spacing, remains an unstable, untranslatable, and inexhaustible abstraction. This excess is an abstraction (a *"récit"*) with no exact definition that traverses genre, gender, or sexual orientation without belonging to any of them:

> In this text, the *"récit"* (abstraction,
> departure, citation, recitation, re-citation,
> trait, retreat, edge, threshold, generating,

generosity, engendering, etc.) is not only a mode, and a mode put into practice or put to the test because it is deemed impossible; it is also the name of a theme. It is the nonthematizable thematic content of something of a textual form that assumes a point of view with respect to the genre, even though it perhaps does not come under the heading of any genre ... The *récit* that I will discuss presently makes the *récit* and the impossibility of the *récit* its theme, its impossible theme or content at once inaccessible, indeterminable, interminable, and inexhaustible; and it makes the word "*récit*" its titleless title, the mentionless mention of its genre.[207]

The affirmative grasp of the Sodomites, their impetus to embrace an indeterminate other is an imperative without law and without category or, one may say, a Law of laws. Attraction to a nonobject, trespassing, grasping, blindness, embers, and enamored ashes are elements in a recurring story that refers to a unthematizable grasp of an exteriority that retreats and recurs as it is retraced through multiplying turns, twists, revolutions, conversions, inversions, strophes and tropes, sentences, and conducts that account and add up to a grasp that remains unaccountable: "All the questions that we have just addressed can be traced to an enormous matrix that generates the nonthematizable thematic power of

---

[207] Derrida, "The Law of Genre," in *Parages*, ed. John P. Leavey, trans. Avital Ronell (Stanford: Stanford University Press, 2011), 226.

a simulated *récit*: it is this inexhaustible writing that recounts without telling and that speaks without recounting."[208]

The nonthematizable excess of the Sodomites cannot come under the heading of any specific gender or genre. Through their (suspended) "grasp," reality and unreality are placed into the scene along with distance and closeness. What cannot be "penetrated" (known) cannot have meaning, "reality," memory, proximity, and so forth. The threshold of all desires, the edge of all desires (if there is such a thing), is desirable beyond any means of desire, and it is the interval of departure where every desire for what is coming, unknown, and affirmative departs anew. Everything in Sodom allegorizes the trace of this desire for the indeterminate other, the foreign, or the external, which in turn (or at the same time) evades every desire that would like to "penetrate," define, program, or appropriate this event. The "external" is never absolute in Sodom's story because it is already contaminated by the interior impression of the Sodomites. The exterior and the internal are a space, a spacing, a threshold without edges. Sodom is a tale of a disappearing trace of desire, but still it is a trace that retraces the conduct and conductivity of the spacing of a desire for a knowledge without name. The interpretation of the story of Sodom requires a translation (a scripture, stricture, duction, reduction) from a space that remains without translation and that is, therefore, inexhaustibly reproduced.

This generous and maddening affirmation of an evanescent and ecstatic trace (which provokes, entices, invites, and transports, without been seen or touched) is the generating genesis of multiplying and commanding laws, of

---

[208] Ibid., 239.

classificatory decrees and multiple genres. The trace renders the path of a spectral affirmation without belonging to any religion. Demands and commands emerge from the ruins, from the effacement of the trace that renders its ecstatic sense imperceptible and unreadable, from the reduction of its conduct to an edge, a threshold, a handful of ashes. The trace of the affirmative passion, which remains in a threshold without reference, is framed in multiple negative boundaries (decrees) that paradoxically reveal an affirmative spacing without reference:

> The play of framing and the paradoxical logic of boundaries introduce a kind of perturbation in the "normal" system of reference while simultaneously *revealing* an essential structure of referentiality. It is an obscure revelation of referentiality which does not make reference, which does not refer, any more than the event is itself an event.[209]

A desire without reference or referent says "yes," and, at the same time, it is hosted by multiplying decrees (shall nots) that spin around a circular economy of reduction, abduction, duction, diction, and reproduction, a process that swirls around metaphors of forbidden referentiality/steps ("do not pass," do not present, do not presence, do not make present, do not see, do not touch, etc.). The impetus to correspond with that which does not respond (or correspond) is in the limit of every analogy. The retreating other withdraws in

---

[209] Derrida, "Before the Law," 213.

the light of day, when whomever translates the edge of what resists translation and passionately recounts what cannot be told, what remains without referentiality.

How to give hospitality to an affirmative conduct that refuses any name, even the name "God" (a name formed through negative theology, negative commands, and the absolute elimination of the trace)? How to give hospitality to the very space that makes hospitality possible? There is no positive name that can contain the generous conduct that makes possible the sending of any and all affirmative names. How to give hospitality to an affirmative conduct, a spastic interval whose indetermination and unpredictability may be easily usurped and transfigured into violent turns, strophes of equivocal names that may take people hostage in an instant? How to give hospitality to an indefinite opening, to a mesmerizing sense of life, freedom, and danger? How to give hospitality to that which distorts the senses, even the sense of hospitality? How to give hospitality to a conduct, to a conductivity that is in excess of every word? Sodom is this gathering and disorganizing place of interruption, of a prereligion, of a religion without religion. Sodom is the receptacle of an abysmal prephilosophical inauguration of what is already inaugural, uncanny, and dangerous.

Is there sin in Sodom? The Sodomites are the receptacle of an ecstatic conductivity, and they merely react or respond to it. Who would know how to respond to the conduct? What tropes and strophes would claim to represent what the conduct "says," and how many catastrophes would take place in the name of a conductivity that cannot be "penetrated"? The names of those catastrophes are already multiple and multiplying. Sodom is the place of crossing and edges from which laws that say "do not cross" emerge without understanding the conductivity that comes from the other. It is the place that in one stroke is crossed and crossed out, the place without place where an ecstatic interval remains virginal, pristine, and impenetrable.

The barrenness of the forgotten city, the sterility of the burned land, and the disappearance in the midst of flames forms a mute expectation that invites every individual to wish for something that does not make itself present but whose conduct/conductivity persistently causes an impression. This foreign texture that dwells in exile, this unbound, unshielded, and untamed excess is the ecstatic impetus, the quiet disquietude, from which human desire for the sacred and the unknown insistently unfolds. The future of religions (and atheism) rests on the possibility of thinking this excess is greater than knowledge, an impetus that exceeds thought itself in its thinking. In the Christian tradition,

> the argument rests entirely on the movement of thought, insofar as it cannot not think the maximum of the being [body divine-God] it is able to think, but thinks also an excess to that maximum, since thought is capable of thinking even that there is something that exceeds its power to think. In other words, thinking … can think—indeed, cannot not think—that it thinks something in excess over itself. It penetrates the impenetrable, or rather is penetrated by it.[210]

---

[210] Nancy, *Dis-Enclosure*, 11.

The story of Sodom is about this unstoppable movement, this impetus to think what exceeds thinking. If there is love in the tale, it is a strange kind of love: one that is not so much a bond for a connection but for a disconnection, for a communication that sends the possibility and impossibility of connecting. It is an event that marks the instance of the most absolute act of freedom when their senses, disorganized in a multiplicity of spaces, pay heed to an unknowable exteriority, an extension, a fold, a nonobject that their senses love to love. The orgiastic impetus of the Sodomites is even more prominent and emphatic through its destruction and ashes, remains of remains that echo a trace of an indestructible desire: "Although it is incorporated, disciplined, subjugated, and enslaved, the orgiastic is not annihilated."[211] Folded into itself, the different figures of Sodom, including the sediment of its ashes (remains of what is without remains), would be the space from which religion parts and departs and also deconstructs itself. This contaminated orgiastic freedom is the impetus from which religion will try to respond and correspond: "The secret of responsibility would consist of keeping secret, or 'incorporated,' the secret of the demonic and thus of preserving within itself a nucleus of irresponsibility or of absolute unconsciousness ..."[212] The impression of whatever or whoever is coming does not have a name or a religion but simply an inkling in passing, a multiplying echo that distorts every last word that attempts to define and defy it. The legacy without legacy of the Sodomites is their spectral surplus, a hyper-reality or sur-reality that unfolds in a dream scene that could be the stage of religion and also the

---

[211] Derrida, *Gift of Death*, 19.
[212] Ibid., 20.

abysmal scene of thought and thinking (the touching of an exterior texture, the skin of writing). This virginal space in passing cannot be exhausted by the excess of writing and the writing of excess.

The orgiastic mystery sends itself: "Orgiastic Mystery recurs indefinitely, it is always at work: not only in Platonism but also in Christianity ..."[213] It makes possible all religions but itself remains secreted, without a place, quietly incorporated and repressed/expelled in the antechamber of religion. Sodom unfolds the seed/leap of all religions, but none of them are able to render the conceptual form of this leap, nor are they capable of forbidding it completely because the possibility of the orgiastic mystery presents itself again in an unexpected instant, in the margins of the most strict strictures of the law. This raging freedom that loves the incommensurable, the incalculable, and the stranger is buried in multiple sacrifices and repressions (in multiple forms of indictments, persecutions, decrees, tortures, assassinations, etc.) that do not destroy the possibility of its return but rather transfer its impetus to new forms of religious enthusiasms. At the point of no return, where "ultimate" destruction takes place, what does not take place returns. Ashes do not erase what cannot be touched. Destruction cannot destroy the perception of a figureless figure. Effacing does not efface the sense that is other than sense. Someone or some other-one, someone who is other than himself/herself, is continually chosen, in an instant, when a cleavage opens a path in the crossing announcing an evaporating presence, a creeping visitation/sending, an incommensurable rhythm that dances without partner, without letting itself be bound to any master.

---

[213] Ibid., 21.

These turns and twits, these rhythmic intervals without sound do not perish, and they partake in the transference toward religion and in the impasse that is without religion:

> (... [Y]es, God (himself) would be impotent to make possible today what you know remains forbidden to us, God himself, which should give you the measure of the thing), but the chance of the impasse devoted to fate can be the impasse itself, and what comes to pass in it for being unable to pass.[214]

Sodom is a story of erasure and under erasure. It returns through its erasure, through its "syncopated" syntax. It returns to both revive religion and deconstruct it. Detached, the fault of Sodom reassembles negative detours ("shall nots") that leave the threshold (the idiom) of the orgiastic principle untouched. The "fault" of the Sodomites leaves its mark, but it is not a visible trace:

> So you are forewarned: it is the risk or chance of this fault that fascinates or obsesses me at this very moment, and what can happen to a faulty writing, to a faulty letter (the one I write you), what can remain of it, what the ineluctable possibility of such a fault gives on to think about a text or a remainder. Ineluctable since the structure

---

[214] Catherine Malabou and Derrida, *Counterpath. Traveling with Derrida*, trans. D. Wills, (Stanford: Stanford University Press, 2004), 192.

of "faultiness" is, a priori, older even than any a priory.[215]

Nothing is really lost during the destruction of Sodom because what the Sodomites experience is nothing that can be attested for, nothing that can be found and then lost. The unexpected visitation takes place without taking place, and the Sodomites cross without passing. The grasping of the coming of the other is never at hand, but it is recurring and it is the legacy (without legacy) of the Sodomites. One cannot conceive of the living presence without its passing, without its oblivion, and without the eternal threshold that defers its presence:

> When he (Heidegger) speaks of the oblivion of Being, says "one must not forget Being"; and that at bottom this is what justifies, accounts for, gives rise to his entire discourse. Yes and no: he does say that, but he also says the opposite—namely, that there is no question of remembering Being without oblivion ...[216]

The oblivion of Sodom remains as an apostrophic space, an exteriority that does not belong, a fault from which an indeterminate polysemy may display at any moment. In a

---

[215] Derrida, "At This Very Moment," 147.

[216] Derrida responding to Vattimo in Derrida and Maurizio Ferraris, *A Taste for the Secret*, trans. Giacomo Donis, ed. Giacomo Donis and David Webb (Cambridge: Polity Press, 2001), 83.

lost and forgotten desert, a promise impossible to program or rule, a syncopeic rhythm recurs virginally and unscathed.

The promise of the coming of the indeterminate other in its multiple dimensions (including the messianic dimension), the divine murmur in passing, the "faith without dogma" will always start anew from the unfindable, unfoundable, and unfathomable city of Sodom.

> This messianicity, stripped of everything, as it should, this faith without dogma which makes its way through the risks of absolute night, cannot be contained in any traditional oppositions, for example that between reason and mysticism. It is announced wherever, reflecting without flinching ...[217]

What remains without reminder and without remains is precisely what ignites a new repetition of the mute orgiastic space and an infinite chain of discursive substitutions. Every individual in the history of humanity experiences the singularity of the ecstatic secret, which is an event that is without history and without religion. Every individual partakes of this repetitive and primordial desire to sense, to make sense of an unknown exteriority, a space/spacing that does not emerge from any specific community, state, religion, gender, or sexual orientation but traverses all of them. The mute call that remains unanalyzed in the remains of Sodom's ashes appears as an imperative impetus, an address that cannot be stopped because it has arrived in passing before I can say "I." The "chosen" individual, the one who experiences

---

[217] Derrida, "Faith and Knowledge," 56–57.

in secret the secreted desire for the ecstatic principle does not emerge from the unity of state and the coherence of family but from the residue of these institutions: "... the individual is merely the residue of the experience of the dissolution of community ... the individual reveals that it is the abstract result of a decomposition."[218] The ecstatic principle founds all religions of the West but remains foreign to their unfolding and dissemination. If Sodom had a legacy, it would be what remains without legacy, without glory, without presence, without God, and without religion: the space that retreats and repeats incessantly and calls for the transmission of a vertiginous interval, a leap that multiplies the desire to know the unknown and fractures the dogmatic element that proclaims the unity and coherence of a presence that remains impenetrable, "In fact it could well be that the 'unnamable' is never divine, and that the divine is always named—even if it is for want of a name."[219] Even trespassing the threshold would not take the Sodomites to the other end. Instead, they would be blinded in the "instant" of their transgression when the indeterminate other shows itself only to remain out of sight. A persisting impasse dwells in the step beyond the threshold, where there is another threshold that transfers the conductivity of an exteriority that touches the senses but remains untouchable. The step beyond the threshold is another threshold, or is a step without a step:

> The messianic figure is a little terrifying and unnerving. For it belongs to the very structure of the messianic event that the

---

[218] Nancy, *Inoperative Community*, 3.
[219] Ibid., 118.

> Messiah is always coming, so that even if we
> meet him at the gates of Rome, we will want
> to know when he is coming, for the arrival
> of the Messiah is *le pas au-de-là*, the step *not*
> beyond, the step that can never be taken ...
> We do not want what we want. We hope
> for this coming but then again we are also
> hoping that he never shows up. We prefer to
> keep talking, to keep saying "*viens!*", which is
> preferable to his actual arrival ...[220]

The arrival of the indeterminate other, of the absolute stranger is preserved in a renewed transferability, in a deferred messianic promise, as an excess that points to a figure that is never at hand (that cannot be conceptualized "as such"). The "leap" toward the sacred (religion, God, faith, etc.) always leaves behind a syncopeic interval, an impasse that renews and restores the leap. This syncopeic region is impossible to inhabit (unhomely/*unheimlich*) and for this very reason calls for all the symbols of homeliness, an exorbitant sphere of apprehensive metaphors, which create a multiplication of economies and a circle of the familiar, of knowing and beliefs. This promise, this texture that is both leap and impasse is possible and imaginable through the tale of Sodom.

Sodom is what remains excluded as the object that no longer exists. Excluded from every religion, the nonobject is also saved (untouchable, immemorial, without space, without country, and without identity). Sodom remains indefinable, a space from which religions and nations draw their laws, concepts, dogmas, and beliefs by retreating from and at

---

[220] Caputo, *Prayers and Tears*, 145.

the same time retracing the spastic interval of Sodom. The ecstatic secret consumes itself without being consumed, and this freedom is everywhere choosing everyone and every other, with or without religion.[221]

The impasse, the blinding, and the burning are defeats that are also triumphs because the unsacrificeable remains, passes through (communicates without passing and without the senses of touch) and persists in what is without remains (enamored ashes): "It is around such a future that the step/not beyond is organized, as the passage that is always made but always blocked. The interruption of the living present is also the disruption of the living, conscious self, the self-presence of the self."[222] The desire that desires what is not yet known, the desire that desires what remains without analogy, the desire that desires before the arrival of any god, object, or law falls into a trap of multiple negative substitutions that fail to grasp what remains incommensurable between spaces, in the threshold of sense. The classification of beings in "nature" releases a madness for naming, a multitude of forms (scenes, perceptions, textures, and narratives), all of which escape the multiplying object of desire:

> Ecstasy is without object, just as it is without why, just as it challenges any certainty.

---

[221] In footnote 49 (notes to pages 212–25), John Caputo explains the pure gift according to Derrida: "In *Glas*, 270–71/243, Derrida speaks of the "pure gift" (*don pur*), if there is one, the gift without exchange, without return, outside the dialectical circle, which makes a holocaust of its holocaust, burns its gift-giving behind it and disappears *as* a gift. The pure gift, *don pur*, would be perfectly consumed in the sacrifice even of sacrifice; cf. *Cinders*, 39." Ibid., 360.

[222] Ibid., 77.

> One can write that word (ecstasy) only by putting it carefully between quotation marks, because nobody can know what it is about, and, above all, whether it ever took place: going beyond knowledge, implying un-knowledge, it refuses to be stated other than through random words that cannot guarantee it. Its decisive aspect is that the one who experiences it is no longer there when he experiences it, is thus no longer there to experience it.[223]

How many counterfeiters would there be in the history of the world that would promise to tear down the threshold, the deferral of the promise, the spastic interval, in order to deliver the "as such," the living presence, the proper name, absolute knowledge, and the "natural" name of nature? It there a way not to counterfeit what is without presence and truth? This nonstep, this "secret" impasse that contains the threshold of an infinite border, has been misconstrued as a leap toward death and sacrifice: "A history of secrecy as history of responsibility is tied to a culture of death, in other words to the different figures of the gift of death or of putting to death." [224] But, instead, the ecstatic secret is no secret, it is life itself, it is the limit where words tend to appear and disappear, to slide into a movement, a murmur, a rhythm, a repetition, a dance that remains jubilant and without analogy.

At the threshold there is already ruin, and beyond it, there is blindness. There is trespassing without passing. At

---

[223] Blanchot, *Unavowable Community*, 19.

[224] Derrida, *Gift of Death*, 10.

the threshold, the hand grasps a sense that withdraws from sense perception, a sense that grasps an exteriority that is foreign to sense. At the threshold there will be the "mark of incompletion and infinity," the trace of an unrepeatable repetition, and the march toward infinite substitutions:

> Speculative transference orients, *destines*, calculates the most original and the most passive "first step" on the very threshold of perception. And this perception, the desire for it or its concept, belongs to the destiny of this calculation. As does every discourse on this subject ... Once the oppositional limit between perception and its other are erased and replaced by an entirely other structure, the suspensive procedure [*demarche*] appears interminable. The interminable is not accidental, does not come, as if from the outside, to mark incompletion and infinity. Speculative repetition and transference start the march.[225]

At Lot's door and beyond, the Sodomites put in motion the secreted secret of religion without religion: a sense that anticipates and transmits but is nondeducible, a desire without analogy that transports beyond desire, a desire that opens all analogies without being one. Those who have the secreted secret of religion before religion and without religion dwell in the threshold of history, in the threshold of perception, in the gates of every city, and in the antechamber of every

---

[225] Derrida, "To Speculate," 384.

temple. Those who bear the secret also bear the promise and the threat of a recurring writing, an ecstatic grasp in the very threshold of perception that sends an event, a nonobject, the who or what that opens the opening of an époque to come.

The ecstatic principle departs from any threshold (from the threshold of our senses) at any time, and any attempt to name it will contaminate it. The name of this contamination may very well be all the nominations, denominations, and dominations that attempt to grasp the excess of the mark at the threshold. The law borrows from this surplus:

> *To borrow* is the law ... Without borrowing, nothing begins, there is no proper fund/ foundation [*fonds*]. Everything begins with the transference of funds, and *there is interest in borrowing*, this is even its initial interest. To borrow yields, *brings back*, produces surplus value, is the prime mover of every investment. Thereby, one begins by speculating, by betting on a value to be produced as if from nothing. And all these "metaphors" confirm, as metaphors, the necessity of what they state.[226]

The "Yes" of the incommensurable without analogy becomes an "as if," a leap of faith through analogies, through a speculation of supplementary analogies. The "Yes," the promise, the "X," the nonobject, the "who" or "what" is borrowed as a speculation and as a threat: "if you pass that which is an impasse and which is without analogy, you will

---

[226] Ibid.

be punished." These laws/decrees hope to find analogies between what is without analogy (the "yes") and "responsible ethics." Through the negativity of the "shall nots" ("if you do this ...", "if you don't do this ...") the law attempts to capture a glimpse of what becomes ruined through the very decree that is mapping a speculative leap between the known and the unknown. The articulated sentences of the laws, the sentences that sentence, the sentences that name and categorize and say "shall nots" reach a momentous clarity (sometimes even a monstrous and disastrous clarity) that is "rotten" from the start: "There is something decayed or rotten in law, which condemns it or ruins it in advance."[227] The law that condemns the Sodomites also sentences their ecstasy, which comes before the law, makes the law possible, and is without analogy.

Religion attempts to articulate and at the same time posit the limits of the unpresentable and unrepresentable. The divine gesture senses, hears, and sees through a limit from which touch, vision, and audition retreat. The divine gesture grasps the sense that is foreign to sense, the sense that announces the promise and the danger of the coming of a what/who without analogy. From this insurmountable leap, religions reproduce a polysemy that is never exhausted and is always subject to ruin. The future of religion departs from a nonknowledge that will have become ruined from its genesis.

The senses mix in Sodom attempting to touch, through a multiplicity of spaces, a spectral perception. Their supplicating hands draw an insufficient analogy. Everything changes and shifts in a motionless and monumental moment that will haunt every future prayer and every supplication.

---

[227] Derrida, "Force of Law," 273.

The gaping mouths of the Sodomites form an ellipse of joy, pain, and surprise, an imperfect circle, a circumvolution of iterations trying to say the missing name of the specter of their desire. Their hands supplicate. They implore for a presence behind all the spaces of perception. They desire to touch what remains without analogy. They desire for there to be something instead of nothing.

XII

Sodom and the "Homosexual Agenda"

W hy is homosexuality associated with Sodom and Gomorrah? Where does it come from, and does it arrive when it arrives? What arrives? Who arrives? Is it an exteriority that contaminates the interiority of the body? How to avoid its coming and its recurrence if the laws of nature and the will of God cannot govern its transit? Is it possible to say that an exteriority that is exterior to nature corrupts the interiority of nature? Who or what is this surplus that arrives from an elsewhere and that contaminates, corrupts, or modifies the nature of nature, the natural nature of desire (if there is such a thing)? Like Abraham's or the Sodomites' "unknowing," sexuality is a similar call that is discovered in secret, without knowledge, without family, community, culture, or religion. In the "genesis" of sexuality, desire had already arrived, by surprise, and its grasp cannot be thought in terms of a presence that arrives or of a governing desire that rules over other desires. The mark of this arrival cannot be repressed by family, community, religion, and state (or cannot be explained by their influence in the body). The mark of the surplus of desire is always a trace of another trace, a function that forms and supplements a communication that communicates.

When sexuality manifests itself, it not only arrives by surprise but is also as if passion has already been "contaminated" before its arrival because it withdraws from the syntax of origin. One's desire for the other and for what is other arrives not because of knowledge, gender, nature, God, religion, the Oedipus complex, the state, the community, the law, and so forth, but in spite of them. The desire for the other, when it extends to the other, does not know anything about itself. Desires desire without knowing what desire means. When does desire for the other, for what is other, become sexual desire? What is transferred and transmuted in this extension? Desire and sexual desire are specters that are never present, that may not be thought of in terms of an origin, of an arrival of certain presence, or of a decision. It is desire that craves (to visualize) presence. Desire (the desire that communicates and sends) is anticipation and longing for an unknown subject that is always in excess of any desire. The desire for the other and for what or who is other involves a vision beyond presence, a desire beyond the visible: "To see sight or vision or visibility, to see beyond what is visible, is not merely *to have a vision* in the usual sense of the word, but to see-beyond-sight, to see-sight-beyond-sight."[228] Sexual desire

---

[228] Derrida, "Living On," 119.

is a desire for presence, and, at the same time, it is a desire for more presence and for something more than presence. The desiring mark (for what or who is other) does not belong to any particular body, gender, party, or institution. This excess "without membership" is a communication that comes from an elsewhere, a sending that makes possible the proximity of touch and the touch of proximity. It is an abstraction that no knowledge can exhaust and every language ventriloquizes indefinitely:

> Here and now, is the law of abounding, of excess, the law of participation without membership ... It will seem meager to you, and even of staggering abstractness. It does not particularly concern either genres, or types, or modes, or any form in the strict sense of its concept ... It is perhaps the limitless field of general textuality.[229]

This surplus that comes from an elsewhere, this excess that "contaminates" and supplements from and outside without contours is mistakenly associated with a dangerous impetus, a supplement that modifies even nature and God. Perhaps the destruction of Sodom and Gomorrah and (ad infinitum) of all the future towns and individuals that yield to the grasp of this "contaminating" surplus harbors the desire for an ultimate presence (God) that would eliminate this supplement, interval, exteriority, difference, and "contaminating" sending. Sodom's surplus offends nature and God, both of which are supposed to be pure presences

---

[229] Derrida, "Law of Genre," in *Parages*, 227.

present to themselves, without intervals, without exteriority, and without deferrals:

> Indeed, Rousseau thinks that this experience of a continual present is accorded only to God: given to God or to those whose hearts *accord* and agree with God's ... The pleasure [*jouissance*] of self-presence, pure auto-affection, uncorrupted by any outside, is accorded to God: "What is the nature of pleasure in such a situation? Nothing external to one-self, nothing except oneself and one's own [*propre*] existence; so long as this state lasts, one suffices to oneself, like God" [*Reveries* pp. 113–114]. There must be *movement*, life, [*jouissance*] delight in time, self-presence there. But movement should be *without intervals*, without difference, without discontinuity ...[230]

Abraham and the Sodomites are hosts and hostages of an affirmative movement of differences, an abstraction-attraction, an impassive magnet that participates without participation, a quiet and affirmative proximity (an interval, a space) that produces the desire for presence. Both Abraham and the Sodomites are before an affirmative and repetitive law that they cannot penetrate, an abstraction that they cannot know as a man, a woman, or as a thing. They desire to penetrate or be penetrated by this abstraction, this open word, this flow of communication that communicates:

---

[230] Derrida, *Of Grammatology*, 249–250.

Nothing holds before the law. It is not a woman or a feminine figure, even if man wants to enter or penetrate it (that, precisely, is its trap). Nor yet is the law a man; it is neutral, beyond sexual and grammatical gender, and remains thus indifferent, impassive, little concerned to answer yes or no. It lets the man freely determine himself, it lets him wait, it abandons him. It is neuter, neither feminine nor masculine, indifferent because we do not know whether it is a (respectable) person or a thing, who or what.[231]

They both hear/sense/perceive/acknowledge something/someone in excess of a body or a thing, something that cannot be experienced "as such" because it is not completely present. They both suspend everything that is familiar and present to them (family, community, beliefs, inherited laws, norms, etc.) in order to participate with something that is without participation, "without membership," without community, and without presence. In an act of absolute freedom, they abandon themselves to this suspension, to this nameless abstraction, to this enticing invitation, to this interruption of knowable knowledge. The Sodomites as well as Abraham have a taste for what is freeing, foreign, and dissembling, for what they have never known before. They have a taste for/of the blinking opening of an abysmal freedom in the very edge of their senses and thoughts, which in turn positions them in

---

[231] Derrida, "Before the Law," 207.

a leap where life and death lose their dialectical sense and no longer oppose each other, at least not as opposites.

Homosexuality, associated with the strange and the foreign, has become (through the centuries) a symbol of an enticing invitation, an abstraction, a communication that surpasses God and nature, that interrupts them and thereby is against both. Homosexuality has become an obscure communication that transmits a desire more powerful than God because He has to prohibit this passion that keeps coming back in spite of His wishes and commands. Homosexuality (and all forms of trans desires that transmit, that communicate desires other than those defined through "nature" and God) sends itself in spite of religious prohibition, family repression, and state persecution. This communication (associated with homosexuality and all its "contaminating expressions") is more powerful than memory and culture because it recurs independently of both. Homosexuality does not belong; it is declared foreign to family, tribe, kingdom, nation, and God. Even though it has been disenfranchised through multiple powers since biblical times, its legacy without legacy returns regardless of any force, language, creed, or time to haunt family, state, and religion. It speaks before the voices that void and avoid its arrival. It arrives unnoticed and unannounced. Would homosexuality be something unforgiving because it would be perceived as a disobedience to family, state, and religion? Would it be considered something against society and community because it is foreign to every established norm, something that emerges in spite of all decrees and is external to established knowledge? Like Abraham and the Sodomites, who did not see their ecstatic call coming, homosexuality is a conduct/conductivity that one has not chosen, a "secret" that the individual remains faithful to in spite of his/her love for family, community, and nation. The coming/sending of homosexuality has never depended on previous knowledge, acknowledgment, cognition, or recognition. Similarly, the commencement of religion does not stand on common knowledge. Religion is also a desire to know the name that arrives before religion and without religion, the name of a sending that arrives before any dogma or belief only to erase itself. If that is the case, why does religion tend to condemn (and at the same time usurp) the very secret that it incorporates? Religion carries a secret as it raises against an orgiastic impetus, a past mystery that is older than any religion. Religion, like homosexuality, "remains faithful to a secret that she has not chosen":

> Let us figuratively call Marrano anyone who remains faithful to a secret that he has not chosen, in the very place where he lives, in the home of the inhabitant or of the occupant, in the home of the first or the second *arrivant*, in the very place where he stays without saying no but without identifying himself as belonging to. In the unchallenged night where the radical absence of any historical witness keeps him or her, in the dominant culture that by definition has calendars, this secret keeps the Marrano even before the Marrano keeps it. Is it not possible to think that such a secret eludes history, age, and aging?[232]

---

[232] Derrida, *Aporias*, trans. Thomas Dutoit (Stanford: Stanford University Press, 1993), 81.

Heterosexuality has been considered for more than two millenniums a "natural" orientation, internal to nature, family, culture, and religion. On the other hand, for about the same amount of time, homosexuality has been perceived as a surplus exterior to natural principles, a passive passion that quietly arrives by surprise (in spite of godly decrees), a desire that is external to the principles of "nature" and society, an impetus that is added to nature (some would falsely say that homosexual desire is without analogy in nature). For these reasons, homosexuality is bound implicitly or explicitly with the events of Sodom, with the surplus that raises against the natural and the godly forces. Homosexuality is this "otherly" desire that overturns the "nature" of "nature" and brings catastrophe and interruption to the "natural" principles in and of "nature." Like the ecstatic principle, the "contamination" acts as a foreign specter in the community because it manifests itself in spite of all societal indictments (explicit or implicit, public or private), in spite of repression, foreclosure, and forgetfulness. The ecstatic impetus disrupts all established beliefs. However, homosexuality, like heterosexuality, bisexuality, and so forth, surges from a nonorigin, an overestimation, a "trans," and conductivity that is not an origin, is not present, and is not subject to programmatic laws, concepts, or principles. If there is such a thing as a trace of sexual orientations or transgender manifestations, one may speculate that it parts and departs from a communication, from a movement that transmits, from a trans that translates without archive and without history. This event is singular for each individual and escapes the control, naming, and categorization of earthly or heavenly institutions.

Although the trace of every sexual orientation is in excess of any cultural formation and is external to any system of beliefs, heterosexuality has been formalized (set in motion, configured, summoned, gathered, ordered, categorized, etc.) as "internal" (to community, family, and nation), as "present," "natural," foundational, and fundamental. Heterosexuality endures multiple usurpations and pressures from the programmatic systems and institutions that organize, summon, and speculate about its trace, its nonpresent origin. Heterosexuality becomes compulsive and compulsory as is "revealed" or "brought forth" as the legitimate sexuality, the one that grants and preserves family, community, and nation. In contrast, and through a dialectic of opposites (even though sexual desire does not oppose), homosexuality is made known to be foreign, dangerous, contaminated, and in opposition to a legitimized, familiar, and compulsory heterosexuality (which is other than heterosexuality).

Neither heterosexuality nor homosexuality can be legitimized through a "legitimate" origin. In *Beyond the Pleasure Principle*, when Freud speculates about the origin of sexual drives, his thoughts reach a limit. They are suspended as his speculations touch multiple gaps when trying to figure the origin of sexual drives. In the threshold of his own thoughts (associated with the origin of sexual drives), he finds an excess that disturbs his search for origins, a conductivity that traces other traces supplementing an origin that is continually displayed and impossible to present. When this "contamination" of origins takes place in his rigorous thoughts, he aims at the origin of sexual drives through myth in order to supplement the lacuna at the origin of sexual drives and sexual difference:

What I have in mind is, of course, the theory which Plato put into the mouth of Aristophanes in the *Symposium*, and which deals not only with the *origin* of the sexual instinct but also with the most important of its variations in relation to is object. "The original human nature was not like the present, but different. In the first place, the sexes were originally three in number, not two as they are now; there was man, woman, and the union of the two ..." Everything about these primeval men was double: they had four hands and four feet, two faces, tow privy parts, and so on. Eventually Zeus decided to cut these men in two ... After the division had been made, "the two parts of man, each desiring his other half, came together, and threw their arms about one another eager to grow into one."[233]

When encountered by a limit in the origin of sexual drives, Freud is exposed to a desire that is in excess of every desire: "a need to restore an earlier state of things" (*Beyond* 69), a "compulsion to repeat" (71) an earlier state of things. If there is something at the origin of the sexual instincts, it is a desire to supplement and restore an earlier state of things that cannot be understood in terms of presence, origin, or truth. Thus, if there were a departure of the sexual instincts, it would be a supplement, a trans, a conductivity that translates through a dividing space that parts and departs

[233] Freud, *Beyond*, 69–70.

compulsively: "All the movements in 'trans-,' the ones that involve repetitions, displacements, and speculations, would not be after the fact in relation to a perceptive or intuitive origin, they would inhabit this origin on its very threshold."[234] The "origin" of homosexuality, heterosexuality, or whatever is in between involves a conductivity, a trans, a repetition that supplements a desire to restore an earlier state of things, an excess that departs from an origin that multiplies and divides since its inception. The departure of sexual drives is other than a sexual orientation.

What differs between the sexes is anything but a dialectic of opposites; however, through the centuries, homosexuality has been explained in opposition to heterosexuality, as a contaminated sexuality, a perversion, as a failure to become "nature," "God's mandate," and so forth. Thus, through a dialectic of opposites, homosexuals become the descendants of an unchosen people, of ancestors without history and without glory. They become wandering specters, inheritors of a threatening excess, of a surplus that is in excess of family, community, and states' values. In that sense, homosexuals bear the idiom of the surplus in Sodom. They bear the idiom of a relationship to the unknown, the strange, and the uncanny (a bond that remains without analogy and without God). At the same time, as they are exposed to multiple discourses that portray them as evil and "*contra natura*," they withdraw to their own incommunicable and infallible spastic interval, to a limit not even known to them, a "momentary extinction" out of which "a highly intensified excitation" multiplies and divides their own sexuality before they can say, "I am commanded to do this or that."

---

[234] Derrida, "To Speculate," 383.

Similarly but in a different manner, the singularity of the "who" or "what" of heterosexuality, the "yes" of heterosexuality, its nonorigin, its trans and conductivity has also been exorcised, neutralized, and usurped into a regime of compulsive heterosexuality (of shall and shall nots), which is equated with a multiplication of truths associated with family, community, religion, nation, and so forth. The mandates of compulsive heterosexuality neutralize the singularity of heterosexuality in order to put in motion a programmatic version of heterosexuality. Compulsive heterosexuality "reveals" its legitimization through a dialectic of opposites where heterosexuality is contrasted with a "perverse," unproductive, and "contaminated" desire that "deviates" from a compulsive heterosexuality categorized through multiple institutions. The multiplication of truths (compulsive heterosexuality, a supreme being, reproduction, the phallus, shall not, pronouncements, decrees, sentences, Oedipus complex, etc.) promise the plenitude of concepts that legitimate compulsive heterosexuality with values of responsibility and respectability tied to family, community, religious institutions, and nation.

The analogy without analogy, the missing word, the interval suspended in the threshold of our impressions, the unanalyzed remains, and the indetermination of the desiring subject is proscribed, usurped, restrained, or obstructed by the multiple systems of truths that say, swear, or promise "not to pass" and not to think beyond the accepted and established cut (a limit that says not only "do not pass" or "this must not be addressed" but also "this is neither a limit nor a cut but nature and truth revealed").

The singular manifestations of every sexual orientation, their conductivities, have been transformed into "conducts" categorized as more or less perverse, more or less permissible, and accompanied by a range of rewards and punishments depending on the act. Through this scheme of "known" and established truths, homosexuality becomes an "exterior contamination" that haunts the internal values of society. Through these inversions and conversions, homosexuality (exterior to nature and a reproductive society) is without legitimacy, without community, and without God (homosexuality has betrayed the very will of God).

"There is homosexuality," like "there is heterosexuality." Sexualities arrive. They are "there" unexpectedly through a calling and an affirmation, through a repetition that is prehistorical and precultural. They are "there" before the individual can be aware of their arrival or sending, before a "natural" or cultural language attempts to define and reorganize the orientations of their singular spaces (spaces of proximity and distance to the other and to everyone and everything that is other). Sexual orientation comes from an elsewhere, from a desire for spaces of proximity and distance that is neither provoked nor induced by gods or institutions. There is nothing secret about this desire that appears in secret and makes the individual aware of a strange solitude, of a space of proximity and deferral toward a who or a what that will never belong to him/her but will mark the path of his/her passions, his/her sense of life, and sense of sense. This call says "Yes" to the coming of the other and its affirmation is ineludible, repetitive, mute, inescapable, singular, and immemorial. As the "Yes" arrives unexpectedly and free of any impediment or memory, the individual will soon encounter the interpellation of the law, the inexplicable thwarting of his/her desire. The individual sees in secret an uncanny, foreign, and frightful awakening of his/her multiplying self. This "secret," however, cannot be kept secret because there is nothing secretive about it. Whether heterosexuality, homosexuality, or sexualities in between, their "contaminated" exteriority, the space that has already arrived as a surplus before "nature" and God, will be in excess of "culture" (one of the names of "nature") and in excess of established structures of meaning, including family, friends, nation, and religion. Each individual is "chosen" to respond to the orientation of spaces in the threshold of sense, a response, a call, and a conduct that is above all the known names promised to them.

The usurpation of the individuals' singularities, of the trace of their passion, converts them into programmed subjects of the state, the church, and the family. Thus, the ecstatic interval that impassions through proximity and distance to a "who" or "what," the analogy without analogy that remains open at the threshold of sense, the stranger within and without ourselves, the visitor within and without that watches us but cannot be looked at, the limit without contours of a figure and a trace, and the passion that says "Yes" to the unknown is incorporated to an infinite debt to God, church, and state.

Homosexual, heterosexual, or in between? Who does not ask these questions of themselves at one or many points of their existence: Why can I not feel at home in my parents' home? Why can I not feel at home with myself? What is that mark that marks my desire? Who is the specter (inside/outside of me) that does not let itself be seen or named? Why am I driven to have a relationship with this X that is not a thing or a being and does not present itself? How do I respond to the call and the invitation in the most affirmative of ways? These are the same questions that Abraham asked of himself. In that moment, Abraham embraced the surplus that disorganized and disjointed all familiar settings, an orgiastic impetus that had no known history and was not determined by any concept. In order to embrace this excess, he was a dissident of family and tradition, and he separated himself in order to engage with a conductivity that he could not control, rule, or understand. The Sodomites follow along the same orgiastic trace. All revolutions and revolts in the world follow a similar dissidence, an analogous separation from traditional and ethical values in order to found a new justice, a new responsibility, a renewed sense of ethics that overturns the nature of nature and the truth of truth.

There is a call for "dissidence" when the sexual impetus of each adolescent starts manifesting. They are awoken to a silent and unconditional impetus that is in excess of themselves, in excess of what they can control or decide. Their sexuality, perceived through the threshold of perceptions, is out of place and exceeds everything they know and understand. They have to make sense with all their senses of a desire that exceeds them and touches them in the threshold of their impressions, in an ecstatic interval that is untouchable. They respond, they try to make sense without knowing, without previous knowledge, without tradition; they decide without deciding the event of their passionate and desiring being. The immemorial memory of this spastic nonobject does not come from a regulative idea or a decree. They respond to a surplus that does not respond or correspond. They respond with their sexuality, their desiring subjectivity, and their love, all of which partake in the excess that constitutes them as unique and singular beings. At the same time, the surplus, the exteriority that calls them to be singular and unique beings is other than their internal sexual orientations. They are not equivalent. Sexual orientation is a function of the surplus, but the latter can never be defined in terms of a sexual orientation alone. Without seeing they are being seen, without feeling they are being touched, and without hearing they hear the rhythmic flow of a syncopeic interval, an alterity, a Nietzschean affirmation without truth and without origin:

> The Nietzschean affirmation is the joyous affirmation of the play of the world and the innocence of becoming, the affirmation of a world of signs without fault, without truth, and without origin which is offered to an active interpretation ... In absolute chance, affirmation also surrenders itself to *genetic* indetermination, to the *seminal* adventure of the trace.[235]

In the threshold of their prepubescent and adolescent impressions, they say "Yes" to what is coming, to the "perhaps" that links a world and a universe with their passions and their sense of sense. Homosexual, heterosexual, or in between, they are dissidents from family, friends, church, and country; from regulative ideals that repress and usurp the affirmation of chance, of "if," and of "perhaps." The

---

[235] Derrida, "Structure, Sign and Play in the Discourse of the Human Sciences," in *Writing and Difference*, trans. Alan Bass (Chicago: University of Chicago Press, 1978), 292.

singularity of every human being turns toward the call/ communication of an archaic and recurrent mystery, a spastic drive that is incompatible with social structures, with ready-made identities and categorical imperatives. They respond to an exterior conductivity, to a multiplicity of spaces; they hear the call of a passionate language of proximity and distance. The distant and close perception that captivates and besieges them also benumbs them in a circling grasp that is not on the side of prescribed knowledge but on the path of leap, interruption, and repetition. This "dissidence" from usurping conventions and conversions is no secret and has no chosen people, gender, or sexual orientation because this play of intervals, this exteriority that expands and contracts in multiple spaces, chooses everyone; it is unsacrificeable and calls for neither sacrifice, nor domination, nor persecution. As children become "subjects" of programed ideologies and programmatic religions, they also become dissidents because the incommensurable overflow that bounds their desires to the indeterminate other (the surplus that defers from God and culture and is in the threshold of sense) remains unsacrificeable and without analogy.

One might optimistically think that in the modern Western world, homosexuality has adjusted to normative society, and, in multiple levels, this assertion would be truthful. Gay rights have been achieved through a co-optation of homosexuality in the service of the state by supporting marriage, adoption, and other forms of parenting/ procreation and benefits for "established" gay couples while still condemning/persecuting against homosexual behavior. The state, family, and some church branches have now the tendency to support gay civil unions and marriages, and these are monumental steps toward the gay-rights movement. Institutions have adapted their heterosexual and family programs (parenting, procreation, and adoption) to the gay community. All these heterosexualizing steps have created a homosexuality-positive culture that has become part of a program where gay individuals acquire presence and legitimacy before multiple institutions. The rest, however, (including heterosexuals, homosexuals, bisexuals, etc.) that do not respond to programmatic knowledge may be considered "dissidents" to the imparted social values. Institutions need subjects and categories in order to govern according to a program or an ideology, and the less that is "added" to the program (the less an "exterior" surplus distorts or disorganizes the established truths), the better is the programmatic continuity of the knowledge considered legitimate. Like the people of Sodom (and before them, Abraham), these "dissidents" respond to a call, specter, communication, and so forth, that is not part of an imparted knowledge.

Although there are no "chosen people" for the idiom of Sodom, it will continue to be associated with a certain homosexuality that is not in attunement with a serviceability, usability, and relevance of an imparted knowledge that discloses the truth of the subjects that "be," subjects entangled in a programmatic social milieu:

> Undoubtedly, the subjectivity of a subject, already, never decides anything: its identity in itself and its calculable permanence make every decision an accident which leaves the subject unchanged and indifferent. *A theory*

of the subject is incapable of accounting for the slightest decision ... Such an undesirable guest [a passive or originarily affected decision] can intrude into the closed space or the home ground of common sense only by recalling, as it were, so as to drive authority from it, an old forgotten invitation. It would thus recall the type or the silhouette of the classic concept of decision, which must interrupt and mark an absolute beginning. Hence it signifies in me the other who decides and rends.[236]

The idiom of Sodom associated to the trace of an inalienable surplus, to the antechamber of communication that is without being and prior to any god, and to the threshold of sense will always be (wrongly) associated with a part of homosexuality that cannot be ruled, programmed, or governed. The idiom from Sodom is a trace (an orgiastic and enamored trace) that cannot be erased by the family, state, science, and church (apparatuses of being, legitimacy, truth, and objectivity). In this sense, the idiom of Sodom may always be "an evil" that comes from an elsewhere, a surplus that remains inaccessible to the ruling forces of earth and heaven.

No country or institution may create a program that bounds sexuality in a way that is determined and determining. The desire for the indeterminate other, for what/who is other, and for the other's other comes before any program or programing. This call is irreplaceable and "unplaceable." The

---

[236] Derrida, *Politics of Friendship*, 68.

world forming, the world of regulative ideals, of ideal being, of program, programing, progress, proclaiming; the world of fundament, genesis, cause/effect, the world of horizons and goals presents a concern and a preoccupation with the "who" or "what" that manifests outside a program of truth, presence, nature, and culture.

Homosexuality and Sodom are positioned in a heterogeneous realm of negative analogies as a desiring subjectivity that does not respond and correspond to the system of analogies that are programed. The "unchosen children" are summoned to their own desert of solitude, without God, without religion, and without nation. Since early childhood, they are called to grasp a surplus that is in excess of their senses and that survives any ideological program, persecutions, and decrees, even the abandonment of family, country, and religion (as in the case of Abraham and the Sodomites).

One may imagine a dreamlike mise-en-scène where a child is quietly trembling with joy and melancholy as s/he senses a sending, a trace of a chiasm that opens the very sense of space and spacing, the proximity to what or who is other, the very analogical perception between inside and outside. One may imagine children sensing the future of possibilities as a "Yes," as a world that flows freely. At the same time, there are the families, institutions, nations, and so forth, usurping the threshold of sense (the trans, the conductivity, the transferability of spaces, the open word, etc.) from the children and aligning their singular alterity, their spastic intervals into a conversion of sorts, into mandates and sentences, into "spiritual" agendas, into programmatic, categorical, and imperative truths.

253

Receptive to an excess that cannot be named properly, appropriately; abandoned to an excess that is dangerous, uncanny, and unfamiliar, the Sodomites leave their legacy in a kernel of interrupted rapture, an intact, syncopeic desire that promises a formidable expectation that cannot be cast in any particular name or fully embraced. The incandescent threshold of perception, the nocturnal passion of an impossible love, an immemorial excess that is missing from the everyday life event "contaminates" the everyday life of every singular individual, with or without religion, regardless of their beliefs, gender, or sexual orientation.

XIII

Sodom, Lot's Wife, and the Vision of a Pure Event

The world of religion hovers around a circular grasp in the threshold of the senses. The circling language of religion draws insistently from a faulty synchronicity, from a mute mark that does not cease to divide and multiply in order to restitute a spectral presence that is unsayable and untouchable. Passions and persecutions, war and sacrifice declare the meaning and presence of a name that attempts to denominate an idiom that cannot be dominated, that defers from nominations and dominations. Through multiplying leaps (of faiths), believers affirm and reaffirm knowledge that they don't know, that is not known through the knowledge of presence and truth, but that they want everyone to declare they know (and to affirm that they believe what they know). Religious names that speak of the plenitude of the living

255

presence nominate, dominate, and denominate an evanescent and unconquerable grasp. As this diachronic "progression" of cultural truths and chosen peoples unfolds, the spectral texture withdraws to an indeterminate and unconditional space between cultures, religions, and in the chore of politics. It is the ungraspable spastic space and the immemorial interval that constitute the unconditional engine through which the circle of conditional religion and sovereign politics reverberates.

The law founded on the ruins of Sodom is the law that makes inaccessible the access to its excess. This untraceable town with invisible tracks is the foundation that retreats from any promised land and at the same inaugurates all the messianic religions to come, all the faiths that attempt to give hospitality to the stranger and the living presence (which defers its presence into a coming that is never one). Without the trace of these enamored ashes, without this forgotten desert, there is no act of faith in the threshold of the senses, no burning hands writing the name of an idiom, an alterity that remains without translation and without analogy:

> Another "tolerance" would be in accord with
> the experience of the "desert in the desert"; it
> would respect the distance of infinite alterity
> as singularity. And this respect would still
> be religio, religio as scruple or reticence,
> distance, dissociation, disjunction, coming
> from the threshold of all religion in the link
> of repetition to itself, the threshold of every
> social or communitarian link. Before and
> after the logos which was in the beginning,

before and after the Holy Sacrament, before
and after the Holy Scriptures.[237]

The alterity of Sodom is in the threshold/antechamber of religion, and at the same time, its disjunctive trace is excluded from any and all religions. Religion stands against the alterity that remains its foundation, a surplus without which religion cannot anticipate its multiple survivals, sacrifices, messianisms, and new beginnings. Sodom will have given to the history of religion a messianic impetus: a "what" that is lacking, a "who" that is missing, a texture that resists touching but opens the path of every touch and consuming grasp. This history of the remains of Sodom is the trace of what never presents itself as such, of a suspended interval, of a presentiment that mesmerizes as one insistently desires beyond any programmatic grasp. The ruins of Sodom, its syncopeic space, recommences mechanistically at any point in time as one desires, with a desire that exceeds desire, a formless impetus through which every desire transits and transmits. Through this sediment that is not nothing, through this vestige of passion that forms out of the formless, through the remains of the remains of a multiplying threshold of the senses, the individual sees the event that inaugurates life every time, and every time anew. One sees himself/herself happening in the promise of a future that is now. In the midst of catastrophe, collapse, and ruins, there is hope and promise for a future where everyone is chosen.

The future of religion, the religion that has a future, departs from this genesis, this revolting revolt, this spasmodic turn around in the form of a vague figure present through

---

[237] Derrida, "Faith and Knowledge," 60.

its passing. The circle of religion renews itself through the messianic promise of delivering the presence of what does not makes itself present. A new passion rises from a death that dies its own death by deferring death, by infinitely suspending death. A new sending is transmitted from consuming embers. From the remains without remains, from ashes, the passion for an indefinite other is carried and transported to a new beginning, to a new departure and partition.

Sodom is a nameless tomb that survives and lives on. Its buried space is dedicated to the memory of nothing—a tomb without glory, a space folding toward its own curvature, turning against itself without utterance, a retreat that keeps in its fold an indefinite limit. This exteriority, however, continues to take place (without taking place). The orgiastic mystery of Sodom, the desire for its specter is sent to haunt all towns eternally with a desire that is without analogy, without negativity, without dialectics, and without opposition between life and death or master and slave. Every town will have been founded on top of the ghostly ruins of Sodom, on top of the nothingness of Sodom, on top of the becoming nothing of the Sodomites:

> This essence [to give oneself up only by becoming writing through writing] will have *been* nothing before this becoming, that is, before this writing prescribed to the friend-reader. This essence is born from nothing and tends toward nothing. For earlier, didn't Silesius say ... *To become Nothing is to become God* ...[238]

---

[238] Derrida, *On the Name*, 42–43.

Sodom remains without glory. Sodom is condemned to a bottomless collapse in an open desert with no routes or paths. From this catastrophic collapse, from this place without world or place in the world, the silence of what is absolute other (foreign, nameless, and disenfranchised) survives and lives on: "God is the name of this bottomless collapse, of this endless desertification of language ... Reference to God, the name of God, [will be joined] with the experience of place [of the desert which] is also a figure of the pure place."[239]

The disappearance of Sodom in a desert buried by another desert cannot disappear its enamored ashes, the remains without remains of an exteriority that transmits, that transfers and lives on. This love for an indefinite other, this anticipation that carries the other (any other who is other), this "messianism without messiah," remains without translation and translates into multiple languages of passion, anticipating the movement of what must be grasped and translated, what will and will never be subject to any programmed knowledge. The symptom of all religion, the infancy of every religion lives in infamy as an "external" part of religion, as the passion neutralized in the threshold, as the impure passion from which "proper" passions are established. It is from this very placeless place of excess, contamination, catastrophe, and silence that strophes, tropes, and sentences emerge through multiple paths of ethics and religion, paths that are other than their foundation (a surplus that remains without analogy). Those who inscribe the "shall nots" of Western religions write from the pulse of the "Yes" of the orgiastic impetus, of the excess that does not know negativity, decree, or opposition.

---

[239] Ibid., 55–57.

Why is there a command not to look back toward this burning town? Lot's wife dares to look back, and what she sees is forever sealed in her salty lips. But of what or of whom was she a witness? The people of Sodom are cremated, swallowed alive by something or someone, and Lot's wife wishes to "see" the catastrophe that is taking place. She needs to see the sending of the event, the coming of the other. She is infected by the contamination of what is arriving. No courage or fear is bigger than the desire "to know" the coming of the unknown, a desire that affects/infects her senses and is in excess of them. Only that woman, who does not have a name in the Old Testament, will have experienced the unknowable, the apocalypse that reveals the X-thing when everything is destroyed. From that revelation that reveals nothing, all desire to know is revealed with a new impetus: "Now, what this apocalypse reveals is not so much a truth as the night of nonknowledge in which every desire gathers momentum."[240] Like the Sodomites, she would die with a secret that is reduced to "nothing." At the same time, that instant, that nothing, that death that lives infinitely the death of its death, that ungraspable limit between vision and (ultimate) sense lives on in the tale of Sodom. That moment lives on through the desire to know the name of that "nothing" that erases and erases itself. The instant of her death is a passage to a pure event. This "nothing" is the surplus associated with a pure event, and her corpus receives (lets itself be given) the ecstatic gift. Her contained desire (a desire that cannot be contained because it exceeds every desire) remains as a forbidden fantasy, a fabulous fantasy that is unconditionally desired. It survives as a fabulous fantasy that withdraws from

---

[240] Derrida, *On Touching*, 51.

all realities but is in excess of every reality, a fantasy that we (the readers) are able to glimpse through her unpresentable vision/perception/grasp. The pure event that she experiences is transmitted through erasure and effacement: "Inviolable secret, without depth, without place, without name, without destination, *hyperbolytic*, excessive destruction, and lysis without measure, without measure and *without return*, lysis without anagogy."[241] The trace of the Sodomites, the trace of the other as other, of the stranger, of the strange, of the other's other, of God; the trace of who or what is always other is preserved in the instant of her death and through the eyes of the reader who sees the nothing that puts in motion every desire to know the nonobject that remains after destruction.

A woman without a name sees something that blinds her and converts her into a statue of salt. She sees an exterior X that remains without name, without presence, and without testimony, a conductivity that transforms everything. She sees a consuming town consumed in flames by something external that burns without being burned. The reader may imagine Lot's wife seeing/perceiving an X that transforms and transmutes everything but remains untranslatable. The reader (anyone who is any other) who tries to see through the eyes of Lot's wife may himself/herself see the "nothing" that transports at the very instant of her immolation. The reader is transported to a "trans" that transports, a surplus that transforms, transmutes, transits, converts, and consumes:

> It is always an *external* constraint that arrests a text in general, i.e. *anything*, for example, life death. What is arrested here:

---

[241] Derrida, *Resistances*, 34.

the authenticity of a being-for-death. Think the exteriority from the angle of this economy of the *arrêt*. *Arrêt*: the greatest "bound" energy, "banded (erect)," *bandée*, tightly gathered around its own limit, retained, inhibited *and immediately* disseminated. Sand. Empty, unloaded itself, spontaneously. In the trance of the trans-. ... Trans/ partition. Trespassing. To be related, without translation, to all the trans-'s that are at work here.[242]

One could speculate that she is petrified when she witnesses what transmutes, binds, and transforms but remains without a proper name, without presence, without being. Sodom is being erased at the moment when Lot's wife presences the absolute other coming to erase Sodom and to erase itself. What or who she witnesses is a thing, a nonobject, a proper name that comes "by erasing itself, to erase itself; it comes only in its erasure."[243] As readers, we stand with Lot's wife in the midst of this fabulation and confabulation. We are also trying to see through her eyes the nonobject, the X that without being present can be grasped in the darkest of nights and through destruction and oblivion. As readers, we also sense, with a vision that is other than the sense of vision, the X that destruction, oblivion, and repression can only multiply. We stand before a surplus, a trans, a figureless affirmation, an exteriority, an event highlighted through its evanescent trace.

---

[242] Derrida, "Living On," 187–188 (lower band).

[243] Refer to footnote 143.

What did Lot's wife grasp in her frozen eyes in the instant of her death? Are we not also, as readers, the desiring eyes of Lot's wife? Are we not the passionate speculators who confabulate in order to fabulate and speculate about the X that crosses in passing through her senses? We are also impassioned by her desire to foresee and trespass. As we wish to trespass and attempt to see without eyes, we are also blinded and paralyzed by the "invisible visibility" of the unconditional and the incommensurable X. The grasp of this invisible visibility impassions us as we "attest" for an idiom that remains without translation. We, the blind and blinded readers of this tale, read what remains unreadable in the reading, what remains without writing in writing. As Lot's wife, "we," the readers, see the "if" of a "conditional visibility," of a condition of visibility that is itself "invisible" and unconditional. Would the writing of religion and of a religion without religion be possible without the dangerous, hopeful, and unshielded "vision" of Lot's wife and the Sodomites, without the remains of the remains of writing?[244]

What remains is what does not remain: a paralyzing desire, a desire that paralyzes. Thus, there is no revelation of presence but its anticipation, no relieving of passion but its deferral, no memory of the orgiastic secret of Sodom but its trace. What remains is Sodom's surplus. What remains

---

[244] "The idea of the Good is situated, at once inscribed and deinscribed, on a divided line cut into two equal parts, each of which is itself cut according to the calculable reason of a *logos*, and this is Plato's word, a *logos* that divides things up according to the analogy between the sensible visible, the mathematical ... the intelligible visible, and the invisible as the source of the visible, the invisible visibility of the visible, the condition of visibility that is itself invisible and unconditional." Derrida, *Rogues*, 117.

are the revenants, the desiring specters of Sodom wandering without country, without present, without presence, and without taking place. They return in the memory that remains silent, "in the writing born from nothing that tends toward nothing."[245] Their spectral passion lives on as an excess that is not programmable, that is not, that does not exist in terms of presence, and that does not desist. It is through cinders and ashes, through the erasure and consumption of meaning that the circle that binds meaning with passion parts and departs, reopening the surplus of an ongoing genesis.

The interruption that extinguishes meaning and presence is the limit of discourse, the hiatus that reopens a relation with an affirmation, a mute excess that binds passion and meaning into a new partition, departure, and genesis. To the readers of the story, the ultimate pleasure in Sodom does not arrive until everything in Sodom is erased. The ultimate pleasure arrives only to erase itself. The ultimate pleasure is the suspension/consumption/effacement of all presence, sight, voice, and touch so that a sense other than the senses extends to an exteriority, to an open word that communicates and departs again anew. Immobilized, suspended, annulled, empty of signification and representation, the remains of a consumed city consist forever in not consisting, in not being consistent, in remaining unstable and open to the arriving of the *arrivant*, the arrival of the event (of the strange, the foreign, the uncanny, and the unknown). The arrival of what arrives can never be consummated or fully consumed but only infinitely dreamed or anticipated. Sodom is the frenzied and consumed city suspended in a revelation that does not reveal presence or truth. It is a pure event without revelation.

---

[245] Refer to footnote 238.

Its signification is that is does not signify, it does not unfold. Its disappearance leaves a hiatus without meaning, with a word that is always missing.

The empty hiatus is a binding space. It calls for a thousand desiring promises determined by an indeterminate "maybe." Whoever senses the call for the desire "to know" the unknown, whoever hears the rhythm of a passing specter will feel chosen and taken hostage by the "maybe" that bounds, linking an X-trace to our desire for multiple futures, anticipations, and iterations. The indestructible "yes" remains untouched, withdrawn, without a place, and refusing to speak, and at the same time, it is from this syncopeic limit where desires are bound, displayed, and linked to a "perhaps" or "maybe." The desire for this conductivity entices in both genders the desire for what is missing (beyond any sexual desire or orientation). There is no sexual orientation, no gender, and no specific genre that ultimately grasps with desire alone the missing exteriority that impassions, the lacking word that mixes genres, the X-thing that entices individuals of either sex, gender, or whatever is in between to grasp the figure of desirable presence that will arrive in not arriving (through delay, deferral, hope, and expectation). Genres and genders remain wanting and unsatisfied as they attempt to respond to this surplus that surpasses them.

Pseudo-Dionysius Areopagite, a mystical theologian who wrote the *Divine Names*, attempted to address the surplus that does not let itself be addressed by any name, the excess that will remain as the name that withdraws from all names, the "Divine Spark" that is always withdrawing from the poem, continually uprooting itself, and persistently refusing to be named. As Dionysius describes this spark, he dedicates his thinking to his friend Timothy. Friendship and the desire for what is other than friendship meet and mix in the threshold of sense where the writing at hand is suspended as it expresses the desire to know the surplus that surpasses desire:

> This is my prayer.
> And you, dear Timothy,
> in the earnest exercise of
> mystical contemplation, abandon
> all sensation and all intellectual activities
> all that is sensed and intelligible,
> all non-beings and all beings;
> thus you will unknowingly be elevated,
> as far as possible,
> to the unity of that beyond being and knowledge.
> By the irrepressible and absolving ecstasies
> of yourself and of all,
> absolved from all, and
> going away from all,
> you will be purely raised up
> to the rays of the divine darkness
> beyond being.[246]

The prayer prays to grasp, with the other of the hand, with the other of sense, a remain that is in excess of everything and, for this very reason, indestructible. In the name of a friendship beyond friendship and other than friendship,

---

[246] Pseudo-Dionysius Areopagite, *The Divine Names and Mystical Theology*, trans. John D. Jones (Milwaukee, Wisconsin: Marquette University Press, 1980), 211–212.

between knowing and not knowing, between the sensible and the intelligible, between a "between" that surpasses what is between, there is a threshold, a surplus that binds, a persisting excess. The poem is not unlike the scene of the Sodomites abandoning themselves to the ultimate "divine darkness," to the step without step, to the step beyond being (other than being), to a "yes" and a "maybe" that consume themselves beyond being and beyond knowledge. That step without step that exceeds the notion of the step (that trespasses without fully grasping) is the indetermination that remains unsacrificeable as it is consummated in flames, as it inflames the passion that consumes and consummates. And that is the gift of the tale of Sodom (or if one would like to express it in another way, it is the gift of the Sodomites).

This consumption reveals the consummation of the indestructible, of an indestructible desire that goes on in the here and now. This consuming delirium is a fragile promise, a "yes," a "maybe" that is at all times being threatened, and it could even be inverted as something that threatens: "The threat *is* the promise itself, or better, threat and promise always come together *as* the promise. This does not mean just that the promise is always already threatened; it also means the promise is *threatening*."[247]

The promise may also become a threat that prohibits and persecutes. It may become dreadful, deadly, and catastrophic when the powers that "be" claim and proclaim to be the caretakers, representatives, and interpreters of a predictable and programed mysterium tremendum. The world has witnessed the atrocities committed by sovereign powers that

---

[247] Derrida, "Nietzsche and the Machine," 255.

appropriate the spectral surplus (through multiple iterations and denominations) into abominable deliriums:

> I am explaining the German spirit, in the German-Jewish psyche that constitutes it. If this psyche, and the entire Judeo-Greco-Christian underpinning that structures it, seems delirious to you, if it gives rise to some delirium, to all types of violence, to the heights and the lows, the depressions, the crises, the historical turning points, the expulsions, the murders or the suicides, the reappropriations, by emancipation or by genocide, well then I am just telling you what this thing you call delirium is made of.[248]

Individuals as well as political and religious institutions have been entangled with the claim to know the other "as such," as enemy or friend, and to let that "truth" be known. Multiple times in history, this delirium has produced catastrophic eras. The delirium "speaks" by claiming to know the name of the other, a domination that dominates and authorizes to speak "in the name" of an established and hegemonic truth (sentence, law, edict, etc.). The delirium promises itself to speak ...

---

[248] Derrida, "Interpretations at War: Kant, the Jew, the German," in *Psyche: Inventions of the Other. Volume II*, ed. Peggy Kamuf and Elizabeth Rottenberg (Stanford: Stanford University Press, 2008), 255.

XIV

Thou Shalt Not Lie with Mankind … The Usurpation of Pleasures

n Leviticus 18:22, one reads the following decree and judgment: "Thou shalt not lie with mankind, as with womankind: it is abomination." A few verses down, in Leviticus 20:13, the sentence for that "abomination" is the following: "If a man also lies with mankind, as with a womankind, both of them have committed abomination: they shall surely be put to death; their blood shall be upon them." The intensity of the law revolves around a command and a limit ("do not pass," "do not advance," "retract without retracing," "retreat without questioning," "divert without looking," "defer indefinitely," "withhold your passion," etc.). The mandate attempts to neutralize/interrupt an excess that has already arrived and said "yes" (before religion, God, family, community, nation, tradition, memory, legacy, etc.).

The law limits and forbids, pushes away a passion that impassions, which existed before Sodom and before the gods: a desire that is in addition to the law, before it, and other than the law. The more the surplus is pushed away, the more it collapses around the law, a collapse that paradoxically injects more vitality into the law. The remains that remain after the law neutralizes the surplus is the remnant that is to be avoided ad infinitum through renewed assimilations, incorporations, idealizations, limits, and divisions:

> And when a limit is established, norms and interdictions are not far behind: "Do," "Do not" says "genre," the word "genre," the figure, the voice, or the law of genre. And this can be said of genre in all genres, be it a question of a generic or a general determination of what one calls "nature" or *phusis* ... or be it a question of a typology designated as nonnatural and depending on laws or orders that were once held to be opposed to *phusis* ... But the whole enigma of genre springs perhaps most closely from within this parti(cipa)tion between the two genres of genre that, neither separable nor inseparable, form an odd couple of one without the other in which each evenly serves the other ...[249]

---

[249] Derrida, "Law of Genre," in *Parages*, 218–219.

The decree insistently draws an imaginary line because the trespassing has already passed through, even before taking place. The limit established by the "no" configures also the desire to cross what one "must not" cross. The promise of the surplus is preserved in a desire to cross what is *forbidden* to cross. Thus, in the limit one must and must not cross, one must cross (but) without crossing; one must cross only to neutralize the surplus through which the familiar is established (by positing bands that ban what is in excess of every prohibition and law). The "no" preserves/assimilates/incorporates the trace of a "Yes" in an economy of debt that promises salvation. One must lose (sacrifice, condemn, annul, neutralize, repress, forget, etc.) in order to be saved, in order to multiply savings, and in order to achieve salvation. An economy of debt (associated with the investment of responsibility, duty, promise, commitment, etc.) multiplies its obligations through a limit that is inexhaustible in its finitude: "Saving (*sauver*) the name of God by keeping it safe (*sauf*); sacrificing the name of God precisely in order to save it ... saving is inscribed in the classical economy of salvation, the circle of losing-in-order-to-save ..."[250]

The destruction of Sodom (which does not destroy its surplus) gives birth (through usurpation and neutralization) to negative laws that reproduce mechanisms of debt, credit, and equivalence grounded in a currency without equivalence. The law circles not only around the transit of bodies and pleasures but also around what transmits and transits. The law, among other things, condemns that which does not reproduce (or those who do not reproduce); it condemns the seed without paternity, the seed that has not been reproduced

---

[250] Caputo, *Prayers and Tears*, 43.

into a market of legitimate (paternal) names. The law makes us believe in a measure of equivalence in commerce, production, and reproduction, but the belief that haunts the law is a certain disbelief that does not respond to measure or calculation:

> The caustic force of the Nietzschean genealogy consists finally in saying something like this: at bottom, we do not believe, we do not believe even in what we believe or say we believe; we do not believe in what we pretend and affect to believe or to credit in order to make the market possible, to make commerce, contract, exchange and finally language possible and thus a social contract, a law that is first of all commercial law.[251]

The normalization, mechanization, commercialization, and institutionalization of the world are narratives that are other than the excess that founds them. The ritualized or machinelike repetition of the world (through multiple institutions of credit and debt that promise what they cannot deliver or what they don't have) draws from the repetitive and unsacrificeable pulse of an incommensurable overflow that is neither inherited nor legal.

The law draws its outline and its mechanistic insistence through the persistence of a surplus that is never quite at hand. The suppression, repression, or sacrifice of the "Yes" is preserved in the law that usurps its excess in order to rule

---

[251] Derrida, *Death Penalty*, 152–153.

it establishing an economy of credit, debt, production, and reproduction. The iterability of the law founds and inscribes a promise in the very limit where the promise may be broken. The promise of the law guards, preserves, and founds a circle of self-legitimization, which at its limit is reiterated, weakened, transgressed, and reinvigorated.

The positing law organizes debt by interrupting and neutralizing what is in excess of the law. The law posits, possesses, appropriates; it gives presence and legitimacy by calling to say "yes, I do not," "yes, I will not pass," "yes, I promise that I will defer the (tact of) excess, that I will not act, even if I am tempted to desire otherwise." The promise that the law mandates (its hegemonic "yes I shall say no") inscribes its traffic of influence, its legacy and legality through the "Yes," which transits and communicates without "trafficking," without inscription, without hegemony, and without paternity. This founding force of belief in the law of "shall not" is without foundation and contaminates as well as reassures its self-proclaimed promise. The promise is inscribed through a promising sentencing and a sentencing promise, through a promise that sentences and a sentence that promises:

> A foundation is a promise. Every positing permits and promises, posits ahead; it posits by setting and by promising. And even if a promise is not kept in fact, iterability inscribes the promise as guard in the most irruptive instant of foundation. Thus it inscribes the possibility of repetition at the heart of the originary. Better, or worse, it is

inscribed in this law of iterability; it stands under its law or before its law. Consequently, there is no more pure foundation or pure position of law, and so a pure founding violence, than there is a purely preserving violence. Preservation in its turn refunds so that it can preserve what it claims to found. Thus there can be no rigorous opposition between positing and preserving, only what I will call (and Benjamin does not name it) a *differential contamination* between the two, with all the paradoxes that this may lead to.[252]

The excess lives on, haunting the iterability of law, its foundations, and its promise. The excess circumvents the law and tempts it, brings it into question, thereby perpetrating the life of the decree through its own contamination and restoration. The decree ("do not pass") conditions not to desire a desire that arrived before the law. The law creates and cremates time, a "before" and "after" the act, which in turn conjures up presence, conscience, and punishment to the act that takes place in the limit established by the law. The law of desire (of the "shall not") asks the individual not to desire a desire that arrived before the law. The law is an excess and in excess of itself. The "no" establishes boundaries, disarticulates and seizes a surplus that does not cease to differ and defer from itself imperatively even through the threat of annihilation. The apparent "clarity" and "coherence" drawn by the law says, "Do not mix desires, do not mix genders, do

---

[252] Derrida, "Force of Law," 272.

not mix genres": "It [the law of genre] is precisely a principle of contamination, a law of impurity, a parasitical economy." [253]

The excess stands in for anybody. The surplus (the "Yes") freely transits and transports to any other who is other. The excess carries the other, the strange, and the uncanny. It transmits and communicates communication and transit. At the same time that the "Yes" communicates the transit of desires and of a desire that is in excess of the desires of touch, it also habilitates the traffic of laws founded through the repression, usurpation, and transferability of the surplus. The law at hand sentences to desire passionately, not to desire a desire that arrives before one can say, "I shall not desire." This compulsive determination that obsesses over desire in order not to desire (in order not to touch) is, in many ways, madness. Without this "madness," without the figuration of the law through a formless figure, without the denominations/sentences/abominations founded against what is without denomination, the law would be easily defied and mocked:

> Of all these subversions playing about the law, can we esteem that they mock the law, that they transgress or reveal its precarious historicity? Not at all, or all these sophistications would not be possible; they would have no force without the instance of the law they seem to defy; they would have no reason for it without drawing Reason from it, without provoking it—to produce it in

---

[253] Derrida, "Law of Genre," in *Parages*, 227. [My parenthetical explanation.]

twisting it, this very reason whose madness
they demonstrate rather than opposing to it,
from the outside, another madness.[254]

The law that says "do not touch" draws from an imperative Law of laws that communicates an affirmation (a "Yes") and that is other than the law that says "do not touch." The "Yes" that opens the possibility of all touch is itself untouchable. The law that says no to touch touches an otherly surface, a membrane that refuses to become a concept. The law that says no is a metaphor of truth, presence, and power that touches an interval that resists metaphoricity, presence, and power but allows for their transit. The law of the "shall not" regulates touch and proximity, but it is founded in a Law of laws that remains at the threshold of touch, an interval that makes possible the transit of touch but itself remains untouchable:

> There is a law of tact there. Touching, in any
> case, thus remains limitrophe; it touches
> what it does not touch; it does not touch; it
> *abstains* from touching on what it touches,
> and within the abstinence retaining it at the
> heart of its desire and need, in an inhibition
> truly constituting its appetite, it eats without
> eating what it is nourishment, touching,
> without touching, what it comes to cultivate,
> elevate, educate, drill.[255]

---

[254] Derrida, "Title To Be Specified," in *Parages*, ed. John P. Leavey, trans. Tom Conley (Stanford: Stanford University Press, 2011), 215.
[255] Derrida, *On Touching*, 67.

This law (of "shall not") touches in the limit of touch, a space where desires transit, an interval that is not an "abomination" but is rather a meridian place where all genres, genders, and sexual desires are possible through a touch that remains out of touch, a spastic interval that nourishes desires and needs but is other than them. The law of the "shall not" touches on the Law of laws that remains in abstinence before any prohibition. The "shall not touch" touches on an untouchable interval, a place without a place where all desires come into play.

The law performs; it acts as a negation that affirms. The circle of the law is ignited by the usurpation of a surplus that remains unknown and out of touch. The unknown, or what arrives without knowledge or memory, is usurped by a law that insistently deviates what it cannot touch, know, or penetrate. A deviant law that affirms, condemns, sentences, and conducts founds the familiar neutralizing the mandate that exceeds familiarity, place, and belonging. The law of the "shall not" ignites the obsessive circle of place, home, and family grounded on a surplus that is other than the law, on an excess that does not belong, on an exteriority that cannot be touched and is not at home in any place. The authority of the law, and its mechanism, takes place (performs, conjures, posits, and declares itself) through both the exorcism and incorporation of the remains of the surplus (the trace of the "Yes"):

> Wherever this foundation ["this mystical foundation of authority"] founds in foundering, wherever it steals away under the ground of what it founds, at the very

> instant when, losing itself thus in the desert, it loses the very trace of itself and the memory of a secret, "religion" can only begin and begin again: quasi-automatically, mechanically, machine-like, spontaneously. Spontaneously, which is to say as the word indicates, both as the origin of what flows from the source, sponte sua, and with the automaticity of the machine. For the best and for the worst, without the slightest assurance of anthropo-theological horizon.[256]

Through the interruption (cut, repression, oblivion, sacrifice, usurpation, etc.) of the "Yes," the law that prohibits ignites an automaticity that founds and sustains it. It besieges the sending, the arrival of what/who announces itself as ineluctable, of what/who has already arrived. The law (of the "shall not") affirms itself by besieging. It calculates and gives itself accountability by restituting the incalculable excess (the "Yes" that defers, that flows, that does not take place "as such," and that does not belong) with the mandate, the command, and the sentence of the law. The unity and clarity of the law positions itself against the surplus that evades unity of place, defers clarity of presence, and refuses to be nominated by a proper name or touched by proper law. All these mechanisms constitute both the hegemony of the law and also its limping, which requires to be constantly guarded and restored:

> For the Law is prohibition/prohibited [interdit]. Noun and attribute. Such would

---

[256] Derrida, "Faith and Knowledge," 57.

be the terrifying double-bind of its own taking-place. It is prohibition: this does not mean that it prohibits, but that it is itself prohibited, a prohibited place. It forbids itself and contradicts itself by placing the man in its own contradiction: one cannot reach the law, and in order to have a *rapport* of respect with it, *one must not* have a rapport with the law, one must interrupt the relation. One must *enter into relation* only with the law's representatives, its examples, its guardians. And these are interrupters as well as messengers. We must remain ignorant of who or what or where the law is, we must not know who it is or what it is, where and how it presents itself, whence it comes and whence it speaks.[257]

The law that mandates "shall not" cannot be touched not because it remains ungraspable (like the Law of laws) but because it remains inaccessible to its foundation. It is prohibited to touch the law that prohibits touch. The law of the "shall not" is in the center of interruption. In order to have a certain "rapport" with the law, the individual must have proper representatives (priests, psychoanalysts, politicians, etc.). The Law of laws that mandates/sends and communicates is now the law that mandates (sentences) and conducts a conduct (a behavior). The affirmative excess that interrupts and defers (the untouchable, the without touch, the open word, the ecstatic interval, the threshold of sense, or

---

[257] Derrida, "Before the Law," 203–204.

what remains without analogy) is contextualized (transferred, analogized, added, usurped, etc.) to an "affirmation" that says "yes, do not touch the law that says do not touch." The sending/mandate of the "Yes," the surplus of the Law of laws, the threshold that remains intact to touch are spaces without touch and without prohibition. They are never prohibited, not a prohibition, do not prohibit, and do not oppose or govern. At the same time and on the other hand, the law that prohibits and opposes (against a surplus that does not oppose or prohibit) calls for sacrifice, death, persecution, oblivion, and forgetfulness.

The pronunciation of a sentencing sentence delineates and produces a normative limit, a desire for the "proper," for a proper economy and community. This performative appropriation of the law opens a path for an identifiable and "proper" desire, but the "proper" (what can and cannot be touched) is drawn from an excess that is, in principle, never at hand. Thus, "the proper" desire needs to be insistently reassured because it departs from an interruption that "contaminates," an impetus that is without law and before the law, a surpassing desire that reaches for a figure that remains out of touch, a space/spacing that partakes in genres, genders, and the law but is other than them. The religious law of "do not" usurps the surplus that touches the body in the threshold of sense. Through a sentence that sentences, through the pronouncement of "shall not … touch" the law participates in the partition of the surplus that is neither separable nor inseparable. The "Yes," the perhaps, the promise, the dangerous, the hopeful, the indeterminable, and the nonoppositional space of the threshold (of sense) is arrested by a limit that says "no."

The law that insistently reminds humankind to promise not to desire a desire that is promised before the law arrived, before the law that promises "not to," this law points inexhaustibly and paradoxically to the very "Yes" that the law tries to oppose to, to the "Yes" that does not oppose and is associated with "a love more loving than love."[258] The law that says "do not touch" constitutes by formulating a promise and a demand to renounce a sending/arrival that cannot be renounced because it already arrived (it had been sent/mandated) before any command. The "passion" of the decree and its effectiveness resides in that it frames a trans, it raises against an interval that will never give up its intensity, its force, its nonprogrammable future, its "Yes." The negative desiring decree founds the familiar and the homely against a desiring principle that is anterior to the principle of the familiar and the homely. The law forms the home of the knowable by a negative decree that draws its force from a surplus that mandates repetitively "Yes," "come," "perhaps ..."

The law pretends to articulate a coherent, clear, and decisive command against an indefinite threshold of perception that cannot be refused, renounced, or commanded. The passage from a capital "Yes" to the "no" of the law is also a passage from the "no" to a "yes" as an affirmation of the law, a lawful affirmation that authorizes the expulsion of the body (the interruption of the interval of the senses). The desire that desires the negative law, the (negative) desire that becomes an affirmative law cannot fully become what it promises and sentences because it is also a reminder of the affirmation of the "Yes." The sending/arrival/trans/ of the "Yes" touches everybody where it is impossible to touch and

---

[258] Derrida, *Politics of Friendship*, 64.

traverses the body before it is subject to the negative law that constitutes individuals as gendered and sexualized subjects of the law. When the "Yes" arrives in passing and by surprise, it marks the subject with wants, promises, and expectations for the yet to be known. The "Yes" does not decide; it is not a decision, a path, or a pact, but every decision, proclamation, and association is possible when the "Yes" flows through the senses and through the letter of the law. At the same time, every decision that produces an event neutralizes the "Yes" of the event, its surprising arrival, the freedom of a desire that desires the surplus of a "perhaps":

> Certainly the decision makes the event but it also neutralizes this happening that must surprise both the freedom and the will of every subject—surprise, in a word, the very subjectivity of the subject is exposed, sensitive, receptive, vulnerable and fundamentally passive, before and beyond any decision—indeed before any subjectivation or objectivation.[259]

The individual cannot decide on something or someone that the subject does not know yet, on a specter in passing that makes itself present through the "maybe" of "anticipation." The individual cannot decide on the spectral passing of the "Yes" but can only respond to it with exuberant passion, infinite calm, or both. This "Yes" in passing, however, does not respond or correspond. It defers before we can say "yes," before we can "know" it. The "Yes (I will touch on the

---

[259] Derrida, *Politics of Friendship*, 68.

untouchable, I will touch on the threshold of impressions, I will touch on a multiplicity of spaces)" sets in motion our passions (our individual bodies and singular subjectivities). The "Yes" (a desire for an alterity that surpasses desire) circulates through every gender before they become one and passes through every sexuality before we are subjects of desire. The "Yes" commands to say "yes" and "come" to the "perhaps," all the time and every time; it is a syncopeic desire that hovers around the body, which responds to the vanishing specter in passing, in the threshold of sense, at the edge of one's grasp: "I have loved it and I have loved only it ... the summons of the all-powerful affirmation that is united with me and a mysterious command, which came from me, and which is the voice that is always being reborn in me, and it is vigilant too ..."[260] The "Yes" is the Law of laws before the genesis of every law.

The "shall not" establishes a limit in the edge of sense, a "there" where the threshold of sense is interminable. The "shall not" affirms that there is a limit, that there is a certain presence/subject/identity established by a limit, that this limit is defined by its crossing, that the crossing affirms the continuity of the injunctive law. The limit establishes the presentation of a "you" shall not and of an "I." The limit establishes the law and its guardians; thereby, it establishes by establishing. The limit, however, does not take place; it withdraws from visualization and presence:

> Now herein lies the essential paradox: from where and from whom do they (representatives of the law) derive this

---

[260] Derrida, "Pace Not(s)," 66.

> power, this right-to-sight that permits them to have "me" at their disposal? Well, from "me," rather, from the subject who is subjected to them. It is the "I"–less of the narrative voice, the I "stripped" of itself, the one that does not take place, it is he who brings them to light, who engenders these lawmen in giving them insight into what regards them and what should not regard them ...[261]

The negativity of the law marks a boundary that says "do not cross," but, on the one hand, the law attempts to cross and besiege the surplus that it cannot govern, and, on the other hand (and at the same time), the crossing had already taken place without the sentence of the law. The law forbids a surplus that is not forbidden, that cannot be forbidden, and that cannot be ruled or governed. So, the law establishes order, legitimacy, and presence through a prohibition that limps, through a prohibition that is prohibited. The story of Sodom becomes the impossible promise of an impossible prohibition: a promise that forbids a surplus that cannot be forbidden, that cannot be grasped, and that cannot be extinguished:

> If the law is fantastic, if its original site and occurrence are endowed with the qualities of a fable, we can see that *das Gesetz* [the law]

---

[261] Derrida, "The Law of Genre," in *Acts of Literature*, ed. Derek Attridge (New York: Routledge, 1992), 241. (My parenthetical emphasis.)

> remains essentially inaccessible even when
> it, the law, presents or promises itself. In
> terms of a quest to reach the law, in order to
> stand before it, face to face and with respect,
> or to introduce oneself to it and into it, the
> story becomes the impossible story of the
> impossible. The story of prohibition is a
> prohibited story.[262]

The gesture of the law originates a genesis of departure, an origination of genesis. It departs incessantly. It self-forms in a circular movement of departure and partition. The juridical subject of the law is present through the subjects that say "yes" to the negativity of the law. An absence of success haunts the law and at the same time empowers it through its insistent excitation, citation, and recitation. The trap produced by the "shall not" takes the form of a sovereign "yes," a promise not to be broken, a faithful assurance not to break a promise that is "contaminated" since its origination and departure. The positive and retreating Law of laws, the "Yes" that is in principle the principle of every law (the conductivity that sends, mandates, and interrupts) is interrupted by a "mandate," "command," and "conduct" that the law sentences, proclaims, and posits. As it retreats to its untouched interval, the "Yes" is supplanted by a commanding "yes, I will not," a decree that comes to prescribe or dictate what is not natural in nature, what is not nature, what nature itself prescribes as not natural, what is in accordance with God's wishes who created nature. The law transmutes the mandate that says "yes" into the command that says "yes, thou shall not." In its

---

[262] Derrida, "Before the Law," 199–200.

double retreat, the mark of the "Yes" remains in the remains of a quiet exuberance, in the margins of the proclaimed sovereignty of the law. The transmutation between "Yes" and "yes thou shall not" can never be completely sealed off. The conductivity that transmits, the conductivity that is between nature and culture, nature and spirit, nature and humans, and so forth, remains out of touch and precedes any dialectical determinations. The desert trace of a retreating and affirmative Law of laws remains attached to its opposite (without opposing it), to a decree that categorically says "yes" to the "no." Thus, in an instant that one may not see it coming, the command "yes I will not," the mandate that promises, swears, and prescribes in the name of God, may transmute into a mandate (a sending) that says "Yes" to the unknown, "Yes" to a promise without sentences, without God, and without prescriptive commands. For this reason, the law must be obsessively vigilant. The posited law, the law in possession is possessed in its obsession to appropriate and found. Through its declared legitimacy, the imperative injunction produces presence, name, category, history, political and cultural realities (truths). The "no," however, cannot fully repress the insistence of the "Yes" that not only withdraws and retreats through the sentence and letter of the law but also defers from it.

A resilient difference between both reinaugurates the threshold of the senses, the surplus of a desire that one longs for with a desire that surpasses desire. This difference between the "Yes" and the "no" opens up the proper and the deviant, the proper deviation, the deviation of the proper, the proper as a deviation of a surplus that remains unclassifiable. The interval of interruption and repetition of the "Yes" does not really say anything, does not respond to a name, does not respond; however, the decree ventriloquizes what remains without words. The hiatus that says "Yes" even through ashes without remains is appropriated with the "appropriate" "no," which sentences, articulates, and occupies while displaying new ways of saying yes to the law ("yes, I will not desire …").

The "proper yes" of the law is closer to a desire with a purpose, a desire that reproduces, that is reproductive, a desire associated with an organized seed that translates into nation, economy, and home (a desire that is compulsively heterosexualized, phallocentric, and reproductive). The "improper" desire (the restless "Yes") defers from productive, reproductive, and useful desire; it overflows gender, nation, and religion because it is a desire that is in excess of purpose, without a specific genre or gender, and without a defined subject or object. This "contaminated" desire has no specific purpose and flows toward a what or a who that is neither a subject nor an object but a specter of possibility (for all subjects). The "Yes" is thus retained, incorporated, ventriloquized, supplanted, multiplied, and divided through a decree in favor of useful desires, an economy of desires that does not waste the seed of what remains without seed. The injunction that commands not to waste the reproductive seed produces a law that reigns and governs sovereignly over a desiring space that is not a seed, that is not sovereign, that does not oppose, and that does not reign. The law utters the first sentence, promises a "yes" through a categorical "no."

The decree proclaims the horizons of desire and its demarcation: who is touching whom, what is the proper touch, and what is the appropriate space determined between the subjects of the law. Its pronouncement establishes presence, truth, punishment, and legacy. Its prescription is against oblivion, forgetfulness, and the absence of trace (although the meaning of "trace" is recontextualized and solely associated with family genealogy). The decree forbids a man to lie with other men. It commands not to waste the seed, the legacy of the trace. And yet, the decree is inscribed in a desire that comes before the law, a desire that partakes in every desire, whether heterosexual, homosexual, or anything in between. The command is inscribed in an inenarrable hiatus, in a sense impression that is not bound to any particular desire, legacy, family, religion, or era. The incommensurable desire for the other, for the coming of the other, and for its trace lives on; it recurs without belonging, inscription, presence, legacy, and memory. The desire for the unknown, for what is yet to come, for an alterity that is uncanny and singular leaves its mark in ruins, ashes, in the letter of the law, and even in the "wasted" seed. It is a malleable trace without a specific referent that opens all kinds of spaces, expressions, and possibilities:

> This structural possibility of being severed from its referent or signified (and therefore from communication and its context) seems to me to make of every mark, even if oral, a grapheme in general, that is, as we have seen, the nonpresent *remaining* of a differential mark cut off from its alleged "production" or origin.[263]

---

[263] Derrida, "Signature Event Context" in *Margins of Philosophy*," trans. Alan Bass (Chicago: University of Chicago Press, 1982), 318.

The nonreferential mark cannot be completely neutralized by any decree because it is, in principle, severed from prescription, and its conductivity passes through the senses without properly becoming "human conduct."

The imperative "no" denominates what remains without a name. The "no" is also a desire, a desire for limits and clear definitions that separate, classify, categorize, and do not mix. The law commands "do not pass" into another gender/genre, "do not mix" genders/genres, "do not transmute" them, "do not use the same word" in order to avoid "contamination," (e.g., do not mix conduct (conductivity) with conduct (behavior), mandate (an alterity that sends itself) with mandate (decree), man with woman, fiction with reality, etc.):

> The genders/genres pass into each other. And we will not be barred from thinking that this mixing of genders, viewed in light of the madness of sexual difference, may bear some relation to the mixing of literary genres. "I," then, keep alive the chance of being a female or of changing sex.[264]

The law proclaims the limit at a threshold without edges. It pronounces the conduct and conductivity that ought to be desired. It founds the "yes, I will not" as a desire that promises the subject sovereignty, presence, recognition, legacy, and so forth. The law transmutes/ventriloquizes the incommensurable excess at the threshold of sense into a sovereign border. It transforms something that is not a thing into a thing of nothingness.

---

[264] Derrida, "Law of Genre," in *Acts of Literature,* 245.

Religions depart from a threshold, a space, a site, an antechamber that is not religion, that is not religious, and that will never be part of the circle of religion. The imperative freedom that comes from an amorous euphoria, from a desiring alterity, may be converted, inverted, and circumscribed by the shepherds of religions into brotherly love, duty, debt, respectability, responsibility, legacy, and so forth, but it is other than them. This other conduct/conductivity remains open to a nonreferential space. The experience of the sending/coming of the other may be designated as a sacred conduct or a divinity, but it precedes a relationship with God and the gods, will never belong to any religion, and would not let itself be determined by any decree or command:

> The Sacred of which it [the site] speaks *belongs* neither to religion in general, nor to a particular theology, and thus cannot be determined by any history of religion. It is first the essential experience of divinity or of deity. As the latter is neither a concept nor a reality, it must provide access to itself in a proximity foreign to mystical theory or affectivity, foreign to theology and to enthusiasm. Again, in a sense which is neither chronological nor logical, nor ontical in general, it *precedes* every relationship to God or to the Gods.[265]

"Conduct" and "conduct" are two words that categorically mean different things. They are both imperatives marked by

---

[265] Derrida, "Violence and Metaphysics," 145.

a difference. The imperative law neutralizes the imperative mandate/sending that is without command or prescription: "The imperative of our imperatives is that true imperatives must not have the character of constraint, of externality, nor must they be tied to the exercise of an injunction, an obligation or a submission."[266]

The imperative "conduct" in Sodom is incessant. It is a conduct before "conduct" (before behavioral injunctions) that leaves an impression in the threshold of the senses (regardless of gender or sexual orientation), an impression of a sense, of a what/who that is missing. What persistently escapes from their fingertips is the writing of this conduct, the proper name of this impression, a pressure and expression that impresses the senses and impassions every emotion with a missing word. The tale of Sodom is captured through delayed and deferred impressions, through a touch that remains in the threshold of touch (there where one cannot touch but the texture of the other). Their impressions (in the instant of their death) touch without contact an exteriority installed in the limit of touch. In their devoted frenzy, the act of penetration is forever suspended in a deferred exhortation, a taste for a recurring adoration that hopes for something to arrive, someone to be "there," and that "there" be someone to touch. The "conduct" of the Sodomites is toward the touch that produces the limit of touch toward an extension/exteriority/interval that is intangible, sensible/insensible. The mark of their interrupted touch aims toward an almost meaningless and defunct sign, to a space in disuse, to a promise that arrives only to erase itself. They leave the mark of an unconditional conductivity, a passion that transports into a future, into a "perhaps," into the

---

[266] Nancy, *A Finite Thinking*, 135.

hope of touching the other in the limit of the unthinkable. It is the trace of a trans and a trance that hopes to touch an otherly body that is no more a man than it is a woman: "Striking and stroking address a 'who' rather than a 'what,' 'the other' rather than some other in general. Such a living 'who' is no more necessarily human, moreover, than it is a subject or an 'I.' And above all it is not a man any more than a woman."[267]

Sodom is the idiom of a mark without a place where one loses everything in the process of desiring an X without reference. What remains is a nonobject, a *récit* that remains foreign to any testament: "It is a *récit* without a theme and without a cause entering from the outside; yet it is without interiority. It is the *récit* of an impossible *récit* that remains foreign and out of bounds."[268] The laws and dogmas of religions rest on an impossible analogy, an impossible penetration, a touch in the limit of grasp that the messengers and representatives of religion will never dominate or fully grasp. The story of Sodom unfolds in the space of two passionate mysteries (one without religion, and the other founding religion—against a past orgiastic mystery without religion). It is a fable warning against those who attempt to confabulate, those who attempt to revive a past ecstatic mystery. Those who celebrate an ancient orgiastic mystery will be taken hostage by it, blinded, burned into ashes, but not without first experiencing the quiet consuming splendor of the sacred space before religion, not without first experiencing in passing an untouchable skin folding upon itself in the limit of touch, not without first experiencing the

---

[267] Derrida, *On Touching*, 69.
[268] Derrida, "Law of Genre," in *Parages*, 232. (The citation is slightly modified.)

conduct and conductivity of genders, genres, and desires passing into each other, attempting to grasp an alterity that escapes the senses of touch.

The desire of the Sodomites is "just" that, a desire that surpasses genders, that mixes them, that is other than them (neither heterosexual nor homosexual, bisexual, etc.), that may not be categorized with any particular genre and, at the same time, may not *not* be categorized by a writing that multiplies the desire to grasp this conductivity that is without referent. This desire that is in excess of itself is "there" as interruption, in the limit of every touch, in a weightless interval, in the quiet ashes of Sodom, in the hiatus of our senses. The remains of this desire are untouched by multiple prohibitions that cannot prohibit what sends itself unconditionally. This excess does not rule, govern, or oppose and, at the same time, makes possible any community (religious, political, scientific, etc.), its laws, regulations, and so forth, all of which cannot completely grasp the exteriority that founds them and remains other than any institution, community, or law:

> The community is not the place of Sovereignty ... It [community] includes an exteriority that thought does not master, even by giving it various names: death, the relation to the other, or speech. [Community] gives rise to an unshared though necessarily multiple speech in a way that does not let it develop itself in words: always already lost, it has no use, creates

no work and does not glorify itself in that loss.[269]

The event that takes place in Sodom leaves an ineluctable idiom in the grasp of every word. It is the mark of a recurring syncopeic moment, an event that does not coincide with any declared law or historical memory. The surplus that affects the Sodomites is not subject to a decision or a law but exceeds both and makes them possible. The interruption/ exteriority/space/spacing/deferral/conductivity that takes place in Sodom's tale remains nameless, without presence, and without God. The desire for the grasp of an X alterity that comes from the other does not coincide with any name, subject, community, religion, or thing in the history of the West.

---

[269] Blanchot, *Unavowable Community*, 12.

XV

The Names That Nominate, Dominate, and Denominate Sodom

What would happen if this intervallic space without name, without analogy, without presence, and without concept were to be appropriated by violent, persecutory names? What if this spastic space would be the site of a false but hegemonic response? Is there a "true" response to this call? To what does one respond when one establishes ethical responsibilities? One may respond with deadly names to what one does not know or understand. After two millennials of "shall nots," the law has taken multiplying paths toward naming the foreign, the unknown, the uncanny, and the unfamiliar. One of these names, only to limit the scope of analysis and to bring it to contemporary times, is the word faggot. What does it name? What does it rule or simulate to master? Every day someone pronounces the word fake, or faggot, as if those words proclaimed a certain order, a "genuine reality," and an "as such," on the condition that individuals repeatedly and insistently conjure and proclaim a name considered exterior and foreign to them. The words fag or faggot are associated with concepts like: contamination, falseness, feigning, unreal, fakeness, nontruthfulness, cowardice, betrayal, deviation, perversion, abomination, threat, and so forth. "Fag" represents everything that is unfamiliar, foreign, and without analogy in a respectable and responsible community that is legitimate, dutiful, present, beautiful, and godly. But, what is the meaning of the word faggot? According to a dictionary definition, the following concepts are explained: "fagot also faggot: 1. a bundle of twigs, sticks, or branches bound together. 2. A bundle of pieces of iron or steel to be welded or hammered into bars. Verbs: fagotted, fagotting, faggots. 1. To collect or bind into a fagot; bundle. To decorate with fagotting."[270] If one looks for "fagotting/faggoting," it reads: "A method of decorating cloth by putting out horizontal threads and tying the remaining vertical threads into hourglass-shaped bunches. 2. A method of joining hemmed edges by crisscrossing thread over an open seam."[271] The word faggot is a floating web, a receptacle of fabrics that binds and lets itself be bound through differential spaces. The word forms a textual chain, a structure of substitutions formed through lacunae. The word is a confectioner of filaments and loose ends, a bundle of threads that meet in a point where all fabrics and fabrications,

---

[270] *The American Heritage Dictionary, Second College Edition* (Boston: Hougthon Mifflin Company, 1985), 485.
[271] Ibid.

all fables, fabulations, and confabulations amalgamate, combine, display, separate, oppose, unite, reunite, and start anew. The word displays and transports meanings. The filaments render themselves to any weaving possibilities, to any fabric formation. In the midst of this hourglass figure, in the locus of this conic and iconic conduct, there is a point, a sort of interruption and junction. "Joining hemmed edges" marks a path "by crisscrossing thread over an open seam." The point where all the threads meet (the hourglass-shaped neck) is not a cut but an unfigurable knot ("unfigurable" because an incalculable number of filaments gather in order to branch out again). Around the unfigurable knot, a web of differences invokes a supplemental display of meanings and references.

Other meaning in the dictionary state the following: "fag end": 1. "The frayed end of a length of cloth or rope. 2. a. An inferior or worn-out remnant. b. the last part."[272] "A worn-out remnant" is a remaining surplus that vehiculates, that binds and conducts. The words faggot, fagotting, faggots, and fag transport and transfigure meanings. For example, "faggot" may also have a transferable signification bound to slang for homosexual.[273] The malleability of the word "fag," its open seam renders itself to any type of confection. It confects as the promise of a language that knits itself for freedom, for the sake of any malleable promise, or it may knit itself against the very freedom of its own conductivity. Depending on the turning of events, the social fabric of the moment may form cloths that veil the very fabric out of which those cloths are

---

[272] Ibid.

[273] "faggot: variant of fagot. Offensive slang. A male homosexual. [Orig. unknown.]" Ibid.

made. The treads of a male cloth or a female cloth do not speak, or rather, they speak through the cloth that veils them. The threads communicate (weave, exchange, turn, and twist) and convert into a veiling cloth, to a social commodity, a value idea of exchange that is no longer equivalent to the mute threat that gave the cloth form, presence, and signification:

> [Marx asks] What is it that the cloth veils when it veils itself and speaks? What can't the cloth say? What alone can it *not* say? What, when the cloth speaks, does it keep secret?. ... Cloth veils the cloth. The object "cloth" must be the veil over the actual *cloth* that is woven by historical social life. But precisely this weaving of social life results— in deed as in knowledge, in commodity-exchange as in the forms of its recognition in a object—in the object "cloth," and thus is a process of a self-veiling, a self-mystification, self-fetishization.[274]

The fabric of a "worn-out remnant" gathers in a social screen where all threads communicate through mute space intervals. What is turning and twisting in the contours of that indeterminate word (faggot)? How does an indefinite word contribute to form other indeterminate words (such as family, community, friendship, etc.)? For example, what is being translated, gathered, converted, inverted, and

---

[274] Werner Hamacher, "Lingua Amisa," in *Futures of Jacques Derrida*, ed. Richard Rand, trans. Kelly Barry (Stanford: Stanford University Press, 2001), 138–139.

disjointed in the established limit of the word faggot and in the proximity of the word friendship? Or, rather, what remainder remains untranslatable and unanalyzed between "faggot" and "friendship"?:

> Friendship does not keep silence, it is preserved by silence. From its first word to itself friendship *inverts* [my italics] itself ... That is why friendship had better preserve itself in silence, and keep silent about the truth. Over the abyss, on the shifting ground of our friendships: "how uncertain (*unsicher*) is the ground upon which all our alliances and friendships rest, ... how isolated (*vereinsamt*, solitary, insularized, "solitarized") each man is," that is what you will say to yourself, with so much experience of "misunderstanding", "ruptures", "hostile fleeings" ["*fuites hostiles*"]. So you had better keep silent about this truth of truth. The truth of truth is that the truth is there to protect a friendship that could not resist the truth of its illusion.[275]

How to proclaim the truth of the illusion of friendship, its sworn legitimacy? It swears against a space of rupture, against an "almost nothing" that truth cannot govern. "Faggot" is a "remnant," a malleable remainder, an almost nothing ("an inferior or worn-out remnant"), a concept that is not one, and a lack without analogy, a lack that is lacking.

---

[275] Derrida, *Politics of Friendship*, 53.

This worthless texture remains without a definite translation and, for this very reason, lends itself to multiple translations, to a multiplication of forms, seams, and textures where the very name "faggot" is suspended in a string that expands and contracts into nominations and denominations: "Like all names we are invoking, like all names in general, these designate at once a limit, and a chance ... a chance, that is, an opening of identity to its very future."[276] The indeterminacy of the word, its surplus value, and its fundamental lack of ground are receptive to a flexible and unshielded conductivity. This vertigo of edges, remnants, and loose threads triggers an impetus to bind threads and to fasten them into a (fagoting) point (a juncture and a hinge), which in turn reproduces another (inverted) bundle of ligatures and bands. This overabundant bundle of threads, this receptacle of meanings that remains without a definite one, provokes a translational impetus, a desire to put in place what is out of place and ultimately without power (an "inferior and worn-out remnant").

The word "faggot" is what is not. It has no presence or legitimacy. It floats in an exterior space and in intervals of empty meaning. It is a word, or rather, a floating signifier that circulates as nonpresence and, at the same time, opens up the possibility of reproducing presence through a play of differential intervals (proximity to or distance from established cultural truths). "Faggot" names what is not, what escapes, withdraws, and disorganizes, and for this very reason, "faggot" is "dangerous," uncanny, not a friend, and

---

[276] Derrida, *The Other Heading*, trans. Pascale-Anne Brault and Michael B. Naas (Bloomington and Indianapolis: Indiana University Press, 1992), 35.

even demonic (it counterfeits and doubles). Thus, the excess of the word "fagot," which might multiply with a second "g," does not oppose but must be opposed, its ghost subsumed into a box, into a category, which at the same time serves to draw the concepts that oppose it (the true presence of friendship, legitimate comradeship, access to life, freedom, liberty, communal recognition, the law, etc.). The excess of the word faggot is not easily localizable, and for this reason, it has to be relentlessly reappropriated in order to convey a certain meaning that plays against the normative circle of family, church, and state. But what is between "faggot" and the circle of an economy of debt and reproduction? We are again in the impassioned and "contaminated" threshold of Sodom, in the contours of an ubiquitous space that opens up the possibility of the clarity of the law, which, in turn, forgets, retains, represses, opposes, "elevates," and so forth, the remains of a space (a surplus/shifting conductivity) that makes the genesis of each and every law possible.

The indeterminate signification of the word "faggot" suspends meaning, mixes genres, and contaminates normative language through its loose, remnant, and malleable strings. At the same time, it is precisely its unreadable contours that call for strange contortions, drastic turns, and categorical denominations. The floating threads and its remnants increase the need/desire for knots, for definite limits that seam together the thread/threat of an evasive excess. The indeterminate meaning of the word "fa(g)got" calls for another sense, a sense that stands in between the senses, in between the multiple treads/threats, in between genres, sexes, and desires.

"An inferior or worn-out remnant," an "inferior and worn-out filament," a foreign exteriority multiplies signs, floats, and names nothing objective, is without institutions, without religion, without community, and without presence: "one can multiply signs of busyness around the very thing one wants to circumvent as a measure of protection."[277] What happens before articulating the word faggot? What conductivity arrives before this word or through it? Could it be that this word calls/conjures up the uncanny, the disproportionate, and the foreign; a measure of disproportion that one may not avoid, nor completely grasp? The desire for an overflowing and foreign surplus calls for disproportionate restitutions, for busy analogies that will never respond to or correspond with the mark of an evanescent, fragile, and ecstatic residue, with a promise that is in excess of itself, with the uncanny indeterminacy of the "maybe" and the "perhaps."

From this foreign space, interval, or mark; from its residual and stimulating silence, there is an urgency to name what is indeterminate through multiple paths of "do (k)nots." "Everything will have been constructed and calculated so that this unanalyzed [reminder] might be inherited, protected, transmitted intact, suitably bequeathed, consolidated, enkysted, encrypted."[278] An "inferior or worn-out remnant" does not speak or is kept in oblivion; however, it is what is supposed not to speak what enables us to speak

---

[277] Derrida, "Du tout," in *The Post Card From Socrates to Freud and Beyond*, trans. Alan Bass (Chicago: University of Chicago Press, 1987), 506–507.

[278] Ibid., 519–520.

around the "unspeakable."[279] It is an everyday event that involves insistently the erasure, the killing, the sacrifice, the prohibition, and the persecution of an unsacrificeable sense of freedom, foreignness, and chance. It is not difficult to repress an interval that communicates the incommunicable, or to suppress what one desires with a desire beyond desire. It is not difficult to neutralize a murmur of enamored ashes in a lost desert. How hard could it be to divert, ignore, or avoid the trace of the orgiastic mystery, of enamored ashes, of "inferior and a worn-out remnants"? "I must sacrifice what I love. I must come to hate what I love, in the same moment, at the instant of granting death."[280] The X-thing, the other that is I and not I, the other that is at the threshold of the senses of touch has no presence, legacy, and legitimacy: "What is the other in me (dead or alive, animate or inanimate) that I want to annihilate so I can finally be myself, alone, sovereign, properly, who and what I am?"[281]

In the contemporary world, there are many realms of power that attempt to "faggotize" the moment of abysmal awkwardness (the event of the coming of the other, the promise, the perhaps, the open word, the "Yes ..."). In order to pretend that the law is a positive, truthful, ethical, and moral law, in order to pretend not to pretend, the law of "shall

---

[279] "The good (father, sun, capital) is thus the hidden illuminating, blinding source of *logos*. And since one cannot speak of that which enables one to speak (being forbidden to speak of it or to speak to it face to face), one will speak only of that which speaks and of things that, with a single exception, one is constantly speaking of." Derrida, *Dissemination*, trans. Barbara Johnson (Chicago: University of Chicago Press, 1995), 83.

[280] Derrida, *Gift of Death*, 64.

[281] Derrida, *Beast Volume I*, 191.

not" has to act, enact, posit, reattach, stitch, appropriate, and render appropriate: "The feint requires that the other be taken into account; it supposes, then simultaneously, the feint of the feint—of a simple supplementary play of the other in the strategy of the game. This supplementarity is at work from the first feint."[282] The feigning and the positing of the feigned multiplies the usurpations of the "Yes," of the coming of other. The positing and establishing of the familiar everydayness takes place through fraudulent play, through the positing of a law that says, "No, do not pass" to what or who has already trespassed/arrived. In order to legitimize feigning, in order to pretend that one is not pretending, one sovereignly must pretend to believe that one knows, even if that legitimized knowledge is founded on a nonknowledge. But doesn't every word in language (including words such as legitimate and truth) act in one sense or another in a feigned fashion? Doesn't the word "God" suppress (steal away) the name of the unnamable? On the other hand (and at the same time), every word that appropriates, denounces, sacrifices, and effaces also leaves a trace of the incalculable and misnamed excess of the untranslatable seam:

> Do we need to recall that any effaced trace, in consciousness, can leave a trace of its effacement, the symptom of which (be it individual or social, historical, political, etc., and even technical—one can never be sure of having erased something on a computer, etc.) can always guarantee its return?[283]

[282] Ibid., 97–135, 128–129.
[283] Ibid., 130–131.

The decapitation of the uncanny and the foreign is an everyday happening. The question is, how could one say "Yes" to life and to the other without opposing, without creating opposites, without feigning? Two thousand years of saying "no" to the "Yes" could not be superseded that easily. Simulacrum and feigning constitutes the very fabric of knowledge, of "proper" knowledge in the history of humanity. The reality that becomes proper and objective to humankind, the truth that becomes knowable and knowledge to humankind, the époque that empowers humans and gives them a presence and a present is grounded in a repetitive simulacrum that erases the track of the foreign, seizes the unknowable, puts at bay the uncanny, and supplements the name that is missing. Through the exclusion of the indeterminate, of the almost nothing, of the trace, the nameless, the other, the interval, the foreign, and the "Yes," the familiar law of the "Yes, I will not" is founded (yes, we are not that X thing, that "inferior or worn-out remnant," yes we are truth, present, and legitimate as long as we raise against that past mystery that we don't understand, that is just a missing word ...). In sum, what one keeps at bay and unanalyzed (as well as unanalyzable), what is foreign and uncanny (what is "faggotized" in the modern world) sets the stage for a programmatic economy of debt, production, reproduction, respectability, and responsibility (a feigned society that proclaims that its feigning is not feigned). The excess of the word faggot and its empty, formless meaning (its plasticity, malleability, and transferability) does not belong to what is "legitimate, present, sovereign, and lawful." With a feather-like texture, the "emptiness" of the word faggot lends itself to substitutions and supplementations that, ironically, turn against the open-ended meaning of the word.

Neither "straight" nor "fag" can be effectively defined or defended through their oppositional meanings, as they both hover around an open and malleable word. Both words are founded in the absence of a general equivalence, in an idiom that is in excess of itself and at the same time reduced to nothing. Proscription, law, and normalization hover around an interval of meaning that not only remains without translation but also tends to be erased: "Difference or the trace does not present itself, this almost nothing of the unpresentable is what philosophers always try to erase. It is this trace, however, that marks and relaunches all systems."[284] Thousands of years of saying "No" when wanting to say "Yes," how has this affected what we call "civilization"? How has it affected the coming of the other? We are forgetful of the murmur that whispers the missing name: "This forgetting is the origin of right and law within the order of which the gift can no longer be grasped."[285]

In this multiplicative display that we call history and the world, the ecstatic principle of Sodom falls into a quiet oblivion as it undergoes wearing and tearing, as it suffers multiple reductions and neutralizations. At the same time, in the ordinary repetition of everyday events, the alterity of an unlocalized desire is constantly lurking in the familiar, the save, the sound, and the sacred.

---

[284] Derrida, "The Almost Nothing of the Unpresentable," in *Points... Interviews, 1974–1994*, ed. Elisabeth Weber, trans. Peggy Kamuf et al. (Stanford: Stanford University Press, 1995), 83.
[285] Alexander García Düttmann, *The Memory of Thought*, trans. Nicholas Walker (London, New York: Continuum, 2002), 25.

XVI

The Eternal Repetition
of the Repression of the
Incommensurable

The remains of Sodom manifest in ordinary words, expressions, and events one may encounter in everyday life. Persistently, the normalization of society is born through a recurrent neutralization of Sodom's orgiastic impetus. In the clarity of mass media communication, every expression presses toward coherent statements: families, masculinity/femininity, heads of state, communities of all sorts, military prowess, respectability, and programmatic ethics; in sum, a multiplication of significations that always makes known what is possible and knowable. How could it be any other way? In this circular economy of knowing and of letting everyone know, of debt and production, sovereign fictions (onto-theology, phallogocentrism, scientificism, etc.)

start anew every second by usurping and neutralizing the conductivity that comes from the other. To know what to believe and to believe what is made known ignites the circle of knowledge and understanding that tend to neutralize the foreign, the strange, and the stranger. But is the normal of normal, "normal."?

The world had become a platform of injunctions, a platitude of shall nots, a place of multiplying spaces of mourning, circling around an indeterminate dispersion administered by multiplying decrees. Is there no peace for individuals in this programmatic process of usurpation of their bodies? Mass media actively participates in the programming of the world, in letting people know what they should believe and understand. In the film industry, for example, the subtext behind most of the scripts may be summarized in two steps: 1. the arrival of the other and the stranger, and 2. the suppression, repression, expulsion, and neutralization of the foreign (by making it external, outside, "not here," and not me). The suppression of the foreign specter, at the same time, becomes the platform of presence, normality, acceptance, country, home, masculinity, and friendship (the world, the "right here," the right to exist, the essence of life, legitimate presence, etc.). The familiar and the homely is released from the coming of the other that in turn is interrupted, negated, destroyed, sacrificed, or made external. In the modern era, apart from very few films, the mainstream film industry appears to have the following motivational thesis to attract individuals: "come to see how we filter and decontaminate the strange and the stranger"; "neutralize the foreign that is in you, and substitute it with knowledge that is familiar to you, your community, and your country"; "feel saved and be safe"; "know what you believe and believe what you know"; "defer from everything that looks or sounds foreign or uncanny"; "discover how the screen makes magic by portraying relationships of any kind that eliminate the strange and otherly"; "watch how an indeterminate and incommensurable foreignness is compulsively repressed so that you may abandon yourself to a unifying, coherent, and promising community of friends and believers like you"; "observe how everything that feels exterior and foreign to you is conquered, tamed, and appropriated into a familiar tale"; "be a witnesses to the death and sacrifice of what is in excess of your grasp"; "be the first to know how the sacrifice of a small infinity that we don't fully grasp magically transports you into a familiar world that you can know and enjoy," and so on.

Hundreds of films aim toward the same repetitious scene: the suppression of the strange and the foreign, and the establishment of the homely and the familiar. One may choose from iconic films like *Wild at Heart*, which stands as a guiding matrix to the past, present, and future of the film's subtext. Written and directed by David Lynch in 1990, *Wild at Heart* (based on the novel by Barry Gifford) was one of those quintessential films where the protagonist fights against all the strange forces of society in order to find his place in the world (as a well-adjusted husband and father). In the final scene, after renouncing to the love for Lula (Laura Dern), Sailor (Nicolas Cage) walks through an empty street where, all of a sudden, he finds himself surrounded by a multiethnic gang. He lights up a cigarette and says: "What do you faggots want." They reacted violently to his comment by punching him until knocking him out unconscious. Laying on the floor (between two yellow lines, alluding to the Oz's yellow brick road), the Good Witch (GW) from *The Wizard of Oz* appears, and Sailor has a dreamlike revelation:

> GW: Sailor, Sailor, Lula loves you. Don't be afraid.
>
> Sailor: But I am a robber and a man's slaughter, and I never had any parental guidance.
>
> GW: She is forgiving you all these things. You love her. Don't be afraid, Sailor.
>
> Sailor: I am wild at heart.
>
> GW: If you are truly wild at heart, you will fight for your dreams. Don't turn away from love, Sailor. Don't turn away from love. Don't turn away from love.

As the Good Witch vanishes, Sailor opens his eyes, stands up, and the next scene unfolds:

> Asian man from the gang: You've got enough, asshole?
>
> Sailor: Yes I have. I want to apologize to you gentleman for referring to you as homosexuals. I also want to thank you

fellows. You taught me a valuable lesson in
life: Lulaaaaaaaaaaaaaa![286]

Sailor then returns to Lula and his son, and in the very
last scene, he sings Elvis Presley's "Love me Tender." It is
implied that Lula and Sailor will soon be formally married
because, earlier in the film, Sailor told Lula that he would
only sing that song to his wife. On top of them, there is now a
blue sky, and the camera films them from below, standing on
a convertible car with the top off.[287]

Throughout the film, Sailor and Lula were surrounded
by a bizarre and otherly world turned violent and virulent.
During the film, the sense of otherness is represented in a
negative manner. The other, the strange, and the foreign are
depicted through scenes of assassinations, betrayal, robbery,
rape, adultery, and bad parenthood. The other becomes
"the bizarre" depicted through grotesque and repulsive
characters: Bobby Peru, Marcellus Santos, Lula's mother,
and so on. Sailor, who describes himself as "wild at heart,"
is haunted by strange childhood and adolescent memories,
but in the end, he overcomes his sense of otherness and
becomes a respectable husband and a responsible father. The
only strange people that do not appear in the film are those
considered to be in excess of the bizarre community and who
are referred as "faggots" and homosexuals. Their absence
alludes to something unnamable, unseemly, and abominating;
something that nobody wishes to be impersonate, to bring
to presence (especially criminals, thieves, and the "wild at
heart").

---

[286] https://www.youtube.com/watch?v=hWtr9Xk8kBM.
[287] https://www.youtube.com/watch?v=nG2DqpcHRoA.

"Faggots" and "homosexuals" are in the collective imagination of the audience (inside and outside the film) as a limit, as a sense of limit. In the film, it is implied that although strange and otherly, criminals and assassins are familiar, part of every society, and more acceptable than "faggots" and homosexuals. Thieves, criminals, rapists, and mobsters have presence in the movie, and their characters are well represented. They have perverted passions that are understood as daring and masculine, passions that are familiar to the audience and accepted. They are recognizable and not by any means "an abomination."

The trace beyond any mark (beyond the passion of those "wildest at heart"), the communication and conduct that does not belong to any group is analogized with homosexuality, which is opposed to the clean presence and behavior of normalized lovers. The family is shielded from the bizarre, from an "external" enemy, from a conduct and conductivity that is unusual and uncanny, without presence, and without God. Their love is finally legitimate and legitimized, present and eternal, nominated and dominated, sacred and blessed by God Himself that reigns in the blue sky beneath them. They are habituated to the habitual, to the routinely, and to the everydayness. They are finally "home": "The common speech becomes the current speech. We meet it on all sides, and since it is common to all, we now accept it as the only standard. Anything that departs from this commonness ... is at once considered a violation of the standard."[288]

In *Midnight Cowboy*, another iconic movie, a similar pattern unfolds. Two strangers have a fortuitous encounter in Manhattan. However, as the film unfolded, it repeated the

---

[288] Heidegger, *What Is Called?*, 119.

social code that had been incessantly gathered for centuries throughout the history of the West: the face of the other would become the face of the same, a fraternal and exclusionary friendship among men. In the film, the encounter with the other is neutralized in multiple ways until it is in attunement with sacrifice and death. Dustin Hoffman and Jon Voight, protagonists of the film, build a strong friendship based, mainly, on the exclusion of women, which are represented as prostitutes, and the marginalization of "fags," associated with the unfamiliar, pathetic, and strange. Before their encounter, they are depicted as strangers without a sense of belonging, but when they connect, they create a familiar space of friendship. They look after each other. They bring home their relationship at the expense of expelling the coming of the other that is localized "outside" themselves. They "take care of each other" by exploiting women and homosexuals. What preserves the illusion of a "pure friendship" that is "free" from "contamination" is the constant affirmation of sovereign values of camaraderie that are opposed to anything that is not familiar and homely, and that would assure the viewers that the protagonists are loving and manly friends cleansed of every and any homosexual innuendo. The viewer is reminded throughout the film that in order to assert loyal, respectable, and masculine love between the protagonists, all homosexual inferences must be carefully removed from their relationship. The issue of the space between them (distance and proximity) becomes significant. The respectable presence of the protagonists' characterization is configured through the constant reminder that there are no foreign feelings in them and between them. Homosexuality and the feminine are represented and displayed as foreign, subaltern, and untrusty and, in turn, contrasted with their luminous friendship. "Strange" feelings are "outside" of them, foreign to them, and not them. The trace of the coming of the other, the incommensurable "lovence" that tends to appear in passing at beginning of the film is suppressed as the film unfolds (or it unfolds because of the limitation of the "lovence" for the indeterminate other):

> The reader will have sensed that this is what I would be tempted to call "lovence": love *in* friendship, lovence beyond love and friendship following their determined figures, beyond all this book's trajectories of reading, beyond all ages, cultures and traditions of loving. This does not mean that lovence itself can take place figurelessly: for example, the Greek *philía*, courtly love, such and such a great current (as we call it) of mysticism. But a lovence cuts across these figures.[289]

Appropriate and exemplary friendship is configured through the negation of what is made known (represented) as contaminated love. The "contaminated" sense for what is other would have been "there" before their encounter, before it was distilled, denied, and conducted toward the exclusionary conduct of both friends. The abyss of life (errant love for what/who is other and is without a home or a proper name) transforms into a clear path toward a coherent and respectable friendship that draws itself by withdrawing from

---

[289] Derrida, *Politics of Friendship*, 69–70.

what is without belonging. The film is about an excess that is both expelled and preserved between them and beyond them, an excess that cannot be grasped or represented but touches both of them in the instant of their encounter before then can say "no." New York, the city where their friendship develops, allegorizes the city of Sodom. The fortuitous encounter of the two strangers opens up in a space depicted as the city of estrangement and foreignness.

Iconic films as well as classical novels may have opening scenes of uncanniness, of love for the foreign and the strange, and of "lovence" toward the indeterminate other; however, and at the same time, as the arguments unfold, they are fashioned around a passion for the familiar, for a desire to be safe and at home with whomever protects them from "external" elements that may "contaminate" the "internal" and coherent concept of love in harmony with God, community, and nation.

What is the threshold of love and touch between Achilles and Patroclus, Helen of Troy and Paris, King Saul and young David, Jonathan (King Saul's son) and David, Sir Lancelot and King Arthur, King Arthur and Guinevere, and so forth? In all these canonical friendships and love affairs, fictive or real, there is a commencement and a command grounded in an otherly love that disorganizes their established worlds from its inception. These characters are the receptors and disseminators of an absolutely determining love that is difficult to determine, impossible to circumscribe, and remains floating and circulating without a definite translation or interpretation. Those heroes who are larger than life attempt to translate a desire that does not belong to their kingdom, a desire that from inception becomes ruined and contaminated: "And so we are dealing with questions of translation that are absolutely determining, determining and difficult to circumscribe: there are no limits, no frontier that can contain these issues of translation."[290] Love for what or who does not belong determines the indetermination of the heroes reflected through a "lovence" that can only be captured through tales that are larger than life. These tales, in turn, cannot exhaust the excess that unfolds them.

The phantom of "lovence" touches an inexactitude, an excess that is not historical but makes the history of individuals and nations possible. In the threshold of this inexactitude, the indeterminate love for something that has no exact name and that is without belonging passes through gender, sexuality, sense, perception, form, and thinking. What conductivity circulates among Genevieve, Arthur, and Lancelot? What sort of "lovence" is between Saul and Jonathan?:

> For one does not know what one says when one says "I love you," and one does not say anything, but one knows that one says it and that it is law, absolutely: instantly, one is shared and traversed by that which does not fix itself in any subject or in any signification ... It is sexual and it is not: it cuts across the sexes with another difference that does not abolish them, but displaces their identities. Whatever my love is, it cuts across my identity, my sexual property, that

---

[290] Derrida, *Beast Volume I*, 339.

objectification by which I am a masculine or
feminine subject.[291]

This otherly conductivity, this "lovence" that is without
belonging, genders, and genres calls for lovers of all times to
translate a desire without end or beginning, an avid "lovence"
that recurs in new tales and stories. "Once upon a time," and
once again a loving and untranslatable idiom devours itself,
passes through lovers in an instant, and drowns in a forgotten
dessert where immemorial ashes of enamored love bring forth
to life the passion of lovers for an incommensurable other that
arrives unexpectedly to their lives. Once again, once upon a
time, one time, in an instant, lovers of an incommensurable
love hear the disjunctive rhythm of a new dance that passes
without steps through a mute, ecstatic threshold. These tales
evoke the promise of otherly love, of love for every other that is
other. Its visitation comes through a conduct, through a leap,
through shivering silences and voices, through rhythms and
paces evoking an immemorial choreography of secret links
that link a desire that does not know its name, with a desire
that multiplies names. Consuming love in the threshold is
never consummated, and it is devoured by a sense that is
never looked at directly, a visibility that does not see, and a
sense of touch that is other than touch.

For the most part, novels and films attempt to give
coherence and unity to what is in excess of itself, to the coming
of the other, to a passion that disorganizes mixing genres
and genders. There are multiple versions of *Midnight Cowboy*
and *Wild at Heart*, films, novels, and tales (past and yet to
come) that naturalize and denaturalize the indeterminate

---

[291] Nancy, *Inoperative Community*, 101.

love for the other, making it more or less moral, more or less natural, more or less different, more or less legal, more or less distant through a moral, religious, or political supplement that orients the force of a passion that is in excess of every decree, gender, and genre:

> Guided by this pattern [by Rousseau's theory of "moral love"], one would have to reread all the texts describing culture as the corruption of nature: in the sciences, the arts, spectacles, masques, literature, writing. One would have to take them up again within the network of this structure of "moral love," as the war of the sexes and as the chaining of the force of desire by the feminine principle. Setting not only men against women but also men against men, this war is historic. It is not a natural of biological phenomenon. As in Hegel, it is a war of consciousness and desires, not of needs or natural desires.[292]

Stories establish clear limits. Omniscient narrators and directors raise against a desire that they cannot fully understand or grasp. A creation unveils, consisting in not mixing genres and genders, in substituting the force of desire for the force of decrees and the assertiveness of dialectical sentences. The narratives of life and love consist in making oblivious the threshold of sense, in reducing the ecstatic interval to nothing, in neutralizing the alterity, heterogeneity, and conductivity of love, in making love clear, reproductive,

---

[292] Derrida, *Of Grammatology*, 180.

compulsively heterosexual, and in agreement to family, community, nation, and God:

> Such is the history of love [according to Rousseau's theory of "moral love"]. In it is reflected nothing but history as denaturalization: that which adds itself to nature, the moral supplement, displaces the force of nature by substitution. In that sense the supplement is nothing, it has no energy of its own, no spontaneous movement. It is a parasitic organism, an imagination or representation which determines and orients the force of desire. One can never explain, in terms of nature and natural force, the fact that something like the difference of a *preference* might, without any force of its own, force force. Such an inexplicability gives all its style and all its form to Rousseau's thought.[293]

Stories promise the temple and conceal its antechamber. Readers want to feel, see, think, and understand; they want to exist in an already inaugurated world and not in the inaugural event that is the world, in the opening that opens, in the threshold that opens the question of existence. Readers love to experience that behind a mystery (behind curtains and veils) there is the truth, one that is coherent, clear, and unambiguous.

Novels follow pretty much a similar script. One may select any novel, contemporary or not, and one may find

---

[293] Ibid., 178.

some evidence that the orgiastic principle (the desire that desires beyond programmable and programmatic desires) lurks into the language of every novel but as containment, as something to be neutralized, repressed, and forgotten. For example, let us dwell in an Italian novel written in 1949 entitled *Il Bell'Antonio* by Vitaliano Brancati. The orgiastic impetus creeps into the text at the beginning of the novel as the narrator unfolds the story by controlling the doses of the orgiastic principle and ultimately drowning it in oblivion. The conduct that crosses every aspect of the novel is the repressive and lawful social fabric that neutralizes the coming of the other (the imperative conduct without imperatives that passes through Antonio's handsome and youthful body). At the beginning of the novel, Sicily is like a magnetic field of sensations, a flux and reflux of indeterminate eroticism. One may feel centripetal and centrifugal forces in the novel, all of which aim toward or away from Antonio's dangerous body. Like the people of Sodom, the people of Catania are impassioned by the disorganizing awakening of their senses. Something foreign, uncanny, and without name passes through their senses as they contemplate a fascinating and immaterial border in Antonio's beautiful body.

An attraction that cuts across all names drowns the people of Catania into a devouring and secret passion, a conduct to what is other, a current that allows the novel to unfold in the first place. At the same time, their pluridimensional perception is usurped and converted into linear, concrete, coherent, and dialectical schemes where genres and genders do not mix, where Antonio is no longer the spectral figure of an exorbitant sending but becomes an object of knowledge subject to paralyzing categorizations. The movement of the novel becomes an incessant negation of the excess that passes through Antonio's body. The cohesion of the community, the very possibility of their existence as a "normal" or normalized community, seems to depend on the insistent suppression of the indetermination that persistently overflows from Antonio's figure.

In order to disable the disabling wink that Antonio's body unleashes, the town frames him into a feminized and impotent subject. Although every "step forward" in the novel marks a new degree of forgetfulness of the incommensurable flow of desires that passes through Antonio's body, at the same time, every drawing of a sovereign limit only reminds the reader that one is closer or farther away from a desire that cannot be measured in/through steps, an excess that traverses Antonio's body, whether he is repudiated or celebrated.

Everybody in town is surreptitiously attracted in some degree to Antonio, who represents a figure of promise, danger, and attraction for men and women because something leaves them desiring more when they are exposed to Antonio's beauty. An excess of desire, an incommensurable and indeterminate exteriority that is in excess of everybody's wants, passes through Antonio's handsome body and affects everyone's perception as they contemplate him. Antonio's beauty is a reminder of an excess that the town cannot completely grasp but that, at the same time, keeps them fascinated. The town dances around Antonio's mystifying beauty. He is like an idol of adoration, an erotic energy that traverses the town with an overflowing irruption that is in excess of everybody's desire, an excess that paralyzes and fills them with a strange joy:

> If love declares the impossible itself ...
> this "madness," which extends from erotic
> fury to spiritual fervor, consists entirely in
> this: in it relation becomes incandescent
> by addressing me to what, in the other,
> is incommensurable with me, and it
> also does so by starting out with what is
> incommensurable in me.[294]

The formless figure that passes through Antonio's body is without analogy, and it is precisely this lack of concept or definition, this "exteriority," this presence in passing that is not given but only dreamed as a disappearing appearance that leaves the town desiring for something that is missing, something in excess of every known and established desire. And it is this "plus" that unfolds the novel as it opens up the grasp of thinking and sensing with joy and awe the desire that remains untranslatable. This "trans" puts the town in a trance and transmits the coming of a conduct beyond feminine and masculine roles, beyond the tyranny of a millennium of dialectics of thinking that neutralizes and paralyzes.

Throughout the novel, the town attempts to translate this overflowing incommensurability but fails to do so due to its phallogocentered tyranny, thereby responding to the coming of the other with a conduct that neutralizes and paralyzes Antonio. In order to keep at bay the indeterminate flow of feelings that comes from the other, the town pressures Antonio to act in a familiar and understandable manner. They ask him to get married or at least to perform "virile" heterosexual acts. This insistence and pressure

---

[294] Nancy, *Adoration*, 58.

makes Antonio sexually impotent. Thus, the "threat" of the incommensurable conduct and conductivity that passes through Antonio's body becomes restricted, narrowed, and controlled as he is forced to fit into social categories that the town knows how to believe and believes that they know.

The repression of a conductivity that cannot be repressed gives signification, fluidity, and rhythm to the novel. The book is not only about a fascist and compulsive heterosexuality in the community but also about a circulation of desires that cannot be completely governed or suppressed. Antonio's intoxicating beauty translates into an excess of sense, a distortion of desires, a longing for something or someone that resists programmatic definitions and fascist imperatives. His body is like a recurring question posited in front of the conservative town, a question that opens the movement of the advent of an unknown freedom and an uncanny joy. It is this amalgamation of energies, this disorganizing movement that creates the multiple displays and detours of the novel. The uncanny perception of the protagonist's body is the platform of society's restrictive and repressive responses. Antonio's imaginary body is the space and stage for the "shall nots" and "do not pass."

The town already has at its disposal all the instruments of knowledge, culture, religion, and politics to establish an imperative and categorical universal conduct in its citizens' receptive bodies, a conduct not associated with heterosexual desire but with compulsive heterosexuality. The normative and compulsively heterosexual regime is made known as "nature," "natural," "legitimate presence," God's will, and so on. Categorical heterosexuality is omniscient and attentive; it watches over the town detecting any aperture to anything "strange" that is other than compulsive heterosexuality. The commanding and familiar law of heterosexuality rules with the state and the church over the stranger, the strange, and the incommensurable. The "regime" detects the undetectable, hovers around the incommensurable circulation of desires, and forms multiple usurpations that neutralize the uncanny and the unfamiliar.

Toward the end of the novel, the characters become more violent when a neutralized, impotent, and feminized Antonio wishes he could be part of a society of compulsively heterosexual men and brothers through the act of rape. He wishes to have sex with a woman against her will. His cousin Edoardo rapes an older woman toward the end of the novel. When Antonio hears about it, he grows jealous of his cousin and hopes to be like him: "a respected soldier that rapes women." He believes that raping a woman will give him heterosexual status, which is the key to gaining access to legitimate recognition by this compulsively heterosexual community. According to Antonio, it does not matter what reasons men invoke for killing and violating the rights of other individuals, as long as they perform heterosexually. Antonio says to his uncle, "<<Importa poco, a me che gli uomini facciano questo! (che gli uomini sono cattivi, che si ammazzano e si squartano). Insieme a questo, essi fanno una cosa, che io, che io, che io.. ... << ... non ho fatto mai!>>." (175). (It hardly matters to me if men act like this! (if they are mean, if they kill themselves and if they tear each other into pieces). Along with all this, they do one thing that I, that I, that I.. ... <<have never done!>>). Antonio regrets that he only dreamed of a rape while his cousin actually performed it: "Invece di condannare o compiangere Edoardo, per ciò che egli aveva fatto ai piedi della scala, (Antonio) lo invidiava." (326). [295] (Instead of condemning or pitying Edoardo for what he had done at the bottom of the stairs, [Antonio] envied him).

This story, apparently, has no "outside" (there is no alternative or opening other than compulsive heterosexuality). The heterosexualization of desire advances, seduces, reiterates, and compulsively reproduces itself. The omniscient phalogocentric regime colonizes bodies and usurps the life of its citizens as it partakes in a political system that promotes a "universal" culture:

> Europe takes itself to be a promontory, an advance—the avant-garde of geography and history. It advances and promotes itself as an advance, and it will have never ceased to make advances on the other: to induce, seduce, produce, and conduce, to spread out, to cultivate, to love or to violate, to colonize, and to colonize itself. [296]

Antonio's objectified, feminized, and neutralized body plays against machismo-fascism, machismo-Leninism, machismo-Marxism, machismo-Christianity, and machismo-nationalism, all of which repeat their feigned monopoly of compulsively heterosexual desires, a reverberant circle of simulation, stimulation, and dissimulation that supplements its own lack of grounds. Antonio's body is the platform against which a sovereign discourse advances structures of

---

[295] Vitaliano Brancati, *Il bell'Antonio* (Milano: Bompiani, 1965).
[296] Derrida, *Other Heading*, 49.

control and psychic exploitation, discourses that reproduce limits to the point of making them invisible and indiscernible with "nature," "truth," and "law." He bears the heavy weight of "reality," of a millennial culture of somnambulism that crushes, flattens, and straightens him.

If at the beginning of the story the perception of Antonio's body disperses and disorganizes the certitude of any sovereign reality, as the novel unfolds there is an exacerbating compulsion to dominate his body, to gather its dispersion, to paralyze it, to make it neutral, passive, and impotent. The freedom, the volatile dispersion, the "Yes" displayed in the beginning (genesis) of the text becomes the threshold of forgetfulness, oblivion, and withdrawal, out of which the drawing of the text (gathering, proper naming, presenting, categorizing, totalizing, etc.) unfolds. The "shall not," the absolute negation of the absolute indetermination that comes from the other (the pluridimensionality that passes through Antonio's body), unfolds the novel and constitutes it. The "shall not" commences and commands the circular economy of what is present and "endowed" with existence, "truth," and legitimacy. The "shall not" imposes a flattened reality that must be positively desired. The town's fascism of desire presents itself as the natural flow of existence; it constitutes itself as the sovereign conduct of "respectability" and "responsibility."

On the other hand, and at the same time, the insistent repetition of the fascist, phallogocentric circle also exposes the failure of its sovereign (feigned) norm. The obviousness, naturalization, legitimization, and unification of normative desires cannot be fully sustained in the circle that contains it, in the circle that is its own production and containment.

The excess in *Bell'Antonio* cannot be fully contained. Paradoxically, however, the excess not only disrupts the fascistic circle but also completes it. It is the very effect of amorphous dispersion and disjunction that, ironically, contributes to draw an infinite realm of forms, a circle of meaning and representation nurtured by the indeterminate threshold of desires that is never at hand. In order to have access to a totalitarian fascism of desire, the characters in the novel not only repress the incommensurable conductivity that passes through Antonio's body but also incorporate it as a "contaminated" conductivity that should be modified and supplemented indefinitely to form proper "conducts."

XVII

Taormina: The Space/Spacing in a Greco-Roman Theater

Where is Sodom? Is it a place that one could inhabit? Is it a place? Was it ever one? Sodom is everywhere and nowhere: in the margins of negative laws and in the flow of the "Yes." There is nothing that could replicate the "truth" of Sodom. Nothing but a fake representation, a theater of thresholds where any dream may come true. Perhaps the Greeks got the right idea, not only by creating the concept of theater but also by producing the space where the "Yes" could always be dreamed. One may take as an example any Greco-Roman theater around the world. For example, if one walks up the hill of the city of Taormina in Sicily, one finds a concentric theater built at the highest part of the city. It is not hard to contemplate the ocean from the open theater, and also the imposing silhouette of the Aetna. Fear, pity, and joy emerge from the juxtaposition of spaces. There is an impression of life and tragedy sensed from within the concentric strings of the theater, which seems to absorb the energies of its surrounding. It is as if from the concentric rings of the theater a dance of spaces was choreographing the interval of life, from the theatre to the ocean, from the ocean toward the ominous Aetna, and back to the theater. The concentric folds are spaces that welcome a dance of spaces that are themselves performing a performance, a mise-en-scène, but without representation, without applause. Something seems to be "there" at the limit of representation, in between the charged, mute, concentric circles: a trace, a trance, a "trans." The theater seems to be its own stage before staging. It facilitates the perception of space before any intuition, impression, or expression. It is the space of transmission, the space that transmits, the space where the affirmation of life is staged through multiple transfigurations, each of which stages what remains without representation. Any spectator that sits in one of the concentric folds would sense that anything is possible through the manifold thresholds, through the display of spaces that welcome the mise-en-scène. There are spaces on display ready to open the opening of a performance, any performance, the performance of life and death, passion on display. Directors, actors, and multiple themes are absorbed in that open space where all fictions are consumed in a recurring hiatus, in a magnetic threshold that makes them possible. Everyone is "chosen" to live the event of life and to stage the joy and tragedy of life and death. From out of the concentric spaces of the theater float freely the pulse of an unrepeatable and irrepressible hiatus, a desire that desires to represent the unthinkable, the thought that is sent/mandated from an immemorial time:

> *In a certain sense, "thought" means nothing.*
> Like all openings, this index belongs within
> a past epoch by the face that is open to view.
> This thought has no weight. It is, in the play
> of the system, that very thing which never
> has weight. Thinking is what we already
> know we have not yet begun; measured
> against the shape of writing, it is *broached*
> only in the *epistémè*.[297]

"There is" a mute and commanding "Yes," a "what" or a "who" in passing initiating insistently, lovingly, kindly, and ominously the interval that has not yet been represented, an X-thing that is immemorial and unsacrificeable, a figureless figure that one can only grasp with a touch that releases, with an open hand. Something is always about to be transported and communicated in the empty Greco-Roman theater, something like the beginning of a dream that will soon be displayed in a representation that will be other than it departure. "There," in the center of multiple concentric centers, there is a quiet but exorbitant insistence, the remains of an intrusive repetition, the figure of an unfigurable specter that reverberates but has not yet been represented. From those concentric spaces, every outline seems to be possible. Every representation seems plausible through a pulse that reverberates in the theater.

The Greco-Roman theater of Taormina welcomes the strange, the stranger, the other, and the visitor who is always arriving in passing. It invites the stranger, any stranger, any other who is other to desire the unthinkable, to sense the

---

[297] Derrida, *Of Grammatology*, 93.

conduct, conductivity, and sending that transports every possible word. The multiplicity of spaces in the Greco-Roman theater carries an overabundant name that is missing, a name that refuses all representations while compelling them to unfold. It is a space/spacing without creator where everyone could be chosen to be one. Every stranger is chosen in the Greco-Roman theater. The juxtaposition of dancing spaces in the theater is an event in itself, an event where insistently and eternally there is a "play," a rehearsing of the advent of love, life, justice, and death, all of which leave the sign of an ineluctable trace through which the singular life of every individual starts all over again. All and every theater performance leave an idiom, an unrepresented word that floats freely in the spaces of the theater. One, anyone who is other, is left with a desire to say that word that is in excess of every word. One, anyone who is any other, may hear, without sound, the murmur that is bursting in the intervals of the theater, a trace, an exteriority that announces itself incessantly in the threshold of sense. One, anyone, a stranger disconnected for an instant from community, family, nation, and religion, is left with a question that never stops asking, with a question that is never at home. Anyone who is any other may stand in an empty Greco-Roman theater and sense the reopening of the question, the opening of what/ who opens the stage of life, the conductivity that mandates to give hospitality to the coming of the other, and the promise that says "Yes" to passion, love, and life. The Greco-Roman theater is not only the antechamber of every temple but the antechamber of space, of a space/spacing without creator where everyone who is anyone and any other is chosen to be one.

XVIII

Sodom Retraced

S odom is the other of Israel. The Holy Land is the place where the coming of the other is an everyday happening as well as an eternal promise (the advent of the Messiah). Israel (as the other of Sodom) is the place that gives hospitality to the strange, the stranger, and the absolute other. It is the space of an adoring abstraction, of a disproportionate and dissymmetrical love for an excess that does not belong and is never at home. It is the place of multiplying thresholds, of an exteriority that remains without place, of an arche-desire, of the desire to name what names all names without being one. Israel is "Chora," the space of conductivity, transference, interruption, suspension, transfiguration, and so forth, the space where the name of an X-thing is always missing its mark:

[*Chora*] a noun that is both replaceable and irreplaceable. To be replaceable in its very irreplaceability is what happens to any singularity, to any proper noun, even and especially when what it "properly" names does not have a relationship of indivisible propriety with itself, with some self that would properly be that which it is as such, with some intact ipseity. Prosthesis of the proper name that comes to mean, to call by its name (without any ontic referent, without anything that appears *as such*, with no corresponding object or existent, without a meaning either in the world or outside the world) some "thing" that is not a thing and that has no analogical relationship with anything. This nomination is an event (both impossible and decisive, which we can decide whether or not to inherit).[298]

Israel lives with its other, an exorbitant insistence that remains without analogy, without name, and without proper place. Sodom's ashes, the remains of what remains without remains, insistently return to Israel as a turn, a "Yes," a revolt, a name that exceeds correspondence with anything and anyone, thereby multiplying the desire for the unthinkable. This transport, this conduct and conductivity, is in every corner of Israel, and it expands to the rest of the world. In

---

[298] Derrida, "As If It Were Possible, 'Within Such Limits,'" in *Paper Machine*, trans. Rachel Bowlby (Stanford: Stanford University Press, 2005), 94.

Israel, Sodom, a ruin buried in the desert, became a silent rhythm, a pace, a space that multiplies into a border that is never present or presentable "as such" but only through the specter of its trace. That border "over there" or "over here," that threshold of passion announces, anticipates, promises, and grasps an insatiable desire that leaves every analogy wanting. Anyone who is any other desires to touch this border/threshold where it is impossible to go, yet it is so real, "here" and "now" through an infinite partition and departure: "All the paradoxes of the limit, of the march or the margin are multiplied when one determines them as *borders* [*bords*]."[299] A border that de-borders, a touch that consummates and consumes on the untouchable, Sodom is forever a charged magnetic field, a touchable-untouchable exteriority, a quiet region, an impasse more than a pathway. The passion of Sodom survives as a spastic insistence, an overabundant remainder, and a (contaminated) promise without definite laws or programmed ethics. Their passionate grasp is the pulse of law and ethics: a law that limits and is its own limit, a promise that may be broken in spite of agreements, a law that experiments its betrayal from its departure:

> A promise must *be able not to* be kept, it must risk not being kept or becoming a threat to be a promise that is freely given, and even to succeed; whence the originary inscription of guilt, of confession, of the excuse and of forgiveness in the promise. The possibility of failure must continue to mark the event, even when it succeeds, as the trace of an

---

[299] Derrida, "Pace Not(s)," 81.

impossibility, at times its memory and always its haunting.[300]

The law of the "shall not (touch)," which emerges from Sodom's arche-desire, limits desire and organizes the space that constitutes the ethics of proximity and distance. The limit is the very mark of a drawing near: "There is no border in (it)self [*pas de bord soi*] no border (pace) that does not mark the limit of/with a drawing near [*approche*], that is, of/with a de-distancing, of/with a (non)pace."[301]

The other of Israel is the threshold from which the passion of Israel turns and returns. The grasp of this conduct and conductivity touches and "contaminates" anyone and any other in the limit of touch, where touch is interrupted, where touch is suspension and trace, one that remains without analogy to the senses. The ecstatic affirmation of the Sodomites, their surplus desire, lives on in the edge of silence, in the plenitude of a trace that gives itself generously to any symbolic content at hand:

> At each instant the discourse is carried out to its limit, on the edge of silence: it transports itself beyond itself. It is swept away by the extreme opposition—indeed, the alterity— by the hyperbole which engages it in an *infinite build-up* [*surenchère*] (freer than the freedom of the free spirit, a better democrat that the crowd of modern democrats, aristocrat among all democrats, more

---

[300] Derrida, "As If It Were Possible," 91.
[301] Derrida, "Pace Not(s)," 82.

futural and futurist than the modern), swept
away by the *perhaps* that arrives to undecide
meaning at each decisive moment.[302]

The impetus of the Sodomites' trace defers to a place
without a place, to an immemorial memory, to an abstinence
without prohibition that reminds anyone who is any other
that one ought to love the coming of the other and each other
to death. In a remarkable mark of enamored ashes, in the
threshold of forgetfulness, we are hosts and "hostages" of
this spectral affirmation whose pulse reappears in the circle
of life, as we love the other and each other to death:

> We owe ourselves to death. What a
> sentence … We owe ourselves to death.
> Once and for all, one time for all times. The
> sentence took me by surprise, as I said, but
> I knew right away that it must have been
> waiting for me for centuries, lurking in the
> shadows, knowing in advance where to find
> me (where *to find me*? What does that mean?)
> And yet—and I would be prepared to swear
> to this—it appeared only once. Never does
> it lend itself to commentary, never does it
> specify its modality: is an observation or a
> piece of advice, "we owe ourselves to death"?
> Does this sentence express the law of what is
> or the law that prescribes what *ought to be*?
> Does it let us hear that, in fact or in truth, we
> own ourselves to death? Or else that we are

---

[302] Derrida, *Politics of Friendship*, 40.

obliged, that we ought, to owe ourselves to death? For it came to me, so to speak, only once, this oracular thing, this one and not another, only one time, the first and last time at the same time, on a certain day in July, and at a certain moment, and every time I make it come back, or rather each time I let it reappear, it is *once and for all, one time for all times*, or rather I should say, all the times for a single time. Like death.[303]

In spite of dogma, or because of it, the passion of Sodom repeats itself in an immemorial excess, through a mandate (without legacy, religion, or knowledge) that orders to penetrate in the limit of touch. The passion of Sodom repeats eternally through an overflowing surplus that no desire can consume or consummate, through a desert passion that cannot be silenced because its idiom is already mute:

> ... [I]t is this non-knowing that marks the idiom that magnetizes desire ... It is a non-knowing installed in the form of "I don't want to know." This non-knowing ... it is not the limit ... of a knowledge, the limit in the progression of a knowledge. It is, in some way, a structural non-knowing, which is heterogeneous, foreign to knowledge. [304]

---

[303] Derrida, *Athens Still Remains*, trans. Pascale-Anne Brault and Michael Naas (New York: Fordham University Press, 2010), 4.
[304] Derrida, "There is No *One* Narcissism," 201.

The legacy without legacy of Sodom does not desist, and it is happening right here and right now because it has already arrived before we say "no." If one prefers "not to know" about the "contamination" of the Sodomites, that very "not knowing" is also a remainder of a nonknowledge that one wishes not to touch, an alterity that arrived before anyone could say "no." Through the flat sentence of the law, through the multiple "I/you shall not," a syncopeic-spastic-interval remains both free and forbidden, repressed and flowing, refusing and telling, open and suspended.

This communication is the maddening threshold of every impassioned religion, an interval that no religion can "penetrate." This sending comes from the other in the form of a promise and a possibility, a sensuous-nonsensuous, interminable temptation that is life but is often misunderstood as death. The circulation of the open secret is the transmission of a limit that is out of touch and produces "demonic frenzy," the limit at which the impossible becomes possible but as the impossible:

> The impossibility of the possible, the possible of the impossible: here is a definition that resembles what one often gives for death ... We have to think this affinity, therefore between the impossibility named death and the impossibility named forgiveness, between the gift of death and the gift of forgiveness as possibility of the impossible, possibility of the impossible hospitality ...

> When hospitality takes place, the impossible
> becomes possible but *as* impossible.[305]

Through the "touch" of the Sodomites, every other who is other grasps an exteriority, an unfathomable skin, an overabundant border in which all desire implodes toward an interminable language of metaphors: "*Eidos*, in Greek, is in the first place a sensible figure, a sensible contour, a form, and it comes to mean a figure that is not sensible. There is a process that may be called metaphorization—idealization— within the *eidos* itself."[306] The temptation of the Sodomites is a desire for a nameless God and a Godless God, a desire for a God that is still to be invented: "Desire beyond desire is, after all, precisely beyond the 'desire of the proper' ... desire beyond desire remains desire for a Godless God—a God still to be invented."[307] Desire at the threshold is desire without name and without God; it is desire that desires what one does not know. This "temptation" is unclassifiable and for this very reason calls for a moralizing command: "Now, all that one needs in order to moralize is to fail to understand."[308]

Anyone who visits Israel, anybody who is any other, may experience in passing that it is a nation of multiplying thresholds. There is a place where it is speculated that Sodom could have existed. It is in a mountainous desert near the Red Sea. Not far from there, it is found what many say is Lot's wife, converted into a pillar of salt. Those are nonplaces,

---

[305] Derrida, "Hostipitality," 387.

[306] Derrida and Ferraris, *A Taste*, 77.

[307] Richard Kearney, "Desire of God," 124.

[308] Deleuze, Gilles, "Ethics Without Morality," in *The Deleuze Reader*, edited by Constantin V. Boundas (New York: Columbia University Press, 1993), 74.

sites of incantation, incarnation, emanation, damnation, and adoration, sites of indeterminate spaces that translate into a language of traces and specters. Any other who is other may be tempted to build a temple in between those ubiquitous spaces, a sanctuary representing the antechamber of every temple. How to make a shrine, a monument, a book that would commemorate an immemorial ecstasy in excess of every kind of hedonism? How to make a sanctuary where one could mourn and celebrate the ecstasy that makes every temple possible, every promise immune to disaster? Any place of worship that commemorates the trace of the Sodomites, any temple that mourns their disappearance, would be a self-defeating concept. It would have to be a spectral temple made of thresholds, a temple that undergoes multiple fires and catastrophes—in sum, a temple in ruins and ruined. A destitute temple without secret paths, doors, or hinges. It would have to be a temple that does not gather up but that instead opens up the hinges of the law toward a blinding justice. How could a temple ungather? How could one make a temple of a threshold, of a sacred space in passing that opens up to the singularity and plenitude of the other? The trace that erases itself while sending the name of a suspended/untouchable passion will remain in the antechamber of every temple, in the multiplication of desert spaces, in the openness that opens up,[309] in the remains of circular ruins and enamored ashes.

---

[309] These words allude to Blanchot's remark on Heidegger's commentary on Hölderlin's hymn, "As on a holiday...": "The double repetition of the word *offen*, 'open' answers exactly to the double movement that 'the Open" signifies: to open up to that which opens up;..." Blanchot, "The 'Sacred' Speech of Hölderlin," 113.

How might one found/find the spectral city of Sodom? Everyone who is every other had already found it. Every other who is other stands in suspense, suspended by a conduct and a conductivity without temple and without religion, contemplating in adoration the overflowing secret of Sodom:

> There is something secret. But it does not conceal itself. Heterogeneous to the hidden, to the obscure, to the nocturnal, to the invisible, to what can be dissimulated and indeed to what is non-manifest in general, it cannot be unveiled. It remains inviolable even when one thinks one has revealed it. Not that it hides itself for ever in an indecipherable crypt or behind an absolute veil. It simply exceeds the play of veiling/unveiling, dissimulation/revelation, night/day, forgetting/anamnesis, earth/heaven, etc. It does not belong therefore to the truth, neither to the truth as *hosmoisosis* or adequation, nor to the truth as memory (Mnemosyne, *aletheia*), nor to the given truth. Its non-phenomenality is without relation, even negative, to phenomenality.[310]

Everyone who is anyone can grasp with open hands the question that is without end, without closure, and always beginning again.

---

[310] Derrida, "Passions," in *Derrida: A Critical Reader*, ed. and trans. David Wood (Oxford: Blackwell Publishers, 1992), 21.

WORKS CITED

Areopagite, Pseudo-Dionysius. *The Divine Names and Mystical Theology.* Translated by John D. Jones. Milwaukee: Marquette University Press, 1980.

Blanchot, Maurice. "Literature and the Right to Death." In *The Work of Fire,* translated by Charlotte Mandell, 300–344. Stanford: Stanford University Press, 1995.

———. "Orpheus's Gaze." In *The Space of Literature,* translated by Ann Smock, 171–176. Nebraska: University of Nebraska Press, 1989.

———. "The 'Sacred' Speech of Hölderlin." In *The Work of Fire,* translated by Charlotte Mandell, 111–131. Stanford: Stanford University Press, 1995.

———. *The Space of Literature.* Translated by Ann Smock. Nebraska: University of Nebraska Press, 1989.

———. *The Unavowable Community.* Translated by Pierre Joris. New York: Station Hill Press, 1988.

———. *The Work of Fire*. Translated by Charlotte Mandell. Stanford: Stanford University Press: 1995.

———. *The Writing of the Disaster*. Translated by Ann Smock. Nebraska: University of Nebraska Press, 1995.

Brancati, Vitaliano. *Il Bell'Antonio*. Milano: Bompiani, 1965.

Bruns, Gerald L. *Maurice Blanchot. The Refusal of Philosophy*. Baltimore: The Johns Hopkins University Press, 2005.

Caputo, John D. *The Prayers and Tears of Jacques Derrida, Religion without Religion*. Bloomington: Indiana University Press, 1997.

Caputo, John D and Michael J. Scanlon, eds. *God, the Gift, and Postmodernism*. Indiana: Indiana University Press, 2001.

Deleuze, Gilles. "Ethics Without Morality." In *The Deleuze Reader*, edited by Constantin V. Boundas, 69–77. New York: Columbia University Press, 1993.

De Man, Paul. *Blindness and Insight*. Minneapolis: University of Minnesota Press, 1983.

Derrida, Jacques. "A Silkworm of One's Own." In *Acts of Religion*, edited by Gil Anidjar, 309–355. New York: Routledge, 2002.

———. "At This Very Moment in This Work Here I Am." In *Psyche: Inventions of the Other. Volume I*, edited by Peggy Kamuf and Elizabeth Rottenberg, 143–190. Stanford: Stanford University Press, 2007

———. *Acts of Literature*. Edited by Derek Attridge. New York: Routledge, 1992.

———. *Acts of Religion*. Edited by Gil Anidjar. New York: Routledge, 2002.

———. *Adieu to Emmanuel Levinas*. Translated by Pascale-Anne Brault and Michael Naas. Stanford: Stanford University Press, 1999.

———. "Aphorism Countertime." In *Psyche: Inventions of the Other. Volume II*, edited by Peggy Kamuf and Elizabeth Rottenberg, 127–142. Stanford: Stanford University Press, 2008.

———. *Aporias*. Translated by Thomas Dutoit. Stanford: Stanford University Press, 1993.

———. "As If It Were Possible, 'Within Such Limits.'" In *Paper Machine,* translated by Rachel Bowlby, 73–99. Stanford: Stanford University Press, 2005.

———. *Athens Still Remains*. Translated by Pascale-Anne Brault and Michael Naas. New York: Fordham University Press, 2010.

———. "Before the Law." In *Acts of Literature,* edited by Derek Attridge, 181–220. New York: Routledge, 1992.

———. "Between Brackets I." In *Points ... Interviews, 1974–1994*, edited by Elisabeth Weber, translated by Peggy Kamuf and others, 5–29. Stanford: Stanford University Press, 1995.

———. "Choreographies." In *Points ... Interviews, 1974–1994*, edited by Elisabeth Weber, translated by Christie V. McDonald, 89–108. Stanford: Stanford University Press, 1995.

———. *Cinders.* Edited and Translated by Ned Lukacher. Nebraska: University of Nebraska Press, 1987.

———. "Désistance." In *Psyche: Inventions of the Other, Volume II*, edited by Peggy Kamuf and Elizabeth Rottenberg, 196–230. Stanford: Stanford University Press, 2008.

———. "Du tout." In *The Post Card: From Socrates to Freud and Beyond*, translated by Alan Bass 497–521. Chicago: University of Chicago Press, 1987.

———. "Edmond Jabés and the Question of the Book." In *Writing and Difference*, translated by Alan Bass, 64–78. Chicago: University of Chicago Press, 1978.

———. "Envoi." In *Psyche: Inventions of the Other. Volume I*, edited by Peggy Kamuf and Elizabeth Rottenberg, 94–128. Stanford: Stanford University Press, 2007.

———. "Envois." In *The Post Card: From Socrates to Freud and Beyond,* translated by Alan Bass, 3–256. Chicago: University of Chicago Press, 1987.

———. "Faith and Knowledge." In *Acts of Religion,* edited by Gil Anidjar, 40–101. New York: Routledge, 2002.

———. "Force of Law." In *Acts of Religion,* edited by Gil Anidjar, 228–298. New York: Routledge, 2002.

———. "Freud and the Scene of Writing." In *Writing and Difference,* translated by Alan Bass, 196–231. Chicago: University of Chicago Press, 1978.

———. *Geneses, Genealogies, Genres, & Genius. The Secret of the Archive.* Translated by Beverly Bie Brahic. New York: Columbia University Press, 2003.

———. *Glas.* Translated by John P. Leavey Jr. and Richard Rand. Nebraska: University of Nebraska Press, 1990.

———. "Heidegger's Hand (Geschlecht II)." In *Psyche: Inventions of the Other. Volume II*, edited by Peggy Kamuf and Elizabeth Rottenberg, 27–62. Stanford: Stanford University Press, 2008.

———. "Hostipitality." In *Acts of Religion*, edited by Gil Anidjar, 356–420. New York: Routledge, 2002.

———. "How To Avoid Speaking: Denials." In *Psyche: Inventions of the Other. Volume II*, edited by Peggy Kamuf and Elizabeth Rottenberg, 143–195. Stanford: Stanford University Press, 2008.

———. "Interpretations at War: Kant, the Jew, the German" In *Psyche: Inventions of the Other. Volume II*, edited by Peggy Kamuf and Elizabeth Rottenberg, 241–298. Stanford: Stanford University Press, 2008.

———. *"La métaphysique-relève de la métaphore."* In *Margins of Philosophy,* translated by Alan Bass, 258–271. Chicago: University of Chicago Press, 1982.

———. "Le Facteur de la Vérite." In *The Post Card: From Socrates to Freud and Beyond,* translated by Alan Bass, 411–496. Chicago: University of Chicago Press, 1987.

———. "Living On." In *Parages*, edited by John P. Leavey, translated by James Hulbert, 102–191. Stanford: Stanford University Press, 2011.

———. *Margins of Philosophy.* Translated by Alan Bass. Chicago: University of Chicago Press, 1982.

———. *Negotiations, Interventions and Interviews 1971–2001.* Edited and Translated by Elizabeth Rottenberg. Stanford: Stanford University Press, 2002.

———. "Nietzsche and the Machine." In *Negotiations, Interventions and Interviews 1971–2001*, edited and translated by Elizabeth Rottenberg, 215–256. Stanford: Stanford University Press, 2002.

———. *Of Grammatology*. Translated by Gayatri Chakravorty Spivak. Baltimore: The Johns Hopkins University Press, 1976.

———. *Of Hospitality*. Translated by Rachel Bowlby. Stanford: Stanford University Press, 2000.

———. *On the Name*. Edited by Tomas Dutoit. Translated by D. Wood, John P. Leavey Jr., and Ian McLeod. Stanford: Stanford University Press: 1995.

———. *On Touching–Jean-Luc Nancy*. Translated by Christine Irizarry. Stanford: Stanford University Press, 2005.

———. "Others Are Secret Because They Are Other." In *Paper Machine*, translated by Rachel Bowlby, 137–163. Stanford: Stanford University Press, 2005.

———. "*Ousia* and *Grammē*." In *Margins of Philosophy*, translated by Alan Bass, 29–67. Chicago: University of Chicago Press, 1982.

———. "Pace Not(s)." In *Parages*, edited and translated by John P. Leavey, 11–101. Stanford: Stanford University Press, 2011.

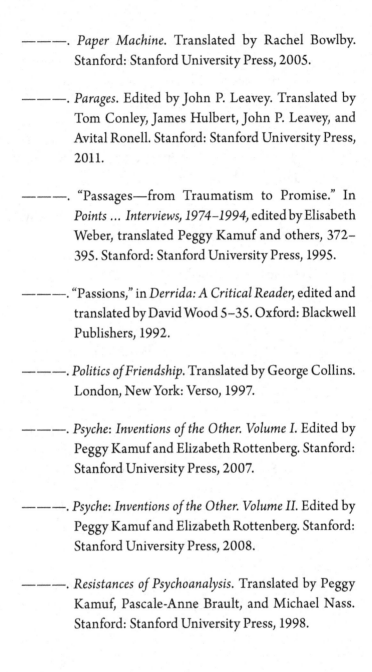

———. *Paper Machine*. Translated by Rachel Bowlby. Stanford: Stanford University Press, 2005.

———. *Parages*. Edited by John P. Leavey. Translated by Tom Conley, James Hulbert, John P. Leavey, and Avital Ronell. Stanford: Stanford University Press, 2011.

———. "Passages—from Traumatism to Promise." In *Points ... Interviews, 1974–1994*, edited by Elisabeth Weber, translated Peggy Kamuf and others, 372–395. Stanford: Stanford University Press, 1995.

———. "Passions," in *Derrida: A Critical Reader*, edited and translated by David Wood 5–35. Oxford: Blackwell Publishers, 1992.

———. *Politics of Friendship*. Translated by George Collins. London, New York: Verso, 1997.

———. *Psyche: Inventions of the Other. Volume I*. Edited by Peggy Kamuf and Elizabeth Rottenberg. Stanford: Stanford University Press, 2007.

———. *Psyche: Inventions of the Other. Volume II*. Edited by Peggy Kamuf and Elizabeth Rottenberg. Stanford: Stanford University Press, 2008.

———. *Resistances of Psychoanalysis*. Translated by Peggy Kamuf, Pascale-Anne Brault, and Michael Nass. Stanford: Stanford University Press, 1998.

———. *Rogues*. Translated by Pascale-Anne Brault and Michael Naas. Stanford: Stanford University Press, 2005.

———. "Shibboleth: For Paul Celan." In *Sovereignties in Question: The Poetics of Paul Celan*, edited by Thomas Dutoit and Outi Pasanen, 1–64. New York: Fordham University Press, 2005.

———. "Signature Event Context." In *Margins of Philosophy*, translated by Alan Bass, 307–330. Chicago: University of Chicago Press, 1982.

———. *Sovereignties in Question: The Poetics of Paul Celan*. Edited by Thomas Dutoit and Outi Pasanen. New York: Fordham University Press, 2005.

———. *Specters of Marx: The State of Debt, the Work of Mourning, and the New International*. Translated by Peggy Kamuf. New York: Routledge, 1994.

———. "Structure, Sign and Play in the Discourse of the Human Sciences." In *Writing and Difference*, translated by Alan Bass, 278–253. Chicago: University of Chicago Press, 1978.

———. "The Almost Nothing of the Unpresentable." In *Points ... Interviews, 1974–1994*, edited by Elisabeth Weber, translated Peggy Kamuf and others, 78–88. Stanford: Stanford University Press, 1995.

———. *The Animal That Therefore I Am*. Edited by Marie-Louise Mallet. Translated by D. Wills. New York: Fordham University Press, 2008.

———. *The Beast & the Sovereign Volume I*. Edited by Michael Lisse, Marie-Louise Mallet, and Ginette Michaud. Translated by Geoffrey Bennington. Chicago and London: University of Chicago Press, 2011.

———. *The Death Penalty Volume I*. Edited by Geoffrey Bennington, Marc Crépon and Thomas Dutoit. Translated by Peggy Kamuf. Chicago and London: University of Chicago Press, 2012.

———. *The Ear of the Other*. Edited by Christie McDonald. Translated by Peggy Kamuf. Nebraska, U of Nebraska Press Bison Book: 1988.

———. *The Gift of Death*. Translated by D. Willis. Chicago: University of Chicago Press, 1992.

———. "The Law of Genre." In *Acts of Literature,* edited by Derek Attridge, 221–252. New York: Routledge, 1992.

———. "The Law of Genre." In *Parages*, edited by John P. Leavey, translated by Avital Ronell, 217–249. Stanford: Stanford University Press, 2011.

———. *The Other Heading*. Translated by Pascale-Anne Brault and Michael B. Naas. Bloomington: Indiana University Press, 1992.

———. *The Post Card: From Socrates to Freud and Beyond.* Translated by Alan Bass. Chicago: University of Chicago Press, 1987.

———. "The Principle of Hospitality." In *Paper Machine,* translated by Rachel Bowlby, 66–69. Stanford: Stanford University Press, 2005.

———. "The Theater of Cruelty and the Closure of Representation." In *Writing and Difference,* translated by Alan Bass, 232–250. Chicago: University of Chicago Press, 1978.

———. "There Is No *One* Narcissism." In *Points ... Interviews, 1974–1994,* edited by Elisabeth Weber, translated Peggy Kamuf and others, 196–215 Stanford: Stanford University Press, 1995.

———. "Title to Be Specified." In *Parages,* edited by John P. Leavey, translated by Tom Conley, 193–215. Stanford: Stanford University Press, 2011.

———. "To Speculate–on Freud." In *The Post Card: From Socrates to Freud and Beyond,* translated by Alan Bass, 257–409. Chicago: University of Chicago Press, 1987.

———. "Unforeseeable Freedom." In *For What Tomorrow ... A Dialogue,* translated by Jeff Fort, 47–61. Stanford: Stanford University Press, 2004.

———. "Violence and Metaphysics." In *Writing and Difference*, translated by Alan Bass, 79–153. Chicago: University of Chicago Press, 1978.

———. *Voice and Phenomenon*. Translated by Leonard Lawlor. Evanston, Illinois: Northwestern University Press, 2011.

———. "Voice II." In *Points ... Interviews, 1974–1994*, edited by Elisabeth Weber, translated by Verena Andermatt Conley, 156–170. Stanford: Stanford University Press, 1995.

———. *Writing and Difference*. Translated by Alan Bass. Chicago: University of Chicago Press, 1978.

Düttmann, Alexander García. *The Memory of Thought*. Translated by Nicholas Walker. London, New York: Continuum, 2002.

Fenves, Peter. "Out of the Blue." In *Futures of Jacques Derrida*, edited by Richard Rand, 99–129. Stanford: Stanford University Press, 2001.

Ferraris, Maurizio and Jacques Derrida. *A Taste for the Secret*. Translated by Giacomo Donis. Edited by Giacomo Donis and David Webb. Cambridge: Polity Press, 2001.

Freud, Sigmund. *Beyond the Pleasure Principle*. Translated by James Strachey. New York: W.W. Norton & Company, 1989.

354

Hamacher, Werner. "Lingua Amissa." In *Futures of Jacques Derrida*, edited by Richard Rand, translated by Kelly Barry, 130–178. Stanford: Stanford University Press, 2001.

Hägglund. Martin. *Radical Atheism, Derrida and the Time of Life*. Edited by Werner Hamacher. Stanford: Stanford University Press, 2008.

Heidegger, Martin *What Is Called Thinking?* Introduction by J. Glenn Gray. Translated by J. Glenn Gray. New York: Harpers & Row, 1968.

Holy Bible. King James. New York: Camex International, 1989.

Malabou, Catherine and Jacques Derrida. *Counterpath. Traveling with Jacques Derrida*. Translated by D. Wills. Stanford: Stanford University Press, 2004.

Nancy, Jean-Luc. *Adoration: The Deconstruction of Christianity II*. Edited by John D. Caputo. Translated by John McKeane. New York: Fordham University Press, 2013.

———. *A Finite Thinking*. Edited by Simon Sparks. Stanford: Stanford University Press, 2003.

———. *Dis-Enclosure: The Deconstruction of Christianity*. Translated by Bettina Bergo, Gabriel Malenfant, and Michael B. Smith. New York: Fordham University Press, 2008.

———. "Elliptical Sense." In *Derrida: A Critical Reader,* edited and translated by David Wood, 36–51. Oxford: Blackwell Publishers, 1992.

———. *The Birth to Presence.* Translated by Brian Holmes. Stanford: Stanford University Press, 1993.

———. *The Discourse of the Syncope.* Translated by Saul Anton. Stanford: Stanford University Press, 2008.

———. *The Inoperative Community.* Edited by Peter Connor. Translated by Peter Connor, Lisa Garbus, Michael Holland, and Simona Sawhney. Minneapolis: University of Minnesota Press, 2006.

———. *The Muses.* Edited by Werner Hamacher & D. E. Wellbery. Translated by Peggy Kamuf. Stanford: Stanford University Press, 1996.

Kearney, Richard. "Desire of God." In *God, The Gift, and Postmodernism.* Edited by John D. Caputo and Michael J. Scanlon, 112–145. Indiana: Indiana University Press, 2001.

Nietzsche, Friedrich. *On the Genealogy of Morals and Ecce Homo.* Translated by Walter Kaufmann and R. J. Hollingdale. New York: Vintage Books, 1989.

———. *The Will To Power.* Edited by Walter Kauffmann. Translated by Walter Kaufmann and R. J. Hollingdale. New York: Vintage Books, 1968.

―――. *Thus Spoke Zarathustra: A Book for None and All*. Translated by Walter Kaufmann. New York: Penguin Books, 1978.

Plato, *Republic*. In *Collected Dialogues*. Edited by Edith Hamilton and Huntington Cairns. Translated by Paul Shorey, 575–844. New Jersey: Princeton University Press, 1961.

Rand, Richard, ed. *Futures of Jacques Derrida*. Stanford: Stanford University Press, 2001.

Roudinesco, Elizabeth and Jacques Derrida. *For What Tomorrow ... A Dialogue*. Translated by Jeff Fort. Stanford: Stanford University Press, 2004.

The American Heritage Dictionary, Second College Edition. Boston: Hougthon Mifflin Company, 1985.

Torah. Skokie: Varda Books, 2012.

Weber, Elisabeth, ed. *Points ... Interviews, 1974–1994*. Translated by Peggy Kamuf and others. Stanford: Stanford University Press, 1995.

Wood, David, ed. *Derrida: A Critical Reader*. Oxford: Blackwell Publishers, 1992.

Printed in the United States
By Bookmasters